The Politics of the
Second Slavery

FERNAND BRAUDEL CENTER
STUDIES IN HISTORICAL SOCIAL SCIENCE

Series Editor: Richard E. Lee

The Fernand Braudel Center Studies in Historical Social Science will publish works that address theoretical and empirical questions produced by scholars in or through the Fernand Braudel Center or who share its approach and concerns. It specifically seeks to promote works that contribute to the development of the world-systems perspective engaging a holistic and relational vision of the world—the modern world-system—implicit in historical social science, which at once takes into consideration structures (long-term regularities) and change (history). With the intellectual boundaries within the sciences/ social sciences/humanities structure collapsing in the work scholars actually do, this series will offer a venue for a wide range of research that confronts the dilemmas of producing relevant accounts of historical processes in the context of the rapidly changing structures of both the social and academic world. The series will include monographs, colloquia, and collections of essays organized around specific themes.

VOLUMES IN THIS SERIES:

Questioning Nineteenth-Century Assumptions about Knowledge, I: Determinism
Richard E. Lee, editor
Questioning Nineteenth-Century Assumptions about Knowledge, II: Reductionism
Richard E. Lee, editor
Questioning Nineteenth-Century Assumptions about Knowledge, III: Dualism
Richard E. Lee, editor
The *Longue Durée* and World-Systems Analysis
Richard E. Lee, editor
New Frontiers of Slavery
Dale W. Tomich, editor
Slavery in the Circuit of Sugar: Martinique and the World-Economy, 1830–1848
Dale W. Tomich
The Politics of the Second Slavery
Dale W. Tomich, editor

The Politics of the
Second Slavery

Edited by
Dale W. Tomich

FERNAND BRAUDEL CENTER
STUDIES IN HISTORICAL SOCIAL SCIENCE

Cover: photo of Ingenio Dolores Abreu in Remedios, Cuba taken by Dale W. Tomich.

Published by State University of New York Press, Albany

For information, contact State University of New York Press, Albany, NY
www.sunypress.edu

Production, Ryan Morris
Marketing, Kate R. Seburyamo

Library of Congress Cataloging-in-Publication Data

Names: Tomich, Dale W., 1946–
Title: The politics of the second slavery / edited by Dale W. Tomich.
Description: Albany : State University of New York Press, [2016] | Series: Fernand Braudel Center
  studies in historical social science | Includes bibliographical references and index.
Identifiers: LCCN 2016005981 (print) | LCCN 2016023474 (e-book) | ISBN 9781438462370
  (hc : alk. paper) | ISBN 9781438462363 (pbk. alk. paper) | 9781438462387 (e-book)
Subjects: LCSH: Slavery—America—History—19th century. | Slavery—Political aspects—History—
  19th century. | Decolonization—America—History—19th century. | Elite (Social sciences)—
  Political activity—History—19th century. | Slave trade—History—19th century. | Antislavery
  movements—History—19th century. | Slave insurrections—History—19th century. | America—
  Race relations—History—19th century. | America—Politics and government—19th century.
Classification: LCC HT1048.P65 2016 (print) | LCC HT1048 (ebook) | DDC 306.3/620973—dc23
LC record available at https://lccn.loc.gov/2016005981

10 9 8 7 6 5 4 3 2 1

In memory of our colleague and friend
Chris Schmidt-Nowara (1966–2015)

CONTENTS

Introduction   ix
Dale W. Tomich

Civilizing America's Shore: British World-Economic Hegemony and the
Abolition of the International Slave Trade (1814–1867)   1
Dale W. Tomich

International Proslavery: The Politics of the Second Slavery   25
Rafael Marquese and Tâmis Parron

Spain and the Politics of the Second Slavery, 1808–1868   57
Christopher Schmidt-Nowara

The Return to the *casa de vivienda* and the *barracón*: The Terms of
Social Action in Slave Plantations   83
José Antonio Piqueras

The Paths of Freedom: Autonomism and Abolitionism in Cuba, 1878–1886   113
Luís Miguel García Mora

Passive Revolution and the Politics of Second Slavery in the
Brazilian Empire   145
Ricardo Salles

The Contraband Slave Trade of the Second Slavery   173
Leonardo Marques

Spaces of Rebellion: Plantations, Farms, and Churches in Demerara
and Southampton, Virginia   199
Anthony E. Kaye

The American Civil War, Emancipation, and Nation-Building:
A Comparative Perspective   229
Enrico Dal Lago

Contributors   253

Index   257

Introduction

Dale W. Tomich

The concept of the second slavery calls attention to the remaking of Atlantic slavery as part of the material and economic expansion of the capitalist world-economy during the first part of the nineteenth century. It refers to both the opening of new zones of slave commodity production—most prominently the U.S. cotton zone, the Cuban sugar zone, and the Brazilian coffee zone—and the decline of older zones of slave production. By emphasizing the social and geographic reconfiguration of slave relations within a new world-economic complex of relations and processes, the second slavery breaks with linear conceptions of temporality and causality, particularly with linear conceptions of the relation of slavery and capitalist modernity. Thus, rather than treating slave relations as premodern or static, it calls attention to their heterogeneity and complexity and views them as continually formed by and formative of the world-economic division of labor.

This book seeks to deepen our understanding of the second slavery by exploring its political dimensions. Although studies of the second slavery have tended to focus on the social and material conditions of commodity production and the reconstitution of slave relations, the concept does not apply simply to the economic history of slavery. Rather, the second slavery reconfigured slave formations in the Americas within the context of a global and regional political transformation marked by the growth and consolidation of national states. Consequently, the concept of the second slavery suggests, and indeed requires, reinterpretation of the history of slavery in its political, ideological, and cultural dimensions as well as its social, economic, and environmental aspects. While the world-economy provides the analytical framework for this book, political action and discourse are regarded here as spatially and temporally complex and multidimensional. A discussion of the politics of the second slavery needs to take into account diverse groups of actors and institutions, exploring the ways that they interact across multiple spatial and temporal dimensions. Accordingly, the chapters of this book examine how the politics of slavery and antislavery shaped the Atlantic political order, the politics of empire and relations between metropolis and colony, the political contention between old and new slave zones, and slavery and state formation in the postcolonial Americas, as well as slave resistance.

Even as the topics are diverse, three key claims shape the second-slavery approach that we pursue in these chapters. First, all politics, even apparently local politics, are grounded in the transnational structures forming the world-economy and interstate system. Second, the all-too-often-assumed opposition between liberal antislavery and antiliberal proslavery must be critically reexamined. Finally, the narrative of a presumed linear movement from slavery to freedom needs to be called into question. In contrast to these prevailing assumptions, the second-slavery approach explores the diverse and contradictory ways that both abolitionism and proslavery politics are constituted and reconstituted within the historical processes of capital accumulation, state formation, and the articulation of liberal political and economic conceptions. This perspective allows us to differentiate apparently similar phenomena and determine their specificity within world-historical processes. It results, for example, in a reevaluation of proslavery politics. From this perspective, the chapters in this book reinterpret old questions and raise new ones. They call attention to the diversity and transnational character of the politics of slavery and antislavery. They seek to open a discussion rather than to provide answers.

The volume originates in a conference held at the Fernand Braudel Center at Binghamton University in 2010. Most of the chapters had their beginnings as papers presented at the conference. I would like to thank Richard E. Lee, director of the Fernand Braudel Center, Anthony Kaye, Rafael Marquese, Ricardo Salles, and Christopher Schmidt-Nowara, as well as Amy Keough, Kelly Pueschel, and Laura Tomich for their assistance in making this volume possible.

Civilizing America's Shore

British World-Economic Hegemony and the Abolition of the International Slave Trade (1814–1867)

Dale W. Tomich

The Congress of Vienna was primarily concerned with the restoration of political order in Europe in the aftermath of the French Revolution and the Napoleonic Wars. Nonetheless, Britain insisted on inserting a provision among the parties to abolish the slave trade. The Congress of Vienna declared that slave trade is "repugnant to principles of humanity and universal morality" and "the public voice in all civilized countries calls for its prompt suppression." This antislavery provision seems almost anomalous given the purpose of the Congress. Why did Britain insist on including it? To address this question, this chapter reinterprets the problem of abolition by examining the politics of British antislavery from the perspective of the transformation of the world-economy. It argues that the campaign to abolish the international slave trade was a key element in linking British strategy in the Atlantic to British strategy in Europe. The Congress of Vienna generalized the British campaign to end the international slave trade and conjoined it to the establishment of the postwar balance of power in Europe. The antislavery campaign was part of the British effort to reorganize and reorder the interstate system while simultaneously bringing the newly independent states of the Americas under its discipline. By this means, Britain attempted to restructure the world-economy around its economic and political advantage and to secure British hegemony over the European world-economy during the first half of the nineteenth century.

Perhaps curiously, the political dimensions of abolitionism have drawn relatively little attention from historians (Alexandre 2000: 65–66; Huzzey 2012: 40–41). Nor has the British antislavery campaign been examined within the analytical framework of the world-economy. The debate over slavery has operated within a binomial opposition between ideological and moral factors on the one hand and economic factors on the other. Within this duality, Britain is privileged as the unilateral agency of antislavery. Whether it is regarded as necessary or contingent, or as the result of economic forces, liberal ideology, or humanitarian concern, the abolition of the slave trade has by and large been treated as an event occurring within Britain and its empire. British abolition is generally viewed as the first of a sequence of events leading, with virtual inevitability, to British slave emancipation, the abolition of the international slave trade, and finally the dismantling of slavery throughout the hemisphere and elsewhere. Such emphasis on the ideological-humanitarian dimensions of the British antislavery campaign or on its economic dimensions has obscured the political interests and motives that led the British state and Britain's ruling elites to support abolitionism. As a result, such interpretations of antislavery at the same time ignore the complex and polyvalent interrelatedness of world-economic processes, and easily fall into a one-sided and linear narrative of liberal capitalist modernity as economic, political, and moral progress.

In contrast, this chapter examines Britain's campaign to abolish the international slave trade during the first half of the nineteenth century in terms of the real and ideal interests of the British state in pursuing abolition of the international slave trade as official policy, not in terms of the moral force of antislavery or the incompatibility of slavery with liberal ideas and values or with industrial capitalism and free trade. It treats the British state's efforts to abolish the international slave trade as part of its attempt to establish hegemony over the capitalist world-economy, and more specifically to create a new international order, institutional framework, and norms of behavior among sovereign and formally equal states of the Atlantic during the so-called Age of Revolution. It is less concerned with ending the forced transportation of Africans to the Americas than with the ways in which the international slave trade and the various anti–slave trade treaties affected interstate relations and their role in the restructuring of the interstate system.

The interpretation of the actions of the British state presented here utilizes the concept of hegemony that has been elaborated by world-systems scholars. Immanuel Wallerstein argues that cycles of hegemonic leadership are a systematic feature of the capitalist world-economy. Hegemony develops when one state accrues such a significant competitive economic, political, military, and diplomatic advantage that it is able to impose its rules on its rivals. The hegemonic state thus becomes a pole of both cooperation and competition for rival states. Such situations of hegemonic dominance are rare and unstable. Nonetheless, they are important because the interests and capacities of the hegemonic power set the parameters for a new cycle of accumulation and innovation that reorders the world-economy (Wallerstein 1984: 37–46). Giovanni Arrighi extends Wallerstein's argument by emphasizing the political and ideological dimensions of hegemony. He applies Antonio Gramsci's concept of hegemony to the arena of interstate relations. In Arrighi's terms, hegemony refers to a state's capacity to combine domination and legitimacy with intellectual and moral leadership in ways that allow it to transform in some fundamental way the mode of operation of the interstate system (Arrighi 1994: 27–31; Gramsci 1971: 44–120).

Thus, this chapter examines how the British campaign to abolish the international slave trade contributed to the construction of British world-economic hegemony during the first half of the nineteenth century. It focuses on how the political and diplomatic negotiation to end the trade gave rise to three interrelated and interdependent dimensions of Britain's hegemonic project: the establishment of an international political order, the establishment of an international legal order, and the establishment of international moral order among the newly independent states of the Atlantic. Viewed from this perspective, the international antislavery struggle at once served as a means to integrate the new American states into the interstate system and to reconfigure the relations of states with one another and with the emergent world market in ways consonant with British interests and power.

The Congress of Vienna and Britain's Hegemonic Strategy

The economic and political organization of the European world-economy had undergone a profound transformation between 1780 and 1815. Haitian and U.S. independence had, in their different ways, destabilized the colonial-mercantilist structure of European domination of the Americas. They initiated a cycle of decolonization that redefined the political character of the region and its relation with Europe. The independence of Britain's North American colonies broke down its mercantilist colonial system and created a significant maritime rival in the Atlantic. The successful slave revolution in the French colony of Saint Domingue removed the world's richest colony from the European world-economy and destroyed the empire of Britain's chief rival in New World. Beginning in the 1820s, independence movements ended Spanish and Portuguese dominion in South America. As the old colonial order in the Atlantic collapsed, Britain found itself in an unprecedented position in Europe. Between 1780 and 1815, Britain emerged as the world's dominant industrial, commercial, and financial power. The mechanization of the cotton industry fundamentally altered the relation between capital and labor and supply and demand, and engendered forces that were to result in unprecedented material and economic expansion and alter the world division of labor (Hobsbawm 1990: 34–154). Further, Trafalgar gave Britain command of the sea. Waterloo left Britain the strongest power in Europe. After 1815, Britain was in a position to reshape the world economic, political, and social order to its advantage, but the British state and the ruling oligarchy had to confront a new set of conditions and challenges to realize its global ambition.

The Congress of Vienna crystallized the new situation at the end of the Napoleonic Wars. As distinguished historian Ludwig Dehio has argued, Britain sought to orchestrate the restoration of the balance of power in Europe, but wanted to avoid direct involvement on the Continent. Instead, it sought to arbitrate continental politics by using its maritime supremacy to control European access to world trade. The emergence of independent states compelled the treatment of the Americas as a distinct issue. Britain's capacity to control the European balance of power and to continue overseas expansion would be jeopardized if it could not establish a stable political order in the Atlantic. The subsequent independence of South American nations only made this problem more urgent (Dehio 1962: 132–223). For Britain's strategy to work, it had to both restore the balance of power in Europe and organize interstate relations among the newly independent states of the Americas in ways that were compatible with British regional and world interests and ambition. These two problems were intimately related to one another. To realize its strategic ambition, Britain had to achieve two political goals in the Atlantic. First, it had to prevent the recovery of European colonial power in the Americas. Second, it had to check U.S. maritime and commercial power in the Americas. The United States was the only challenger to British supremacy in the Atlantic, but at the same time it was outside of European politics and the Congress of Vienna.

British efforts to restructure interstate relations in the face of colonial decline and the emergence of new independent states in the Americas were of course linked to and complementary with British economic expansion and the restructuring of the world market. Contrary to what could be expected from the perspective of mercantilism, Britain's trade with the independent United States was far greater than it had been with the thirteen colonies. During the Napoleonic Wars and Continental Blockade, Britain enjoyed exceptional access to Latin America. After the war, it sought to remove old colonial impediments and gain direct entry to Latin American markets. It promoted the development of national economies and the formation of an international division of labor articulated through the market. Indeed, Britain regarded the market as an entity outside of and above states and the interstate system. Its unfettered operation was to regulate the economic relations among and within states. However, it must also be stressed that Britain's efforts to establish a stable interstate system and market relations in the Americas went hand in hand with further colonial expansion elsewhere. Arguably, the stabilization of interstate relations in the Atlantic was the condition for colonial expansion in other regions of the world (Dehio 1962: 174–75, 190–93). The epicenter of the empire shifted from the Americas to India as Britain engaged in unprecedented colonial expansion in Africa, Asia, North America, and the Pacific.

The International Slave Trade and the Second Slavery

Anti–slave trade initiatives were a regular feature of British diplomacy during the first half of the nineteenth century. The British state's effort to abolish the international slave trade and reorganize the interstate system during the first half of the nineteenth century was a prolonged and complex process that entailed negotiating continually shifting economic, political, and social relationships. Britain's efforts to abolish the trade were at times inconsistent, and British statesmen had to navigate between domestic abolitionist pressure and the political and diplomatic requirements of the international situation. Despite numerous treaties calling for the abolition of the international slave trade beginning in 1814, it took until 1839 to secure treaties with all the major maritime powers with the exception of the United States, and nearly fifty years to secure the termination of the traffic (Temperly 1972: 168). Britain attempted to negotiate the abolition of the slave trade with states that had neither the will nor the interest to do so, and indeed they resented Britain's attempt to impose abolition as an affront to their sovereignty. Further, the impact of Britain's efforts to suppress the African trade on the slave formations of the Americas increased the pressure for agreements in principle and gradualist solutions.[1]

Perhaps more fundamentally, slavery in the Americas was itself dramatically restructured during the first half of the nineteenth century. The abolition of the international slave trade and British slave emancipation were not simply outcomes of the linear continuation of British antislavery or the secular decline of slavery. Rather, the field of action was transformed after Britain abolished its slave trade in 1807. Britain and other actors were faced with a new set of problems, possibilities, and constraints.

As I have argued elsewhere, British efforts to abolish the Atlantic slave trade had to confront the expansion of the second slavery (Tomich 2004, esp. pp. 56–71). The U.S. South, Cuba, and Brazil emerged as dynamic new centers of slave-based commodity production that were of central importance for the expansion of the world-economy and the redefinition of the world division of labor. They were the major sources of supply of the world's cotton, sugar, and coffee as well as important markets for British exports. The formation of the U.S. cotton frontier, the Cuban sugar frontier, and the Brazilian coffee frontier entailed the massive redeployment of slave labor under new conditions of industrialization, urbanization, and the expansion of world markets. These new zones of slave production anchored new commodity circuits linking the Atlantic world. In them, slavery itself was reconfigured, with increasing scales of production, growing pressure to increase the productivity of labor, new technologies of production and transport, and new modes of labor discipline and social control. Even as slave trading operated under new logics and strategies, the Atlantic slave trade—legal and illegal—was the motor of the expansion of commodity production in these new zones of the second slavery. Historically, the plantation zones of the Americas were chronically short of labor. The African slave trade permitted the expansion of staple production into new commodity frontiers by supplying the necessary labor force to the right place at the right time (Wagley 1960; Moore 2000). The volume of the slave trade during the first half of the nineteenth century closely approximated its eighteenth-century peak, but its outlets were overwhelmingly in Cuba and Brazil (Tomich 2004: 56–71). An internal slave trade also played a significant role in the development of Brazil's coffee frontier.

The emergence of these new slave commodity frontiers represented a crisis of the previous colonial division of labor in which competing metropolitan powers attempted to control and manage the sources of production in their Atlantic colonies and to confine trade within politically defined mercantilist circuits in order to promote national development. The old colonial spaces were unable to compete under the new conditions. By the late 1820s and early 1830s, sugar production stagnated and declined in the old slave colonies of Britain and France as well as in the Brazilian Northeast, whether or not they had an active slave trade. This crisis of colonial slavery was accompanied by the nationalization of slavery in the new productive zones. The creation of national slaveries was the result of the independence of the new American states. These new slave zones anchored commodity circuits that were formed through market relations rather than colonial-mercantilist preference. Consequently, while they worked to articulate themselves as national economies that were linked to the world-economy through the market, they were subject to varied pressures, including Britain's efforts to abolish the international slave trade. (Although Cuba remained a colony of Spain, Cuban sugar planters gained increasing autonomy during the first half of the nineteenth century and had to place their product in competitive world markets.) Thus, there was a political crisis of the geopolitical organization of slave labor and slave commodity production, but not a crisis of slavery as such. As the old zones of colonial slavery declined, the "second slavery" transformed the Atlantic as a political economic space. The strategic point of control over the nineteenth-century Atlantic economy would no longer be the sites of production, but rather the transnational flows of commodities, which Britain sought to dominate.

Under these conditions, continuation of a legal, large-scale international slave trade would threaten Britain's intention of establishing a division of labor and staple trade ordered by market relations and stable relations among sovereign states. Renewed prosecution of the slave trade could provide the means for the old colonial powers—France, Spain, and Portugal—to reassert their control over their American slave colonies and to attempt to renew slave production in their colonies. If this were allowed to occur, the slave trade would reproduce the mercantilist colonial division of labor as a preferential space for metropolitan states and capital. If such a mercantilist colonial division of labor were to be restored, it would present a fundamental barrier to the establishment of a liberal world market and political order in the Atlantic.

Thus, if Britain could abolish the international slave trade, the link that conjoined slavery with the expansion of the world-economy would be severed. The raison d'être of slavery for capital accumulation would then be eliminated. While the *slave trade* required the existence of slaves as a commodity, the zones of *slave production* did not. In the absence of the slave trade, the problem of labor in the expansion of these new commodity frontiers would be reduced to the problem of securing an adequate supply of cheap labor, which may or may not be met by slave labor (Beiguelman 1978: 77–80).

Reordering the Atlantic: The Politics of International Abolitionism

To realize its purposes in Europe and the Americas, Britain had to confront the diversity and complexity of geopolitics and the slave trade in the Atlantic world. France, Portugal, and Spain each presented different problems for British strategy. Unlike at Versailles 100 years later, the defeated nation was an integral part of the postwar settlement. Britain had to promote the restoration of France, including its colonies. To establish the Continental balance of power in Europe, Britain needed France to serve as a counterweight to Russia in European affairs. Further, any French government had to contain the threat of social movements, whether in the form of republicanism, Bonapartism, socialism, or nationalism. Consequently, Britain encouraged the restoration of French power under the moderate Bourbon monarchy (Dehio 1962: 176–77). Britain also had to support the Portuguese and Spanish dynasties with their extensive slaveholding colonies. Yet Britain wanted to ensure that France, Portugal, and Spain did not form a pro–slave trade block (Murray 2002: 54). Its long-term goal was to promote Latin American independence and gain access to its markets while transforming Spain and Portugal into European client states. Thus, the requirements of European politics complicated Britain's strategy. Britain was able to secure universal consent to the principle of the abolition of the slave trade at Vienna, but achieving abolition in practice was a much more difficult and complex process that was more effectively pursued through bilateral treaties (Huzzey 2012: 52).

The restoration of France entailed reconstructing what remained of the French colonial empire. After more than two decades of war, revolution, blockade, and foreign occupation, the French Empire was in shambles. France had not only lost Haiti and Louisiana, but its navy and merchant marine were devastated and its port cities were impoverished. Unable to gain access to other overseas markets, France was dependent on the colonial trade. The slave trade and slavery were key elements in the recovery of France's colonies, merchant marine, and navy. Against the opposition of the abolitionists, Britain returned Martinique and Guadeloupe to France, and supported French claims against Haiti. It also allowed France a five-year grace period in which to resupply its colonies with slaves. France followed an aggressively protectionist policy in its remaining colonies to promote the recovery of its port cities and commercial fleet. However, the colonies remaining to France were old productive zones, and the possibilities for their renewal were limited. Under British pressure, the French government outlawed the arrival of slaves to its colonies by 1817–1818, but did little to enforce the law. Further, to defend its sovereignty, France also refused to agree to reciprocal search rights. The slave trade continued unabated. Only after the Revolution of 1830, when the liberal July Monarchy was eager for a détente with Britain, was the French slave trade definitively ended. However, by this time the demand for slave labor had fallen off in the French colonies, and France posed little danger to Britain's Atlantic monopoly (Tomich 1990: 53–61; Kielstra 2000).

Both Portugal and Spain were part of the Vienna agreement. Each was severely weakened as a result of the decades of war and revolution. After the Peninsular Wars they were susceptible to British influence and their ties with their extensive colonial empires were weakened. On the other hand, the need to protect both dynasties inhibited the execution of British policies against the slave trade.

British anti–slave trade policy was one of the important factors differentiating and then gradually dissociating the interests of Portugal and Brazil (Alexandre 2000: 68, 81). This policy was implicated in a broader anticolonial strategy. Britain's goal was to trade directly with Brazil and to integrate it into the world market without the mediation of the Portuguese metropolis. The Napoleonic invasion of the Iberian Peninsula exacerbated these tensions as well as the tensions between Portugal and Brazil. In 1807, the transfer of the Portuguese Court to Rio de Janeiro under the protection of the British fleet shifted the center of gravity of the Portuguese Empire to Brazil while Portugal's role within the empire diminished. At the same time, Portugal itself remained under threat of annexation by Spain throughout the war and became dependent on British military intervention in the Iberian Peninsula. With these moves, Britain gained influence in Luso-Brazilian affairs.

At the Vienna Congress, Britain pressured Portugal to end the slave trade. The emperor in Rio de Janeiro refused any compromise, both because of Brazil's continuing dependence on slave imports and to defend the integrity of the empire in the face of British interference (Alexandre 2000: 71–73). However, the Portuguese representatives in London negotiated an agreement that expressed Portugal's interests within a European context. In return for exoneration of Portugal's debt to Britain and other concessions, they agreed to abolish the Portuguese slave trade north of the equator, to the reciprocal right of inspection of suspected slave ships, and to mixed commission courts that judged the ships brought before it without right of appeal. They also committed themselves to a future treaty that would abolish the slave trade. However, this agreement left untouched the flourishing slave trade between Africa and Brazil south of the equator (Bethell 1970: 149, 159). These agreements deepened the divide between Brazil and Portugal. Brazil remained dependent on the slave trade, and the emperor remained committed to it, to Brazil, and to the integrity of the empire. In Portugal a nationalism oriented toward the continent began to emerge. For Britain, signing the reciprocal right of visit was crucial because after the war it could no longer invoke the right of a belligerent power to interfere with the shipping of another state. It provided both international recognition of some limits to the slave trade and the means to enforce them (Alexandre 2000: 76–80).

With Brazilian independence in 1822 the Portuguese slave trade lost its imperial justification. Independent Brazil raised a new set of issues for British efforts to abolish the slave trade. Britain insisted that Brazil assume Portugal's treaty obligations with regard to the slave trade as the price of recognition (Bethell 1970: 31–32). In 1826, in exchange for recognition by both Britain and Portugal, Brazil committed itself to suppressing the trade north of the equator and to complete abolition of the Brazilian slave trade three years after the treaty with Britain was ratified (Bethell 1970: 58–61). However, Portugal neither signed a treaty nor a passed national law prohibiting the slave trade south of the equator. Consequently, when the treaty abolishing the Brazilian slave trade went into effect in 1830, slavers continued their activity by sailing under the Portuguese flag. Further, those violating the Brazilian law banning the slave trade were to be tried in Brazilian courts rather than the international commissions favored by the British (Bethell 1970: 45–49, 54–62, 69–71). Finally, the new planter elite, led by the conservative coffee planters of the Paraíba Valley, resisted ratification of antislavery treaties with Britain and impeded enforcement of anti–slave trade agreements through control of the legislature and influence in the judiciary (Mattos 1994; Salles 2008). The law abolishing the Brazilian slave trade was in effect a dead letter.

The failure of Brazil to enforce its abolition law compelled Britain to take a more active role in suppressing the South Atlantic trade. Britain's response to the situation oscillated between renewed efforts to establish a legal structure that would allow it to act more effectively against the trade and more aggressive unilateral action (Bethell 1970: 166). Cooperation and coercion at times complemented one another and at times pulled in opposite directions. Britain's efforts to more vigorously pursue slaving ships under the existing treaties resulted in widespread fraud and deception as slavers resorted to false flags and papers—especially Portuguese colors—to avoid the British suppression squadrons. In the absence of bilateral treaties authorizing the British right to visit ships using false colors, Britain lacked legal competence to search and prosecute them (Bethell 1970: 150).

Britain pressed to secure more effective authorization to search suspected slave ships at sea, to oblige other nations to join in the suppression of the trade through naval action, and to establish mixed commissions to adjudicate the cases. It also unsuccessfully proposed that slave trading should be treated as piracy once Brazilian abolition of the trade went into effect. In 1839 the Palmerston Act threatened more aggressive unilateral action against slaving ships sailing under Portuguese colors. By 1842 it pressured Portugal into a satisfactory antislavery treaty, and the use of the Portuguese flag was virtually eliminated from the Brazilian trade (Bethell 1970: 187). However, slave traders rapidly replaced it with the United States flag. The United States was the one maritime power that refused to sign right-to-search treaties, and widespread use of the U.S. flag by slavers undermined British efforts (Bethell 1970: 190–92). Finally, with the establishment of the Anglo-Brazilian commission in Rio de Janeiro, traders also began using the Brazilian flag again, as their chances of acquittal before the Rio commission were very favorable.

Tensions deepened between Britain and Brazil throughout the remainder of the decade, fueled by both antislavery and commercial issues. In 1845 Brazil refused to renew the treaty authorizing both the British right to search vessels flying the Brazilian flag and the Anglo-Brazilian commission in Rio de Janeiro, in the hope of renegotiating a treaty that was more favorable to it. In response, Britain unilaterally assumed the right to seize Brazilian ships suspected of being slavers and to adjudicate the cases in Admiralty courts with the passage of the Aberdeen Act (Bethell 1970: 242–66; Huzzey 2012: 58–59). Under this law, Britain began seizing Brazilian ships on the high seas and aggressively patrolling the Brazilian coast, even entering the harbor of Rio de Janeiro in 1850 and 1851. However, these measures had little impact on the increasing volume of the slave trade to Brazil; Brazil regarded them as an attack on its sovereignty and a threat to its territorial integrity (Huzzey 2012: 58–59). The impasse finally ended in 1851, when as a result of the combination of changing conditions in Brazil and rigorous British external pressure, the government legally abolished the slave trade and effectively suppressed it (Bethell 1970: 363).

The slave trading interest was not as important in Spain as it was in Portugal. However, slave traders of various nations frequently sailed under cover of the Spanish flag. In 1817 Spain, financially distressed and dependent on British loans and subsidies, also acceded to British diplomatic pressure and abolished the slave trade north of the equator in exchange for an indemnity, and in 1820 the trade was prohibited south of the equator as well. In addition, Spain granted British warships the right to inspect suspect slavers sailing under Spanish colors. However, like Portugal, the Spanish government demonstrated little inclination to enforce the ban. With the complicity of Spanish officials, the laws were used to protect the slave trade rather than prosecute it (Murray 2002: 91).

In practice, Spain's position on the slave trade was closely linked to Cuba. After the independence of Spanish America, "always faithful" Cuba was the pivot of Spain's efforts to establish its "second empire" (Schmidt-Nowara 1999). Cuba remained a colony, and Spain itself depended on Cuban revenues. During the 1830s the almost insatiable demand for slave labor on Cuba's expanding sugar frontier was matched by Britain's efforts to secure more effective measures to suppress the slave trade to Cuba. Unlike Brazil, Spain did not allow its antislavery treaties with Britain to lapse, but rather it subverted their enforcement. Cubans, Spaniards, North Americans, Portuguese, and French engaged in the slave trade to Cuba even after it was illegal. As in the case of Brazil, slavers trading with Cuba sailed under Portuguese and U.S. flags to avoid British suppression squadrons (Murray 2002: 91–113). However, unlike the aggressive policy pursued against Brazil, Britain continued to pressure Spain to comply with its obligations. Nonetheless, the slave trade continued unchecked until the American Civil War, when political conditions compelled the United States to also take more effective measures against the slave trade to Cuba (Murray 2002: 298–326).

The United States presented the most difficult obstacle for Britain. The independent American republic was outside of European balance-of-power politics. It was at once a continental empire and a maritime and commercial power that presented Britain with its only serious challenge in the Atlantic. The United States, and particularly the North, was heavily involved in the international slave trade as shipbuilders and financiers. Their involvement with the slave trade, particularly to Cuba but also Brazil strengthened commercial ties with those countries (Bethell 1970: 189–90). The slave South had a disproportionate voice in U.S. politics. Southern threats to reopen the slave trade to the United States and, on various occasions, to annex Cuba, Mexico, Central America, and the Amazon to expand the zones of slave commodity production unsettled British plans to create a stable Atlantic order under British hegemony.

The U.S. government had abolished the slave trade to the United States and made it illegal for U.S. citizens or ships to participate in the traffic. Nonetheless, the United States was extremely protective of its sovereignty and steadfastly refused to sign a treaty allowing mutual right of search with Britain and protected ships flying the U.S. flag. U.S. colors provided cover for a great proportion of slave ships trading with both Brazil and Cuba during the 1830s and 1840s. U.S. ships and crews participated in the slave trade illegally, usually under false papers and at times with the complicity of U.S. officials (Huzzey 2012: 56–57). After negotiations with Britain in 1842, the U.S. government agreed to send a token force to police U.S. ships involved in the slave trade on the West African coast. However, the consequence of this arrangement was that the British navy was still denied the right to search and seize ships flying American colors (Huzzey 2012: 55–56). Only in the exceptional circumstances of the U.S. Civil War did Lincoln grant Britain the right of search for a period of ten years and move to vigorously suppress the trade (Murray 2002; Huzzey 2012: 57). These measures and aggressive British action in West Africa and off the coast of Cuba greatly reduced the slave trade to Cuba and altered the political conditions under which it could operate. The Spanish government began to take measures against the slave trade, though not against slavery itself, and finally outlawed it in 1867. The Atlantic slave trade had effectively come to an end (Bethell 1970: 189–90; Murray 2002: 104–106, 298, 304–22).

The New Atlantic Legal Order

The British campaign to abolish the international slave trade was a key moment in which the interstate system was renegotiated and reformed to accommodate and incorporate the independent states of the Americas. The problem for Britain was to create a new institutional order in the Atlantic and new norms for interstate relations that were consistent with British power and aspirations and that served British interests. Domination and economic pressure alone were insufficient for these purposes. The ways in which Britain pursued its antislavery strategy contributed not only to the political reordering of the Atlantic state system, but to the creation of a stable institutional and normative order among sovereign states. The institutional and normative dimensions of this process encourage us to go beyond the fact of British political domination to consider the ways in which British action shaped the interstate system into what Gerrit Gong calls a "society of states" (Gong 1984: 3–23). Gong's concept implies not that states have the same interests, but that there is a common framework and norms of conduct within which individual states pursue their interests. From this perspective, the fifty-year-long British antislavery campaign not only ended the traffic in human beings across the Atlantic, but it created an interlocking web of treaties, laws, policies, and standards of state action that provided a shared political-legal structure for relations among states and served as an instrument of British world-economic hegemony (Davis 1975: 503–505).

Unlike the previous interstate order, which was organized through European dynastic states and their imperial extensions, the new order was formed by sovereign and formally equal territorial states. The independent states of the Americas made claims to sovereignty in various forms, including both republic and empire, while Cuba remained a colony. In this context, British antislavery may be seen as part of an effort to institute new principles of sovereignty. It helped to integrate the new states into a legal and normative order that was established by consent and mutual agreement, and it brought them under the discipline of the interstate system and world market. British policy effectively promoted the territorialization and nationalization of states. (To the degree that British policy prevented or weakened the reassertion of European colonialism in the Americas, it also compelled European dynastic states to behave as if they were "liberal" territorial states.) This project entailed an international legal order that regulated the relations between states and between state and market. The doctrine of state sovereignty, international law, and securing the consent of participating states shaped the institutional framework of this new international order. If, as Arrighi argues (1994: 53), the new territorial states were controlled by communities of property holders, then states had to possess institutional continuity and the capacity to adjust national and private interests within a stable framework. The operation of markets and the flows of commodities and capital across national borders required that the rights of persons, contracts, and property be guaranteed. Further, sovereign states had to negotiate their relations with one another within a common political and legal framework. It is no accident, then, that the reconfiguration of concepts of sovereignty, balance of power, and international law during the first half of the nineteenth century are contemporaneous with the articulation of the doctrine of comparative advantage. Here, the restructuring of the interstate system entailed the political reintegration of the Atlantic economy and the subjection of sovereign polities and national economies to the discipline of the market.

Thus, international antislavery conventions may be seen as instruments for establishing by consent relations between sovereign territorial states and creating an internationally agreed-upon standard of law. They helped to create a new international legal-political regime in which all states agreed to operate—in essence, new rules of the game in interstate relations. The point that I want to make here may appear self-evident, but it nonetheless carries far-reaching implications. To make the interstate system function and to transform it into a "society of states," Britain had to respect the sovereignty of the new states and secure the agreement of the new Creole (slaveholding) elites. Consent took precedence over coercion. In the entire course of its effort to abolish the international slave trade, Britain proceeded by negotiating treaties and attempting to secure compliance with treaty obligations that had been agreed to in principle. This is not to say that coercion was not an element of the antislavery campaign, or that Britain did not abuse its position. But more often than not, coercion was used to induce consent (Huzzey 2012: 52–64; Bethell 1970: x, 54–55). (Indeed, a strong body of opinion in Britain opposed the unilateral and coercive measures attempted under the Palmerston and Aberdeen Acts.) Britain's insistence that independent Brazil assume the treaty commitments of Portugal, its attempts to secure cooperation in the suppression of the slave trade once it was declared illegal, its efforts to make treaties recognizing the joint right to search suspected slaving vessels on the high seas, the use of mixed commissions or vice-Admiralty courts, and its attempt to equate slave trading with piracy may all be seen as points of contention between states. However, these were not merely instrumentalities for suppressing the slave trade. Issues of sovereignty and international law were also at stake. The resolution of these issues was obtained through conflict and negotiation. They formed part of a pedagogy of sovereignty in the emergent interstate system through which new principles of sovereignty and international law were established.

Viewed from the perspective of the reformation of the interstate system, Britain's strategy of attacking the international slave trade rather than the institution of slavery itself appears not to have been simply a matter of expediency. Rather, it conforms to the conditions of the emergent interstate order. Britain pursued its aims by challenging the external conditions of the American slave regimes while formally respecting the sovereignty of independent states and restraining itself from intervening directly in their internal affairs (Huzzey 2012: 52–65).[2] By dealing with the slave trade rather than with slavery itself, British policy did not touch directly on the domestic social question. Slaveholding elites remained firmly in control of national affairs. This strategy allowed national elites to resolve questions of slavery, race, property, and citizenship in national terms—and a wide range of response was possible—while pressuring them to do so in a manner consistent with the international order. Perhaps more importantly, by not addressing the institution of slavery directly, Britain did not encourage radical responses to the question of slavery that would threaten the economic and political status quo. Suppression of radical challenges to the slave order, whether from Jacobinism, radical republicanism, local antislaveries, or slave rebellion, remained the responsibility of national and local elites.

While this approach empowered slaveholder regimes in the national sphere, those regimes were also pressured to conform to the conservative character of British liberalism in the international arena. Further, by respecting the formal sovereignty of independent states, the emergent interstate order also allowed the social and material division of labor to form, as private actors inside and outside the national state were able pursue their interests through the market. Thus, this strategy did not impair the flow of slave-produced commodities. It gave free reign to British industrial, commercial, and financial superiority and transmuted the formal equality of sovereign states into substantive inequality.[3]

Antislavery and the International Moral Order

Britain's campaign against the international slave trade provided the dimension of moral leadership that is a defining element of Britain's world-economic hegemony. In its effort to reconstruct interstate relations through diplomacy and international law based on mutual interest and formally equal rights among sovereign states, Britain attempted to establish antislavery as a norm of international conduct. Antislavery thus contributed to the construction of the interstate system as a moral order among states. It provided a standard of performance against which nations are still judged today, and is part of what Gong refers to as the "standard of civilization." This shared standard is a defining element of the "community of civilized states." It both enables reciprocal relations among states and provides the criteria for determining which states are within the "community of civilized states" and which are not. Consequently, the "standard of civilization" also provides justification for the "civilizing mission" (1984: 3–93).

Britain's antislavery campaign constructed British moral superiority and mobilized the "standard of civilization" as the criteria for creating a moral hierarchy among states, civilizations, and peoples. Here we may speak of the British state's appropriation of the moral capital of the abolitionist movement. The abolitionist leaders were ideologically constructed as the "saints" and abolitionism became a part of British national identity (Davis 1975: 446–50; Brown 2006: 3). The struggle against the international slave trade was conducted as a moral crusade (Huzzey 2012: 40–41, 64). The moral valuations entailed in the campaign against slavery were implicated in the production of colonial difference. At the level of the interstate system, its classification of peoples, civilizations, and states into categories of "civilized," "semicivilized," and "barbarous" created the criteria that disqualified African polities and peoples from participation in the community of nations and established conditions for "colonial tutelage" (Huzzey 2012: 52–53).[4] Antislavery thus justified the "civilizing mission" and provided the rationale for subsequent colonizing projects in Africa and Asia (Huzzey 2012: 65).

Further, the claims to moral superiority embodied in the antislavery campaign shaped the "standard of civilization" in ways that allowed Britain to apply moral judgments to the internal regimes of American slave societies and the colonialism of others without intervening directly in their affairs. Antislavery was not only a question of slavery, it was deployed as a universal moral and civilizational criterion for the judgment not only of rival states, but of whole societies and peoples (Huzzey 2012: 46). In Palmerston's view, the Portuguese were "habitually addicted to the slave trade." "Of all European nations," he commented elsewhere, they were "the lowest in the moral scale" (Bethell 1970: 109). Similarly, Spanish indifference if not hostility to abolition of the slave trade was evidence of their lack of humanity: "The word is not understood by a Spaniard. . . . Appeal then to the humanity of such a nation in favor of a race which they look upon as mere beasts of the field" (cited in Murray 2002: 99).

Within an international regime of formal political equality between sovereign states, antislavery created a regime of moral and cultural inequality. It established a normative standard for the behavior of states, societies, and peoples. The application of this standard enabled Britain to establish claims to moral superiority and to construct the moral and cultural backwardness of slaveholding societies. Within this hierarchical order, Britain asserted its claim to moral leadership of the reorganized state system. Through antislavery, Britain defined itself as exemplar and arbiter of civilized behavior among states. British liberalism, tempered by the moral fervor of evangelical Protestantism, was construed as the social, cultural, and political standard to which other societies were pressured to conform. Britain was thus able to regulate and manipulate membership in the "community of nations" and assert its hegemony over the interstate system.

Conclusion

The British campaign to abolish the international slave trade played an important role in integrating the newly independent states of the Americas into the interstate system and furthering British hegemony over the world-economy. The campaign ended the trans-Atlantic slave trade and pressured, in diverse ways, national regimes of chattel slavery. However, antislavery, and the fundamental concepts of slavery and freedom embedded in it, were deeply implicated in power politics, understandings of sovereignty and interstate relations, and the formation of an unequal global order. The campaign to end the slave trade operated in distinct but intertwined registers of politics, law, culture, and economy. By establishing structures of international law, normative values, and rules of conduct, antislavery disciplined sovereignty and defined modes of interaction between states. It thus helped to establish a legal-political structure that ordered the relations between sovereign states of the Atlantic and shaped them into a "community of states." However, while it recognized formal equality among states, British antislavery created substantive economic, political, cultural, and moral hierarchies. In so doing, it provided a stable institutional framework that facilitated the flow of commodities across national boundaries and the reformation of the world market. It was the instrument for the diffusion and hardening of cultural and racial difference under the tutelage of the British imperial state and evangelical Protestantism. It produced and reproduced "colonial difference" in diverse contexts and became a mechanism that promoted colonial and neocolonial strategies.

The abolition of the slave trade deserves to be examined as a subject that is both complex and important. To treat it within the simple antinomy between humanitarian concerns and material interest is far from adequate. In many ways such approaches reproduce the problematic of the apologetic imperial histories of the nineteenth and early twentieth centuries that deploy British antislavery to justify Britain's claims that its own colonialism in Africa and Asia was a disinterested and benevolent civilizing mission that benefitted the "backward peoples." Antislavery, abolition of the slave trade, and slave emancipation were major achievements of the Age of Revolution. That antislavery forms part of the standard of civilization and contributes to our conceptions of international law and of human rights is equally important, particularly as slavery becomes more ubiquitous and assumes more diverse forms today. Recognition of these problems obliges us to develop more sophisticated analytical and interpretative frameworks for studying slavery and antislavery, ones capable of addressing the comprehensive scope and complexity of the political transformation of the interstate system and the world-economy of the nineteenth century.

Notes

1. Having secured general agreements to abolish the slave trade and condemning slavery at Vienna and in various bilateral agreements, Britain's strategy was to pressure countries to do in practice what they had agreed to do in principle. Britain thus gained the high ground. The terms of the debate shifted in favor of antislavery. Liberal, antislavery elements formed within the slave zones, and its opponents no longer justified slavery as a civilizing force that saved Africans from barbarism and converted them to Christianity. Rather, they defended it as a necessary evil and adopted a gradualist position on abolition, asserting that slavery, and by extension the slave trade, would have to be maintained out of necessity until an alternative labor force could be secured (Alexandre 2000: 69–70; Bethell 1970: 40–41).

2. Thomas Babbington MacCauley's statement on the occasion of the removal of the sugar duties in 1845 is relevant here: "My special obligations with respect to Negro slavery ceased when slavery itself ceased in that part of the world for the welfare of which I, as a member of this House, was accountable." He refused to turn the fiscal code of the country into a penal code for the purposes of correcting vices in the institutions of independent states, or the tariff into "an instrument for rewarding the justice and humanity of some foreign governments and punishing the barbarity of others" (cited in Eric Williams 1944: 193).

3. See the discussion of "the internalization of the external" (Cardoso and Faletto 1979: 8–28).

4. Palmerston felt that "the Law of Nations governed the relations between European and American states and was not applicable to 'half naked and uncivilized' Africans who

should be compelled to abandon the slave trade where they were too barbarous to sign anti–slave trade treaties" (cited in Bethell 1970: 185–86).

Works Cited

Alexandre, Valentim. 2000. *Velho Brasil, novas Áfricas: Portugal e o Império (1808–1975)*. Porto, Portugal: Afrontamento.

Arrighi, Giovanni. 1994. *The Long Twentieth Century: Money, Power, and the Origins of Our Times*. London: Verso.

Beiguelman, Paula. 1978. "The Destruction of Modern Slavery: A Theoretical Issue." *Review* 2 (1): 71–80.

Bethell, Leslie. 1970. *The Abolition of the Brazilian Slave Trade*. Cambridge, UK: Cambridge University Press.

Brown, Christopher Leslie. 2006. *Moral Capital: Foundations of British Abolitionism*. Chapel Hill: University of North Carolina Press.

Cardoso, Fernando Henrique, and Enzo Faletto. 1979. *Dependency and Development in Latin America*. Berkeley: University of California Press.

Davis, David Brion. 1975. *The Problem of Slavery in the Age of Revolution, 1770–1823*. Ithaca, NY: Cornell University Press.

Dehio, Ludwig. 1962. *The Precarious Balance: Four Centuries of the European Power Struggle*. New York: Vintage.

Gong, Gerrit W. 1984. *The Standard of "Civilization" in International Society*. Oxford, UK: Clarendon Press.

Gramsci, Antonio. 1971. *Selections from the Prison Notebooks*. New York: International Publishers.

Hobsbawm, Eric J. 1990. *Industry and Empire: From 1750 to the Present Day*. Harmondsworth, UK: Penguin Books.

Huzzey Richard. 2012. *Freedom Burning: Anti-Slavery and Empire in Victorian Britain*. Ithaca, NY: Cornell University Press.

Kielstra, Paul Michael. 2000. *The Politics of Slave Trade Suppression in Britain and France, 1814–48: Diplomacy, Morality and Economics*. New York: Palgrave.

Mattos, Ilmar Rohloff de. 1994. *O tempo Saquarema: A formação de estado Imperial*. Rio de Janeiro, Brazil: Ed. Access.

Moore, Jason W. 2000. "Sugar and the Expansion of the Early Modern World-Economy: Commodity Frontiers, Ecological Transformation, and Industrialization." *Review* 23 (3): 409–33.

Murray, David R. 2002. *Odious Commerce: Britain, Spain, and the Abolition of the Cuban Slave Trade*. Cambridge, UK: Cambridge University Press.

Salles, Ricardo. 2008. *E o Vale era o escravo: Vassouras, século XIX: Senhores e escravos no coração do Império*. Rio de Janeiro: Civilização Brasileira.

Schmidt-Nowara, Christopher. 1999. *Empire and Antislavery: Spain, Cuba, and Puerto Rico, 1833–1874*. Pittsburgh, PA: University of Pittsburgh Press.

Temperley, Howard. 1972. *British Antislavery, 1833–1870*. Columbia: University of South Carolina Press.

Tomich, Dale W. 1990. *Slavery in the Circuit of Sugar: Martinique and the World Economy, 1830–1848*. Baltimore, MD: Johns Hopkins University Press.

———. 2004. *Through the Prism of Slavery: Labor, Capital, and World Economy*. Lanham, MD: Rowman & Littlefield.

Wagley, Charles. 1960. "Plantation America: A Cultural Sphere." In *Caribbean Studies: A Symposium*, edited by Vera Rubin. Seattle: University of Washington Press, 3–13.

Wallerstein, Immanuel M. 1984. "The Three Instances of Hegemony in the History of the Capitalist World-Economy." In *The Politics of the World-Economy: The States, the Movements, and the Civilizations*. Cambridge, UK: Cambridge University Press, 37–46.

Williams, Eric. 1944. *Capitalism and Slavery*. Chapel Hill: University of North Carolina Press.

International Proslavery

The Politics of the Second Slavery

Rafael Marquese and Tâmis Parron

The Global Impact of the American Civil War

In January 1867, after criticizing a Catholic Priest, a Brazilian polemicist and supporter of Protestantism offered a global analysis of one of the main challenges faced by the Brazilian Empire: how to handle the fate of slavery in his country, after the Civil War led to its abolition in the United States. He stated that "Brazil and Cuba kept slavery in the shadow of the United States, a powerful nation to which no other people in the world would dare to impose any condition of its political existence. But ultimately the question of slavery was discussed, disputed, and sentenced within that country, and no foreign country demanded the freedom of its slaves; it was a sole decision of that nation: one part submitted the other and slavery disappeared in the United States. Therefore in Brazil and Cuba slavery *has no more reason to exist—it is a question of time!*" ([Abreu e Lima] 1867: 326).

These words are particularly surprising because they clearly expose the limits of independence in a period marked by national sovereignties. According to the author's argument, since Brazil and Spain were not political or economic powers, they could not curb the pressures of international abolitionism; consequently, they should initiate emancipationist legislative processes themselves to adapt to the international order that emerged in the aftermath of the Civil War. The conclusive conjunction *therefore* (a key word in the quotation) assumed that slavery in the nineteenth century was an institution regulated at the national level, but conditioned by the international context. It is an accurate assumption. If states wanted to be sovereign regarding slavery, they should start by recognizing the limits of their own sovereignty.

The interpretation defended by Abreu e Lima did not wither with the passing of the nineteenth century. The historiography on Cuba and Brazil has highlighted for a long time the major role of the American Civil War in initiating a crisis of slavery in both countries. Historians have stressed how the war not only permanently banned the transatlantic slave trade to the Caribbean island, but was also linked to the emergence of the antislavery movement in Puerto Rico and Spain, to the outbreak of the first Cuban war of independence, and in turn to the process that led to the passing of the Moret Law in 1870 (Murray 1980: 298–326; Schmidt-Nowara 1999; Guerra y Sánchez 1971: 589–90, Scott 1991: 65–66). For the Brazilian case, the scholarship explains how the U.S. event directly stimulated the early debates on the project of a free womb law, which was enacted as imperial law in 1871 (Bandeira 2007: 155–61; Conrad 1975: 88–100; Pena 2001; Chalhoub 2003: 139–42; Salles 2008: 79–110). Despite all their different theoretical and methodological perspectives, historians seem to be reaching a relative consensus on the centrality of the American Civil War in ending slavery in Cuba and Brazil and, consequently, in all the Western Hemisphere.

No one has systematically explored, however, the historical process that turned *a* civil war into *the* Civil War—in other words, the process that converted a domestic conflict into a great world event with an immediate and direct impact on a European monarchy and a New World empire. The historiography mentioned above provides part of the answer. Still, by treating Brazil and Cuba as isolated cases, scholars have not fully grasped the role of the wider forces that shaped Atlantic slavery between the 1820s and 1850s. Even recent efforts to evaluate the institution from a global perspective (Drescher 2009: 245–411) offer narratives that juxtapose, rather than substantially incorporate, the local outcomes of slavery in the United States, Brazil, and Cuba, seldom articulating these slave societies with each other or with the global processes that shaped them. We believe that an approach combining international dynamics and regional particularities, without looking at these poles as static and separate units of analysis, can provide a more adequate way to solve the problem presented here.

Herein lies the heuristic validity of the concept of *second slavery*. With this idea, Dale Tomich draws attention to the unified historical experiences of the U.S. republic, the Brazilian Empire, and the Spanish colony of Cuba. Usually considered the century of emancipation, the nineteenth century actually witnessed the heyday of black slavery in the New World, in terms of both the absolute numbers of slaves employed in plantations and the total value obtained through the exploitation of their labor. According to Tomich, "beneath the apparent uniformity of nineteenth-century slave emancipation we find complex and differentiated trajectories and outcomes that are traceable to the position of particular slave systems within the world economy" (Tomich 2004: 57). The changes brought by the advent of an industrial world-economy in the nineteenth century imposed on New World planters the need for continuous growth in the productivity of their slaves, without which they would run the risk of being excluded from the world market. The forces set in motion led to the collapse of the old producing areas in the British and French Caribbean, which had reached the limits of their productive capacity, while opening new opportunities for regions hitherto on the periphery of areas where New World slavery made sense economically. In this process, the destinies of Cuba, Brazil, and the southern United States became closely intertwined: their respective specialization in the large-scale production of sugar, coffee, and cotton reshaped their economies in a broad movement of mutually conditioned influences.

Despite all the richness of his analytical perspective, Tomich has not given due weight to the dimension of power in his original formulation of the concept; to put it another way, he did not explore the role of the political and diplomatic clashes of the nineteenth-century interstate system in making the new historical structure of slavery and producing its subsequent crisis after the American Civil

War. Highlighting the place of slavery in the reciprocal political relations among Brazil, Spain, and the United States will make more intelligible the crisis of the second slavery, which was spawned by the great U.S. military conflict. Our goal is not to assess the effects of the Civil War on other countries, but to explore the international articulations that assured that those effects would be felt in the Brazilian and Spanish monarchies.

At first glance, it may seem unfruitful to draw parallels between the political structures of the United States, Brazil, and Cuba from the 1820s to the 1850s, since they had very little in common. After all, the United States, which had been an independent republic for four decades, was marked by a federal arrangement that remained open to the incorporation of new states (which would result in an aggressive territorial expansion of the republic), and had a representative regime that not only allowed the simultaneous presence of national political parties containing relatively clear programmatic content in Congress, but also gradually evolved into a democracy based on racial distinctions. Brazil, a centralized monarchy that became independent only in 1822, fought against territorial fragmentation and built a representative system that had to cope with the difficulties of maintaining a regular exchange of power between political parties, as well as managing a voting system that involved a large range of actors, from white slave owners to free blacks and mulattoes. Cuba remained a colony, unlike all other continental territories in the Americas.

Thus, how can we approach the political dynamics of the United States, Brazil, and Cuba within a single framework? In addition to the fact that the nineteenth century was marked by the problem of nation-state building, two other key points apparently unified the political trajectory of these three regions: first, the decisive weight of slavery in each political order, and second, the emergence of the international antislavery movement, which was turned into a geopolitical weapon by Great Britain and conditioned their political outcomes.

To examine these points, this essay is divided into three parts. First, we present the local political responses of the United States, Brazil, and Cuba to the emergence of the international antislavery movement headed by Great Britain, which imposed new challenges by tightening the screws of the old, loose Westphalian system of international relations (Arrighi 1996: 47–58). We then look at the efforts to build an international proslavery movement, which aimed at unifying the U.S. Southern, Brazilian, and Cuban planter classes against the threat brought by the transatlantic alliance between British and Northern abolitionists. In the final section, we analyze the limits faced by this international proslavery movement, which were directly connected to the crisis of the historical structure of the second slavery.

Great Britain, International Antislavery, and National Political Systems

At the turn of the nineteenth century, political interactions among the United States, Brazil, and Cuba seemed mild compared to their later intensity. The forces that brought them together were related to the global economy—the opening of new consumer markets (including the United States itself, starting in the 1780s), the rising demand for tropical commodities in the North Atlantic, and the demise of Saint Domingue. Their political convergence accelerated after the decisive impact of the imperial strategies put into practice by Napoleon between 1802 and 1807. With the fiasco of Charles Leclerc's army in Saint Domingue (1802–1803) and the end of the French dream of a slave empire in the Gulf of Mexico, the United States, driven by the fear of sharing a border with French veterans of the Caribbean rebellion and motivated by the economic growth of Kentucky and Tennessee (two new states that exported their products along the Mississippi River), acquired the Louisiana Territory (1803) and became an imperial power (Fry 2002: 26–31; Meinig 1993: 23). The political effects of this transformation were substantial. Its architects, the Republicans from Virginia, concentrated enough power to crush Federalist positions across the country, encouraging the Northern belief that the republic was increasingly being dominated by slaveholders. Economically, the Louisiana Purchase opened vast lands to the cultivation of cotton, allowing the creation of an internal interstate slave trade based on the natural reproduction of slaves.

Without a slave empire in the Atlantic, France adopted a counteroffensive at the end of the period 1802–1807, promoting the Continental Blockade and the invasion of the Iberian Peninsula—an indirect way of regaining control over American dominions. These events eventually gave a new role to the slave zones of Cuba, Brazil, and the United States in the world arena. By stimulating independence in most Spanish colonies, Napoleon's conquest of Portugal and Spain allowed Cuban slave owners to politically project themselves into the structures of the Spanish Empire by reinforcing their loyalty to Fernando VII and becoming one of his few sources of income. Something similar happened in Brazil, the final destination of the Portuguese Crown after the attacks by Napoleon. The American colony, now a key part of the enlightened reforming plan to rehabilitate the Portuguese Empire, became its temporary center in 1808 and its definitive core in 1815. Finally, the Continental System, which led Britain to seize American vessels engaged in trade with France, was one of the sources of the Anglo-American War of 1812—with Southern war hawks gaining a notorious ascendancy over reluctant Northerners during its course.

If, on the one hand, the Napoleonic campaigns for control over the world-system contributed to turning these three slave regions into the political core of their respective states and giving them a new regional and global role, on the other hand, it posed internal and external challenges to the political arrangements that originally seemed to benefit them. Solutions to these dilemmas, gradually worked out during the 1820s and 1830s, were reached within the national structures of the United States, Brazil, and Cuba and Spain. However, in the face of the abolitionist experiences of the 1830s, strongly inspired by universal claims, new arrangements were tested, this time on an international level. Let us consider these two-step answers on a case-by-case basis.

During the Continental Blockade, unilateral searches of American ships by British gunboats and the subsequent impressment of American sailors to the Royal Navy produced a series of retaliations (U.S. trade embargoes against England starting in 1807, and subsequently the Anglo-American War of 1812) that brought anti-slavery rhetoric to the center of relations between both countries and established an important precedent for the U.S. refusal to cooperate in the fight against the transatlantic slave trade, seen as a manifest sign of British imperialism. (Mason 2006: 87–105). During the conflict, the development of antislavery sentiment in the North—on the rise since the Louisiana Purchase—reduced U.S. political heterogeneity (East versus West, small states versus large states, mercantile interests vs. agrarian interests) to a more clearly defined South versus North axis. Unsurprisingly, the creation of new states after Louisiana gained statehood (1812) had to obey the golden rule of bilateral balance, leading to the simultaneous admission of slave and nonslave states, such as Mississippi and Indiana (1817) or Alabama and Illinois (1819). This pattern led to a great dispute over the incorporation of Missouri as a slave state, the so-called Missouri Crisis (1819–21), one of the most serious sectional conflicts before 1850. To avoid dissolving the Union, the radicalization of the pro- and antislavery positions in the federal Congress required a formal agreement between Southern and Northern representatives on the future extension of slavery in the U.S. territory (Mason 2006: 177–212). The Missouri Compromise would profoundly shift U.S. perceptions of their society and their government: slavery was perceived as a geographic, moral, political, and economic divider, while the first Republican Party was increasingly seen as being associated with Southern interests.

Besides the 1820 Compromise, the emergence of the Second Party System (1830s–1850s) contributed to smoothing over the tensions related to slavery that were brought about by the Missouri Crisis. As David Brion Davis suggests, the conflict "contributed to the creation of a national two-party system intended to contain and neutralize the kind of sectional discord that erupted in 1819" (Davis 2006: 279; see also Forbes 2007). Indeed, during this period, Democrats and Whigs organized on a national scale to avoid at all costs the transformation of slavery into a political issue on the federal level. Some historians argue that the balance between the parties secured the exercise of hegemonic power over the antebellum republic by Southern slaveholders (Ashworth 1995: 289–437). This hypothesis seems plausible when we remember that proslavery critics of the Second Party System, such as South Carolina nullifiers and states' righters, demanded a commitment to preserve slavery from both Democratic and Whig leaders to neutralize Northern radical abolitionists.

At this point, the role of Britain in configuring this political framework becomes clear. By placing the slavery issue at the center of Anglo-American relations during the War of 1812, and thus indirectly contributing to the Missouri Crisis, Britain intensified its role as a global antislavery actor in the 1830s. The radicalization of the British antislavery movement (with a transition from the gradual emancipation platform to immediatism), the abolition of slavery in the West Indies (with the beginning of the apprenticeship approved in August 1833), and the founding of the American Antislavery Society in December 1833 generated harsh reactions within the United States. These antislavery forces crystallized in the late 1830s with the establishment of a formal political alliance between North American and British abolitionists, unintentionally strengthening the power of slaveholding sectors within the United States in the 1840s. South Carolinians became the vanguard of the proslavery bloc, although its main political leaders distanced themselves from Jacksonian democracy (Rugemer 2008: 180–221; Maynard 1960; McDaniel 2006: 28–105; Sinha 2000). Great Britain came to be considered the "natural enemy" of the North American republic during most of the antebellum period (Greenberg 1985: 106–23).

Political actors in Brazil and Cuba offered different answers to the challenges faced by slave societies in the Atlantic world. The abolition of the transatlantic slave trade to British possessions in 1807 generated pressures on Portugal and Spain, as early as the following year, to adopt a similar measure regarding their American colonies. This pressure reached a new level after the end of the Napoleonic Wars. With the reestablishment of peace in Europe, the antislavery activism that had been part of the struggle against the transatlantic slave trade became an essential tool of British diplomacy. In the following five decades, its primary targets would be Portugal, independent Brazil, and Spain (basically Cuba). Having explored the links between the politics of slavery in Brazil and Cuba from 1790 to 1850 in a recent book (Berbel, Marquese, and Parron 2010), we will briefly highlight here two moments of their political responses to British pressure.

The first moment is the crisis of the Iberian Atlantic system, from the Napoleonic invasion of the Iberian Peninsula (1807) to the end of the independence wars in the Portuguese and Spanish Americas (1824). At this juncture, the political action of the Brazilian and Cuban planter classes was guided by three clear objectives: to keep the transatlantic slave trade alive, to ensure free connections to the world market, and to maintain their internal social orders. During the first constitutional experience of Cádiz (1810–1814), the main threats faced by Cuban slaveholders were brought by the opposition of liberal Gaditanians (members of Parliament in the Cortes of Cádiz) to the extension of free trade principles to the Spanish American provinces and, especially, by parliamentary plans to stop the transatlantic slave trade and emancipate slaves, which in turn stimulated conspiracies involving slaves and free men of color against slavery and Spanish colonialism. While the restoration of Fernando VII in 1814 stimulated movements for independence and the demise of the slave order in the American mainland, Cuban slaveholders saw an opportunity to obtain effective political and economic gains through direct negotiations with the monarch. The crisis of the Iberian Atlantic system occurred differently in Brazil because of the flight of the Portuguese royal family to America, but its final outcome was similar to that of its Cuban counterpart. During the 1810s, Brazil—elevated to part of a United Kingdom with Portugal and Algarves in 1815—demonstrated that it was possible to maintain the transatlantic slave trade despite British pressure, promoting full free trade and avoiding the social disruption caused by the revolutionary breakdown of the old imperial order. In fact, the policies regarding Brazilian slavery espoused during the reign of D. João VI became a model for Cuban planters, who used it to negotiate their position within the Spanish monarchy during the first absolutist reaction of Fernando VII (1814–1820).

In the second moment (1824–1837), the concentration of political and military power in the hands of the captain-general—granted by the Royal Decree of May 1825—gave the Cuban planters broader channels, which they would use to deal with the dangers of an eventual war of independence, such as the risk of slave revolts or British interference. The measure was implemented by Fernando

VII—restored to the Spanish throne as an absolutist monarch—in response to the demands of the Cuban slavocracy, who opposed the expansion of the colonial public sphere that had occurred during the constitutional experience of the Liberal Triennium (1820–1823). With the return of a representative government in the metropolis in 1836–1837, the so-called regime of omnimodous power (*régimen de las facultades omnímodas*) was perpetuated in Cuba through the active role played by the most important and powerful fraction of the Cuban planter class and the majority of metropolitan deputies, who fought the opposition groups who were willing to replace the regime by a constitutional text that they wanted to extend to Cuba. Thus a peculiar political equation emerged in which colonial proslavery and anticonstitutional groups allied themselves to metropolitan constitutionalists (some of whom were antislavery proponents) to preserve, at the same time, imperial unity, colonial slavery, and the illegal transatlantic slave trade.

Both groups ensured that the representative government on the Iberian Peninsula would coexist with the exclusion of colonial representation in the Spanish Parliament, the consequent suspension of the Spanish Constitution overseas, and the suppression of provincial deputations. While the principles adopted in 1837 generated new political tensions, they also provided the institutional framework for the modernization and growth of the Cuban slave economy. These changes marked the conclusion of the construction process of the "Second Spanish Empire" (Schmidt-Nowara 1999), an arrangement that emerged as a reaction to British antislavery pressure and guaranteed the maintenance of an illegal transatlantic slave trade. Politically, the Second Spanish Empire was characterized by the absence of parliamentary representation for colonial subjects, a racially defined citizenship, and the biaxial composition of "constitutional areas" (the peninsular provinces) and "nonconstitutional areas" (overseas territories). The most striking feature of this pact is that it turned black slavery into its ultimate justification, leading those colonial groups who were eager to participate in a representative regime to link slavery to the restriction of their own rights. Every effort to revise this imperial pact would then have to assume either an anticolonial and antislavery stand or an annexationist proslavery discourse, as particularly evidenced in the reformism of José Antonio Saco and his group.

After the 1820s, the Brazilian Empire presented a notably distinct trajectory from Cuba. Its independence in 1822 opened up a new opportunity for British anti–slave trade interference. Since the Anglo-Portuguese Treaty of 1817, signed by the former king of Portugal and Brazil, the issue had been left untouched at the diplomatic level. In exchange for formal recognition of the new sovereign state, Britain demanded from the new emperor of Brazil, Dom Pedro I, an effective commitment to suppress the slave trade. The issue was solved only in 1826, with the signing of an agreement to end of the transatlantic slave trade. The traffic should be suppressed within a three-year period after the ratification of the treaty by Great Britain, which took place in March 1827. The diplomatic quarrel, which eroded the political capital of Brazil's first emperor and contributed to his down-fall in 1831, was closely monitored by slave traders and planters. The increase in African imports during the second half of the 1820s clearly expressed the coeval apprehension that the traffic in human beings would be effectively ended in 1830.

Empowered by the fall of Dom Pedro I and seeking to reaffirm Brazilian sovereignty, a national parliament approved a penal law in November 7, 1831, that contained draconian measures to combat the slave trade: Africans introduced into Brazilian territory after that date should be automatically freed and returned to Africa; offenders of the law—sellers or buyers—would be subjected to criminal prosecution; and denunciations of illegal landings or possession of illegally introduced slaves could be made by any individual, including the illegally enslaved people themselves. According to the letter of the law, therefore, planters buying Africans in the illegal transatlantic business would be subject to harsh punishments. Although usually reputed to be a "*lei para inglês ver*" (a "law for the English to see," in other words, a law passed for the sake of appearances), the original intent of the November 7 decree was clearly to extinguish the transatlantic slave trade, and contemporaries read it in this way. Between 1831 and 1834, slave landings substantially decreased, to their lowest level in Brazil since the end of the seven-teenth century. The slave trade became somewhat residual.

Soon, however, the great reforms of the Ato Adicional (1834)—a series of constitutional amendments—and the abolition of slavery in the British Caribbean redefined Brazilian politics. After 1835, a profound reversal of the trends described above took place. After a period of downturn, proslavery actors began to voice their views in public spaces, and a broad coalition of former moderate liberals, former supporters of D. Pedro I, and large slave owners of Center-South Brazil—the very basis of the future Conservative Party—advocated the nullification of the 1831 law. In this two-way movement between the demands of the master class and the efforts to woo voters by this new political group, coffee planters from the Paraíba Valley (the most dynamic economic area of the Brazilian Empire in the following decades) played a central role by calling for the reopening of the transatlantic slave trade through direct political pressure and actions in the public space. By bringing this issue to the center of their political campaigns after 1835, the agents of the Regresso Conservador, or Conservative Reaction (later known as the *saquaremas*), indicated to slave dealers and coffee and sugar planters that they would be given a green light to resume the infamous trade. The strategy worked as expected: while nearly 240,000 illegally enslaved Africans were disembarked in ports of Center-South Brazil in the second half of the 1830s, a number that rose to more than 300,000 in the following decade, the *saquaremas* imposed their agenda on imperial policy. The institutional framework that Brazilian conservatives erected between the 1830s and 1850s proved to be as solid and enduring as the biaxial structure of the Second Spanish Empire and the Second Party System of the United States.

International Proslavery

As we have seen, the outcome of the Missouri Compromise, the regime of omnimodous power, and the crisis of the *Primeiro Reinado* (the reign of Dom Pedro I) in Brazil were political events related, to varying degrees, to the problem of expanding slavery in politically unstable scenarios. In all three cases, their respective institutions put the power over the future of the slave system within reach of the owners, in a clear attempt to obtain what may be called the "governability" of slavery. The specific forms of those arrangements, however, were conditioned by the political culture, social composition, and government structures peculiar to each region. In the United States, the congressional initiative was stalled by conceiving of that institution as a divided body that represented a slave society (the South) and a nonslave society (the North). In Cuba, the powers were concentrated in the hands of a military figure placed at the center of a slave-owning class, becoming, therefore, subject to its constant influence. In Brazil, decision-making authority shifted from the executive (initially strengthened by the 1824 Charter) to the legislature, now perceived as the body representing the interests of a slave society.

Before the 1830s, these three slaveholding spaces created legal frameworks and broad domestic arrangements to meet local impasses and the challenges brought by the interstate system managed by Great Britain. Each country certainly looked at the events in the other two and incorporated previous experiences in a cumulative learning process, but there is no explicit evidence of support among them with regard to the international plan. After the 1830s, however, it is possible to identify not only the domestic developments of the Second Party System in the United States, the Second Spanish Empire, and the Brazilian party system under the *saquarema* hegemony, but also the respective articulations of these arrangements with the evolution of the international antislavery movement headed by Britain. More than mutual imitation, the historical actors of the New World slave zones foresaw the construction of coordinated actions against a common enemy. Emulation gave way to cooperation.

The first indication of this new conjuncture was the replacement of the British and French Empires with the U.S. republic as a model of governmental decisions about slavery. On July 17, 1839, during a debate in the Brazilian Chamber of Deputies about the connivance of high *saquaremas* authorities with the resumption of the illegal traffic, Honorio Hermeto Carneiro Leão (future marquis of Paraná)—one of the main leaders of the ongoing conservative reaction and a coffee planter himself in the Paraíba Valley—referred to the persecution of abolitionists in the United States, suggesting that a similar conduct should be enforced in Brazil against those who publicly spoke out against slavery. The abolitionist experience, in other words, should be seen through the North American lens, rather than the British. "With the fury of abolitionists growing in that country in 1835 and

1836," he argued in the Parliament, "states with slaves opposed it, and the people of states without slaves understood that, judging the interests of the slave states to be threatened, they should not be mere spectators, but take the initiative to punish the abolitionists."[1] Although the local circumstances of antiabolitionist mobs in the U.S. North, marked by the desire to strengthen the racial divide between whites and free blacks, were distinct from local circumstances in Brazil with its fluid racial barriers, the speech by Carneiro Leão tried to demonstrate to the local groups who opposed the reopening of the transatlantic slave trade that the proslavery agents in the Brazilian Empire were not alone in the world arena.

The United States not only gradually became the central reference for other slave powers, it encouraged the convergence of actions with Cuba and Brazil. To explore all the relationships between global forces and national political processes on these issues is in itself a broad research agenda. For now, we would like to quickly explore the efforts to build an international proslavery movement during some critical occasions after the British global campaign against the transatlantic slave trade and slavery intensified.

The first moment was when British and North American antislavery movements formalized their transatlantic alliance. As David Turley suggests, "the decade from the mid-1830s to the mid-1840s was the high point of transatlantic abolitionism as a functioning international enterprise" (1991: 196–97). The period of Apprenticeship in the British Caribbean was closely monitored by proslavery defenders and abolitionists in the United States. With final emancipation in 1838 and the formation of a new antislavery society in Britain in 1839 (the British and Foreign Anti-Slavery Society, which expressed its internationalist platform already in its name), ties between abolitionists on both sides of the Atlantic solidified. Meeting in London in 1840, participants in the first World Antislavery Convention supported the aggressive military and diplomatic policy of Lord Palmerston against the transatlantic slave trade to Brazil and Cuba, defended the free-soil principle as an instrument of pressure against the U.S. domestic slave trade, and called for the abolition of slavery in Texas as a condition for the eventual recognition of its independence by Mexico and Great Britain. Two other social forces pressured the

British government. On one side, the British working classes struggled for better living conditions, including open access to colonial commodities, whose prices, under the West Indian monopoly, soared after the crisis that followed the end of the apprenticeship system (1838). On the other side, the West Indian lobby pressured the Crown for strong actions against Brazil and Cuba, which were direct competitors that, in a free-market environment, had a wide advantage because of their unlimited access to enslaved Africans (Drescher 2002: 158–78).

Under the pressure of these three groups (abolitionists, laborers, and West Indian planters), Great Britain adopted a new diplomatic behavior that led to the signing of the Treaty of London in December 1841 (trying to bring France, Russia, Prussia, and Austria to the right-of-search doctrine) and made efforts to include an emancipation clause in the new trade agreement with Brazil to replace the 1810 one (renewed in 1827, its expiration date was in 1842–44). At the same time, the Foreign Office suggested a series of measures to end the shortage of laborers in the British colonies, such as the proposal, made to the United States in 1842, to move American free blacks to the West Indies, or the confiscation of the enslaved Africans illegally shipped to Cuba or Brazil. At that moment, the performance of British abolitionist agitators in Cuba (in the famous Madden-Turnbull Affair) and the convening of a second world antislavery meeting convinced proslavery forces that a broad conspiracy to end slavery in the southern United States, Brazil, and Cuba had been set in motion. It seemed that after acknowledging the economic downturn caused by abolition in the 1830s, Great Britain—impelled by material, nonhumanitarian reasons—decided to confront its direct opponents.

Steven Mitton (2005), Gerald Horne (2007), Edward Rugemer (2008), and Matthew Karp (2011) have recently examined the efforts promoted by agents of the U.S. executive between 1841 and 1845 to build a united front with Brazil and Spain and Cuba to deal with Great Britain's antislavery actions. Rather than list all the diplomatic initiatives of the proslavery triumvirate represented by the journalist and diplomat Duff Green, Secretary of State Abel Upshur, and John C. Calhoun, it is worth drawing attention to the response to their efforts in Cuba and Brazil.

The first event representing the new constellation of forces in the global scenario took place in 1840. A few years earlier, U.S. ships taking slaves from Virginia and Maryland to the Gulf States lost their human cargo after severe weather forced them to stop at some British Caribbean colonies, where the free-soil principle had been enforced since 1833. Since railroads linking the Atlantic Coast to the Deep South had not been built in the 1830s as originally planned (especially after the financial panic of 1837), the coastal route continued to be the best way to supply labor to the cotton frontier. The coastal route should therefore be protected against seizures, it was argued, since these potential losses produced legal uncertainty in trade and raised insurance costs during a period when cotton prices were falling in the world market. John Calhoun managed to unanimously approve a protest motion in the U.S. Senate, stating that the U.S. Congress saw no difference between property in slaves and any other kind of property. The emancipation of U.S. slaves would be taken as a violation of international law and, as such, liable to retaliation. Calhoun knew that, by demanding unanimous approval from Congress, he was crafting a document to show not only to local actors, but also to the international community, the complete consensus of the American republic regarding its domestic institutions (Mitton 2005: 22–55; Karp 2011: 34–44).

It was not simply a coincidence that Calhoun's motion, approved by thirty-three votes to zero (with fifteen abstentions from antislavery representatives) immediately resonated in Cuba. Since 1840, the Spanish government in Cuba had been dealing with the increasingly aggressive tone of British diplomacy, which demanded the emancipation of enslaved Africans illegally disembarked in the colony after 1820—when the 1817 Anglo-Spanish treaty should have been implemented. One response to the increasing antislavery pressure promised to effectively suppress the transatlantic slave trade and prepare a new legal code that would stimulate the natural reproduction of slaves in Cuba. When Captain General Gerónimo Valdés asked twelve of the most prominent colonial slave owners to give their opinion of his project, one of them—Wenceslao de Villa Urrutia—did not hesitate to incorporate the recent maneuver by Calhoun in the United States to interdict the proposal:

The U.S. Senate has just deliberately inserted in one of its minutes related to servants belonging to U.S. citizens the word *slaves*, unusual in its Constitution and in all the Legislative and Federal Government documents, with the sole aim of showing to the powerful nation that tries to undermine and destroy slavery in certain countries that the U.S. Congress considers it a legal institution with all its consequences and that it is ready to support it and defend it against all kinds of attacks. Timely and exemplary action of national dignity that no single abolitionist vote dared to contradict! True Spaniards do not yield to anyone in possession of these qualities, and Cuba hopes that its government belongs to this group. (quoted in Tardieu 2003: 257)

The years between 1841 and 1845 were not easy for Brazil either. The period was marked by a tense renegotiation of the Anglo-Brazilian commercial treaty, which would have expired in 1842 but was extended until 1844. Great Britain's insistence on incorporation of a clause establishing the future emancipation of slaves in exchange for tariff concessions on Brazilian sugar fell like a bomb in the Brazilian Parliament. One representative, attuned to the antisystemic spaces that British hegemony created, contextualized the Brazilian position in the interstate system and suggested that since the country was not alone, it could remain irreducible in the renegotiation without fear of reprisals: "the British armed themselves against the Chinese and won, but should the same happen with Brazil? Would the United States and France consent in this blockade?" At the same time, prominent *saquaremas* such as Bernardo Pereira de Vasconcelos and João Manuel Pereira da Silva employed in their speeches in Parliament and in the Brazilian press the same proslavery arguments being espoused by Green, Upshur, Calhoun, and other Southern ultras to defend rapprochement between the United States and Brazil. The failure of the emancipation experiment in the British Caribbean, the economic collapse of the recently founded Latin American republics that had abolished slavery, and the British perfidy and hypocrisy demonstrated by its actions in Ireland and India were themes mobilized with the same purposes in the U.S. South and the Brazilian empire ([Pereira da Silva] 1845; see also Parron 2011: 208–19, 223–30).[2]

Evidence in the Brazilian diplomatic correspondence sent from London in 1843 shows the existence of mutual influences between the Green-Upshur-Calhoun plans to annex Texas as a means of confronting Britain and the *saquaremas* projects for maintaining the illegal transatlantic slave trade. The Brazilian agent responsible for renegotiating the commercial treaty (without accepting the emancipation clause) mentioned a meeting with a journalist allied to Calhoun and Hammond who was on an unofficial mission to London. Although the Brazilian emissary did not mention his name, his allusions indicated that the informant was Duff Green, who was then working as an "ambassador of slavery" in Europe. According to the Brazilian, Green

> came to me as a former acquaintance, and based on his words I was informed that he had also been charged with the task of talking about slave emancipation with all the influential people he dealt with. He told me that the procedure of the English government in wanting to entice Brazil and Cuba to emancipate their slaves worried too much the American government, which considered this procedure as an illicit intervention that England arrogated in the internal affairs of other peoples. He also told me that in order to avoid the effects of this intervention on the territory of Texas, the President of the United States was ready to present to the Congress a proposal to incorporate this Republic.[3]

In 1844, the argument of national control over the institution also guided the diplomatic instructions that Calhoun sent to the American representative to the Brazilian Empire, justifying the decision to annex Texas. In his letter, Calhoun stated that "it is our established policy not to interfere with the internal relations of any other country, and not to permit any other to interfere with ours." He then concluded: "Brazil has the deepest interest in establishing the same policy," since the "avowed policy of Great Britain is to destroy that relation [between the European and African races] in both countries and throughout the world. . . . To destroy it in either, would facilitate its destruction in the other" (Manning 1932:

127). These North American speeches were quickly incorporated by Brazilians. In a session of the Senate on July 3, 1845, Carneiro Leão unmistakably argued that the United States provided a model for dealing with antislavery voices and developing a positive defense of slavery in Brazil: "One of the elements of the existence of Brazilian society is slavery; this element cannot be destroyed without the destruction and damage of the same society. It should not be tolerated . . . to speak against an institution of Brazilian society that should last for many centuries, because it is expected that this society is governed by Brazilians, whose real and permanent interests will require the conservation of slavery for many centuries."[4]

With this ideological realignment of the world order, a move by U.S. diplomacy may have inflated the confident Brazilian refusal to sign a deal with Britain two days before the expiration of the antislave trade treaty of 1826 (ratified in 1827 and expected to expire in 1845). In the early 1840s, Brazilians had witnessed the dramatic Portuguese experience, which, after the sudden impact caused by Palmerston's Act of 1839, found a peaceful solution for the crisis with the establishment of a bilateral treaty in 1842 (Marques 1999). Its practical consequence was that the Portuguese flag could not be used in the illegal slave trade anymore. From the Brazilian point of view, this defeat had been largely counterbalanced by the signing of the Anglo-American Webster-Ashburton Treaty in 1842, interpreted by many as a victory. Unlike the Anglo-Portuguese treaty, this one prevented British vessels from stopping North American commercial ships—in other words, it did not grant the right of search to Great Britain. The early 1840s showed, therefore, that the old Portuguese metropolis was unable to openly defy Britain, and that the United States appeared to be the only power capable of doing it. To ignore the "perfidious Albion," as Brazil had done in 1845 by refusing to renew the anti–slave trade treaty, did not put at risk the legal corridor opened by Webster-Ashburton, and appeared as an act to reaffirm national sovereignty.

It is not surprising that U.S. capital, vessels, and, above all, the flag had an increasingly important role in the illegal slave trade to Brazil during the 1840s (Fehrenbacher 2001: 156–202; Marques 2010). In the face of this reconfiguration of the slave trade, and obviously aware that commerce—unlike the prescriptions of the liberal creed—depended on state intervention, Britain chose to attack the center of Brazilian imperial power through direct naval pressure (under the provisions of Aberdeen's Act of 1845) and efforts to internationally isolate the country. The weaknesses of an eventual alliance between the *saquaremas* and proslavery sectors in the United States became clear. If, on the one hand, the U.S. flag could protect slavers operating in the South Atlantic, largely because of the pervasive anti-British sentiment in the United States (which had an undeniably proslavery tone), on the other hand, the United States could not formally defend the illegal slave trade to Brazil in the world arena.

The military strategy employed by Great Britain against the South American empire could never be applied to Cuba. This is the other side of the international proslavery movement. Projects to annex the Spanish colony had circulated in the highest levels of the U.S. federal government since the Jefferson administration. These plans had some resonance in Cuba and were incorporated by Juan Bernardo O'Gavan in his defense of the slave trade presented to the Madrid Cortes in 1821. But it was not before the critical years of 1839–1843, when Cuban slaveholders were cornered by the actions of British abolitionists and racially subaltern sectors of the island (slaves and free men of color), that annexationism expanded. The equation seemed simple to Cuban masters: if Spain did not demonstrate the ability to curb the risks of an alliance between British abolitionists and Africans and their descendants in Cuba, their only choice would be to become allied to the largest slave power of the continent (Berbel, Marquese, and Parron 2010: 276–303).

Annexationism as a political movement waned after the Conspiracy of La Escalera (1843) and resurfaced right when Britain launched its decisive attack against the transatlantic slave trade to Brazil (1848–1851). The U.S. desire for the Texas, New Mexico, and California territories was fulfilled in the war against Mexico, which provided a concrete example of the military strength and political skills of the country and revived the hopes of annexationists in Cuba and the United States.

The reasons for the different British treatment given to Cuba and Brazil regarding the suppression of the transatlantic slave trade are clear. In 1852 Lord Stanley explained them to the head of the British Foreign Office, Lord Malmesbury:

"the alternative of giving in the case of Cuba orders similar to those which have been given by Palmerston and recalled by us in that of Brazil, is one approaching so nearly to the declaration of war." The inevitable consequence would be the annexation of the island by the United States. Lord Stanley's statement shows how the inclusion of Cuba in the North Atlantic geopolitical game was an enormous obstacle to ending the contraband slave trade to the island. According to his terms, "the difficulty is how to do this without exciting the jealousy, or encouraging the aggression of the U.S. If you remove the few vessels that occasionally touch at the Havana, you make known your difference to the Americans, and they are thus encouraged in their designs. If on the other hand, you establish a Blockade or anything approaching to one, you excite in America a cry of 'British interference' and instantly it is believed you are going to seize upon Cuba" (Murray 1980: 230–31). Slave-owning groups in Cuba and in the United States were fundamental in creating the field of forces that neutralized British attacks, maintaining the colony within the Spanish orbit despite annexationist pressures: while the slave owners in Cuba flirted with annexation to the United States if Spain yielded to Britain, U.S. slave-owning groups promised to incorporate the neighboring colony if Britain pressed Spain. Although each group had an immediate interlocutor (the Cubans had the Spanish monarchy; the Americans, Great Britain), their union was crucial to protect, through indirect means, the continuity of the illegal transatlantic slave trade to the island.

Something similar happened in the Brazilian Empire, whose interprovincial slave trade was steadily growing after the closing of the contraband slave trade. This internal trade already existed before 1850, but it was only after that year that it made considerable headway in Brazil, rapidly reaching a scale comparable in relative terms to its U.S. counterpart (Slenes 2004). In 1851 a crucial episode concerning the institutional stability of this new commercial branch took place when the Royal Navy seized the ship *Piratinim* as a suspected slaver on the Brazilian coast. The vessel, however, had been employed in the domestic slave trade between Bahia and São Paulo. More than one hundred slaves were freed and taken to the British West Indies, generating great fears about the consequences that the case could have on the Brazilian economy and social order. At the height of the crisis, Paulino José Soares de Sousa—foreign minister of a *saquarema* cabinet at the time—considered using the U.S. flag to protect Brazilian coastal shipping. His threat was not fortuitous: the Brazilian representative evidently had in mind not only the smuggling practices across the Atlantic, but above all the previous U.S. experience in confronting Britain to protect its coastal slave trade carried through the upper South–Florida Strait–Gulf of Mexico route. The action of Paulino Soares, combined with the effective enforcement of a new law against the illegal transatlantic trade by the Brazilian government, led the Foreign Office to retreat (Parron 2011: 245–49).

The U.S. South became, in the first half of the 1850s, the political and demographic model for those who, like the *saquaremas*, conceived of slavery as the best way to insert Brazil into modernity. Speeches in the Brazilian press and Parliament recalled the example given by the United States, which, without the assistance of the transatlantic slave trade, successfully expanded its slave population based on improvement in slave management (Marquese 2004: 286–88). In the Brazilian Council of State, politicians praised the so-called Compromise of 1850 in the United States, which counterbalanced the polemical acceptance of California as a free state with pro-South measures, including a stronger law to surrender runaway slaves and the definition of a safer western border for Texas. In the words of the Marquis of Olinda, a sugar planter in Pernambuco and chairman of a Council of State committee that issued a report analyzing a project of gradual emancipation recently submitted to the government, "there is this people who live in the Northern part of our continent, who have not yet dared to change their legislation on slavery, and who are giving us the most authentic testimony of indulgence that the legislator should maintain with the ideas and interests of the governed; and all this despite the efforts of a huge and well built party seeking for these reforms, reforms that are highly supported by a large part of the nation."[5]

However, contrary to what Olinda had predicted, the Compromise of 1850 did not curb the growing secessionism of domestic politics in the United States. One year after his memorandum, the senator from Illinois, Stephen Douglas, called for the suspension of the Missouri Compromise, leaving to local settlers the power to decide what system should be adopted in the new western territories. The strategy, which sought to eliminate abolitionist pressure on Congress and encourage the settlement of new areas, eventually stimulated the creation of the second Republican Party and the consequent escalation of tensions that led to the outbreak of the Civil War (Schoen 2009: 212).

The radicalization of the militant proslavery sectors of the South—whose international dimension became even sharper—was a key element in this outcome. Its two maximum expressions, although not necessarily convergent, were related to Cuba and Brazil. On the one side, Southern Fire-Eaters renewed the annexationist movement; on the other side, they started a campaign to reopen the transatlantic slave trade to the United States. During the 1850s, especially after 1854 (when the Kansas-Nebraska Act was passed), the annexation of Cuba became a sectional matter, conceived in the Southern states as a means to counterbalance the growing antislavery power in the North. Annexing Cuba—through filibustering, adventures, or purchase—would increase the weight of the South within the Union or lay the basis for the creation of an autonomous slave empire in the circum-Caribbean area. The developments in 1854–1855 produced a profound discomfort in Spain toward Southern designs, especially after all the publicity gained by the Ostend Manifesto, which was leaked to the European press by one of its authors in October 1854. This infamous document, which predicted a war for Cuba if Spain refused to sell it to the United States, would also serve as a propaganda tool for the recently formed Republican Party, which denounced the progress of the Slave Power Conspiracy to Northern audiences. When, in 1859, President Buchanan tried to put the purchase of Cuba on the Congressional agenda again, his project was abandoned because of the negative reaction of Spain (supported by Britain) and the fierce opposition of Republicans (May 2002: 46–76).

The reopening of the transatlantic slave trade, in turn, was impelled by the strong demand for slave labor in the states of the Deep South, which were going through a cotton boom and a railway revolution in the 1850s, and by the radicalized platform of Fire-Eaters, who saw the measure as a means to openly confront the opponents of slavery and thus boost the movement for secession (Takaki 1971). According to some speeches in the South, reopening the traffic could benefit not only the United States, but also Brazil, which appeared as a potential frontier to Southern slaveholders. Such an approximation was facilitated by the consecutive appointment of two Southerners, William Trousdale (Tennessee) and Richard Meadde (Virginia), as U.S. ministers to Rio de Janeiro for almost a decade, from 1853 to 1861. In the *Correio Mercantil*, one of the leading newspapers at the time, would-be novelist José de Alencar wrote that closer trade relations and policies between both countries would give birth to "a great American political thought, which in the future will drive the destinies of the New World and put an end to European intervention" (Alencar 2004: 336). These words would have pleased Calhoun, who had suggested a decade earlier that Brazil and the United States should have a common anti-European foreign policy.

When Meadde formally presented a proposal for an international alliance between the United States republic in the Northern Hemisphere and the Brazilian monarchy in the Southern Hemisphere based on their common institution of black slavery, a Brazilian representative, praising that "rare and notable manifestation" of international friendship, regretted that the Brazilian government thought that "everything had been done through the prudent and delicate answer given by the monarch to that minister."[6] It is not hard to understand why the government's response to Meadde was so "prudent and delicate" instead of dazzling and loud. The memory of the serious military-diplomatic crisis of 1848–1851 was still fresh, and U.S. projects to open the Amazon Valley for North American colonists were certainly unwelcome: what had happened to Mexico, after all, was recent too. Even in the U.S. South, many proslavery advocates rejected projects to reopen the transatlantic slave trade, arguing that it was a risky *boutade*, or venture, for the security of the slave states. This was in fact a correct evaluation. The pro–slave trade campaign and actions led by South Carolina politicians and journalists in 1859 gave impetus to the Republican Party in the North and, therefore, to the presidential election of Abraham Lincoln (Luz 1968; Sinha 2000: 173–80).

International Proslavery and Its Limits

Some of the most ardent Southern proslavery ideologues were responsible for the efforts to build an international proslavery movement. In terms of doctrine, they were the only master class of the Americas who formulated the idea of a hemispheric alliance between slaveholders from the U.S. South, Brazil, and Cuba. Does this mean that we should agree with current assessments that, among all slave societies of the New World, only the U.S. South defended the institution in positive terms?

Our answer is negative. There was in Brazil and Cuba a large set of ideas employed to defend slavery: the idea that bondage produced citizens in Brazil; the perception—contrary to the basic claims of political economy—that slave labor was cheaper and more productive than its free counterpart in regions of open frontier; the perception that the abolitionist experiment in the British West Indies had been an economic failure; the definition of slavery as a tool for progress; the comparisons between the life conditions of slaves and European free workers; the condemnation of British imperialism in the Far East; the denunciations of Irish poverty; the characterization of abolitionism as a radical movement that was equivalent to socialism. By outlining these similarities, it is possible to analyze some of the differences caused by local events and global processes. In the absence of a continuing polarization of the local political arena, such as had occurred in the United States, Brazilian and Cuban spokesmen were not compelled to articulate those ideas in a radical way, as Southerners had done. In the Spanish Empire, the annexationist movement became stronger only when distrust of the central government increased. While it did not sound as extreme as the Fire-Eaters who pledged secessionism in the South, its attitudes regarding how the government should protect slavery were quite the same. In Brazil, on the contrary, where polarization over slavery never took place on such a large scale, the set of proslavery ideas never took the form of extreme political actions and thoughts.

Far from being merely formal, this difference can be better understood when considered in light of the nineteenth-century interstate system. The nature of proslavery discourse in the South and the projection of the United States into the international arena through its successful annexation of other North American territories produced a space of relative autonomy in the interstate system that was vital to the survival of slavery in peripheral countries such as Brazil and the Spanish Empire. It could not have been different: the people who were heard in London (from a militarily relevant state that defeated Britain itself twice) and provided the main input of the Industrial Revolution were not the coffee planters of the Paraiba Valley or the sugar planters of Western Cuba, but the white, Protestant planters who were members of an English cultural community and produced cotton in the U.S. South. While Brazilian and Hispanic-Cuban actors responded to their immediate challengers (especially from Great Britain) through their local presses and diplomatic channels, proslavery sectors in the U.S. South also sought to operate in the international sphere, publishing writings destined for foreign audiences in the hope of reversing the gradual expansion of an antislavery consensus in the West.

To put it in another way: the audacious actions by Southerners—stimulated by their national quarrels, by the centrality of cotton in the industrial world-economy, and by the international strength of their state—assured the stability of slavery in other spaces. The Southern behavior made strong defenses of slavery in Brazil and Cuba unnecessary, since it inhibited emancipation projects in both spaces and, on an international level, curbed the diplomatic pressures against the slave trade and slavery. This observation shows the need to break with the internal-external categories in the analysis of the national state-building processes, since all of them were formed in the unified arena of the modern-world system, which was simultaneously global and local (Hopkins 1982).

A few concrete examples are provided by key proslavery politicians such as Honório Hermeto Carneiro Leão, Paulino José Soares de Sousa, Juan Bernardo O'Gavan, and Wenceslao Villa-Urrutia, who praised the strength of slavery in the United States as a way to confront their opponents in the Brazilian and Spanish Empires. These convergences were also recognized by a resentful Palmerston in the mid-1850s. He confessed that sooner or later Great Britain would have to "give way step by step to the North Americans on almost every disputed matter . . . except the maintenance of our own Provinces and of our West Indian Islands" (Schoen 2009: 218). This was the heyday of the United States slave power. But if this process—viewed with resignation in London—infused the Brazilian and Cuban planters with hope, it also faced some nearly insurmountable obstacles.

In the decade before the Civil War, the two basic modes used to reproduce slave relations on a large scale—the illegal transatlantic slave trade and the expanded natural growth of the slave population—had in the United States a model of maximum efficiency. These actions provided the material basis for proposals of the U.S. proslavery vanguard for an international proslavery movement (most clearly developed, on a theoretical plane, by South Carolina's John C. Calhoun), in which slave countries would help each other against the abolitionist interventionism of European powers. The greatest shortcoming of this ideology, however, resided precisely in the inability of its proponents to formally transform the international proslavery program into a consistent agenda. Its achievements were limited to the contingent practices of each space; proslavery groups from the United States, Brazil, and Cuba never met with each other in world conventions, such as those held in 1840 and 1843, or established an organizational epicenter equivalent to London. Charleston was never capable of attracting the master classes from Brazil and Cuba.

This failure was caused by two limits. The first was the international division of labor itself. The proslavery militants of the U.S. South entered the Civil War motivated by their belief in the power of King Cotton, predicting that the military conflict would be quickly resolved because of the dependence of northern U.S. and European industrial centers on the supply of cotton provided by the South. The logic of competition between the producing zones of raw material in the world market, however, led to the worldwide web of cotton production being reconstituted during the Civil War, weakening the diplomatic and political position of the Confederate States of America. This process involved a potential ally of the Confederacy: along with the growth of the cotton trade in other parts of Latin America, Africa, and Asia, the resumption of Brazilian cotton exports between 1862 and 1865 contributed to the Union victory (Schoen 2009; Beckert 2004).

The second limit was directly related to the first: the place of slavery in the interstate system of the nineteenth century. To cope with Great Britain and the rise of Northern abolitionism, the international proslavery movement that emerged in the U.S. South had an undeniably imperialist nature, generating strong resistance in Spain, Cuba, and Brazil, where local actors had to choose between guaranteeing the survival of their systems of work or their own government regimes. These anxieties were also stimulated by racist Southerners' negative view of Latin peoples. The antislavery internationalist movement was, in this sense, much more effective. The British militancy against the transatlantic slave trade became a powerful weapon for the reorganization of diplomatic relations and the spaces of global flows in a way that the U.S. South could never replicate, subordinated as they became to those same flows.

During the crisis of 1860–1861, Southern proslavery sectors inaccurately assessed the international correlation of forces. The coexistence of slavery in all three American spaces created a stability that was mutually conditioned, but that had not evolved sufficiently to provide a platform for a concerted political action. In its moment of truth, the Confederacy needed its independence recognized by Britain, rather than by Brazil or Spain, monarchies that had little bargaining power in the interstate system of the nineteenth century. The Confederate States of America went to war alone, but when they sank, they took with them the Brazilian Empire and the Spanish rule over Cuba—as well as their dearest dreams of perpetuating black slavery.

Notes

1. *Annaes do Parlamento Brazileiro: Câmara dos Srs. Deputados* (ACD). Rio de Janeiro: Typ. da Viúva Pinto e Filho, 1884, seção de 17 de julho de 1839, t. II, p. 336–37.

2. *Anais do Senado* [AS], 25 a 27 de abril de 1843: 346–96.

3. "Ofícios da missão especial em Londres, 1843, de José de Araújo Ribeiro a Paulino José Soares de Souza, 23 de novembro de 1843 e 28 de dezembro de 1843," Arquivo Histórico do Itamaraty, códice 271/4/6.

4. AS, 3 de julho de 1845: 217.

5. "Extrato de um Parecer da Seção dos Negócios do Império do Conselho de Estado, de 4 de Fevereiro de 1853, sobre um plano para a introdução de colonos no Império," Instituto Histórico e Geográfico Brasileiro (IHGB), lata 824, doc. 18.

6. *Anais da Câmara dos Deputados do Império do Brasil,* Sessão de 4 de agosto de 1858: 36.

Works Cited

[Abreu e Lima, José Inácio de]. 1867. *As bíblias falsificadas ou duas respostas ao sr. cônego Joaquim Pinto de Campos pelo christão velho.* Recife, Brazil: Typ. G. H. de Mira.

Alencar, José de. 2004. *Ao correr da pena,* org. by João Roberto de Faria. São Paulo, Brazil: Martins Fontes.

Arrighi, Giovanni. 1996. *O longo século XX: Dinheiro, poder e as origens de nosso tempo* (Portuguese trans. of *The Long Twentieth Century*; 1st ed., 1994). Rio de Janeiro: Contraponto; São Paulo: Ed. Unesp.

Ashworth, John. 1995. *Slavery, Capitalism, and Politics in the Antebellum Republic,* 1: *Commerce and Compromise, 1820–1850.* Cambridge: Cambridge University Press.

Bandeira, Luiz A. Moniz. 2007. *Presença dos Estados Unidos no Brasil* (1st ed., 1972). Rio de Janeiro: Civilização Brasileira.

Beckert, Sven. 2004. "Emancipation and Empire: Reconstructing the Worldwide Web of Cotton Production in the Age of the American Civil War." *American Historical Review* 105 (5): 1405–38.

Berbel, Márcia, Rafael Marquese, and Tâmis Parron. 2010. *Escravidão e política: Brasil e Cuba, c. 1790–1850.* São Paulo: Hucitec.

Chalhoub, Sidney. 2003. *Machado de Assis, Historiador.* São Paulo: Companhia das Letras.

Conrad, Robert Edward. 1975. *Os últimos anos da escravatura no Brasil, 1850–1888* (1st ed. 1973, *The Destruction of Brazilian Slavery, 1850–1888*), translated by F. de Castro Ferro. Rio de Janeiro: Civilização Brasileira.

Davis, David Brion. 2006. *Inhuman Bondage: The Rise and Fall of Slavery in the New World.* Oxford, UK: Oxford University Press.

Drescher, Seymour. 2002. *The Mighty Experiment: Free Labor versus Slavery in British Emancipation.* New York: Oxford University Press.

————. 2009. *Abolition: A History of Slavery and Antislavery*. Cambridge, UK: Cambridge University Press.

Fehrenbacher, Don E. 2001. *The Slaveholding Republic: An Account of the United States Government's Relations to Slavery*, completed and edited by Ward M. McAfee. Oxford, UK: Oxford University Press.

Forbes, Robert Pierce. 2007. *The Missouri Compromise and Its Aftermath*. Chapel Hill: The University of North Carolina Press.

Fry, Joseph A. 2002. *Dixie Looks Abroad: The South and U.S. Foreign Relations, 1789–1973*. Baton Rouge: Louisiana State University Press.

Greenberg, Kenneth. 1985. *Masters and Statesmen: The Political Culture of American Slavery*. Baltimore, MD: Johns Hopkins University Press.

Guerra y Sánchez, Ramiro. 1971. *Manual de Historia de Cuba* (1st ed., 1938). Havana: Editorial de Ciencias Sociales.

Hopkins, Terence. K. 1982. "The Study of the Capitalist World-Economy: Some Introductory Considerations." In *World-Systems Analysis: Theory and Methodology*, edited by T. K. Hopkins and I. Wallerstein. Beverly Hills, CA: Sage Publications, 9–38.

Horne, Gerald. 2007. *The Deepest South: The United States, Brazil, and the African Slave Trade*. New York: New York University Press.

Karp, Matthew Jason. 2011. "'This Vast Southern Empire': The South and the Foreign Policy of Slavery, 1833–1861." Unpublished PhD diss., University of Pennsylvania.

Luz, Nícia Villela. 1968. *A Amazônia para os negros americanos: As origens de uma controvérsia internacional*. Rio de Janeiro: Saga.

Manning, William R. 1932. *Diplomatic Correspondence of the United States: Inter-American Affairs 1831–1860*. 2: *Bolivia and Brazil*. New York: Simon & Schuster.

Marques, João Pedro. 1999. *Os Sons do Silêncio: O Portugal de Oitocentos e a Abolição do Tráfico de Escravos*. Lisboa: Imprensa de Ciências Sociais.

Marques, Leonardo. 2010. "A participação norte-americana no tráfico transatlântico de escravos para os Estados Unidos, Cuba e Brasil." *História: Questões & Debates* no. 52: 87–113.

Marquese, Rafael de Bivar. 2004. *Feitores do corpo, missionários da mente: senhores, letrados e o controle dos escravos nas Américas, 1680–1860*. São Paulo: Companhia das Letras.

Mason, Matthew. 2006. *Slavery and Politics in the Early American Republic*. Chapel Hill: University of North Carolina Press.

May, Robert E. 2002. *The Southern Dream of a Caribbean Empire, 1854–1861*. Gainesville: University Press of Florida.

Maynard, Douglas H. 1960. "The World's Anti-Slavery Convention of 1840." *The Mississippi Valley Historical Review* 47 (3): 452–71.

McDaniel, William Caleb. 2006. *Our Country Is the World: Radical American Abolitionists Abroad*. Unpublished PhD diss., Johns Hopkins University.

Meinig, D. W. 1993. *The Shaping of America: A Geographical Perspective on 500 years of History*. 2: *Continental America, 1800–1867*. New Haven, CT: Yale University Press.

Mitton, Steven Heath. 2005. *The Free World Confronted: The Problem of Slavery and Progress in American Foreign Relations, 1833–1844*. Unpublished PhD diss., Louisiana State University, Baton Rouge, LA.

Murray, David. 1980. *Odious Commerce: Britain, Spain and the Abolition of the Cuban Slave Trade*. Cambridge, UK: Cambridge University Press.

Parron, Tâmis. 2011. *A política da escravidão no Império do Brasil, 1826–1865*. Rio de Janeiro: Civilização Brasileira.

Pena, Eduardo Spiller. 2001. *Pajens da casa imperial: Jurisconsultos, escravidão e a lei de 1871*. Campinas, Brazil: Ed. Unicamp.

[Pereira da Silva, J. M.]. 1845. *Inglaterra e Brasil: Tráfego de escravos*. Por um Deputado. Rio de Janeiro: Typographia do Brasil, de J. J. da Rocha.

Rugemer, Edward Bartlett. 2008. *The Problem of Emancipation: The Caribbean Roots of the American Civil War*. Baton Rouge: Louisiana State University Press.

Salles, Ricardo. 2008. *E o Vale era o escravo: Vassouras, século XIX. Senhores e escravos no coração do Império*. Rio de Janeiro: Civilização Brasileira.

Schmidt-Nowara, Christopher. 1999. *Empire and Antislavery: Spain, Cuba, and Puerto Rico, 1833–1874*. Pittsburgh, PA: University of Pittsburgh Press.

Schoen, Brian. 2009. *The Fragile Fabric of Union: Cotton, Federal Politics, and the Global Origins of the Civil War*. Baltimore, MD: John Hopkins University Press.

Scott, Rebecca J. 1991. *Emancipação escrava em Cuba: a transição para o trabalho livre, 1860–1899*. (orig. 1985, 1st ed., *Slave Emancipation in Cuba: The Transition to Free Labor, 1860–1899*; Portuguese translation by M. L. Lamounier). Rio de Janeiro: Paz e Terra.

Sinha, Manisha. 2000. *The Counter-Revolution of Slavery: Politics and Ideology in Antebellum South Carolina*. Chapel Hill: University of North Carolina Press.

Slenes, Robert. 2004. "The Brazilian Internal Slave Trade, 1850–1888: Regional Economies, Slave Experience, and the Politics of a Peculiar Market." In *The Chattel Principle: Internal Slave Trades in the Americas*, edited by Walter Johnson. London: Yale University Press, 325–70.

Takaki, Ronald T. 1971. *A Pro-Slavery Crusade: The Agitation to Reopen the African Slave Trade.* New York: Free Press.

Tardieu, Jean-Pierre. 2003. *"Dominar o morir": En torno al reglamento de esclavos de Cuba (1841–1866).* Frankfurt: Vervurt; Madrid: Iberoamericana.

Tomich, Dale. 2004. *Through the Prism of Slavery: Labor, Capital, and World Economy.* Lanham, MD: Rowman & Littlefield.

Turley, David. 1991. *The Culture of English Antislavery, 1780–1860.* London: Routledge.

Archival Materials

Anais da Câmara dos Deputados do Império do Brasil 1858.

Arquivo Histórico do Itamaraty, códice 271/4/6.

Congresso Nacional. Senado Federal. *Anais do Senado* (AS) 1843, 1845.

Instituto Histórico e Geográfico Brasileiro (IHGB).

Spain and the Politics
of the Second Slavery, 1808–1868

Christopher Schmidt-Nowara

The U.S. Civil War set the stage for the formation of a significant abolitionist movement within Spain. In political circles, the U.S. Civil War became a rallying point for domestic opposition to the monarchy of Isabel II and its increasingly despotic political allies. Among those liberals and republicans in opposition, there was widespread admiration for the Republican Lincoln as well as sympathy for the goal of abolishing slavery. Indeed, from the beginning, Spanish advocates believed the North would triumph sooner by immediately abolishing slavery. A recent study of the image of Lincoln in Spain has found that Lincoln the emancipator was more revered than Lincoln the savior of the Union (Boyd 2011). This outburst of support for Lincoln and antislavery in newspapers, poems, and banquets was not completely unprecedented. During the 1850s, American antislavery sentiments were warmly welcomed in Spain, including *Uncle Tom's Cabin*, a work that appeared in multiple translations as well as adaptations to other media, such as the theater (Surwillo 2005). At the end of the Civil War in 1865, Spanish and Antillean liberals and republicans founded the Spanish Abolitionist Society, which consciously adopted and adapted Anglo-American political repertoires (Alonso 2012), including public meetings (called "mitins" in Spanish), petition campaigns, regional chapters, and an ample presence in print through a periodical, *El Abolicionista*, and numerous pamphlets and collections of essays and poems about slavery, abolition, and the virtues of free labor. From its founding until the abolition of Cuban slavery in 1886, the Spanish Abolitionist Society would play a significant role in pressing the Spanish colonial state to bring Antillean slavery to an end, though its influence waxed and waned considerably during those two decades. It is this process, the formation of an organized abolitionist movement in the wake of the U.S. Civil War, that I would like to examine, and I want to suggest what it tells us about the politics of the second slavery. I will begin by comparing three approaches to Atlantic history that help to explain the circulation of ideas and practices, the foundations of abolitionist mobilization, and the economic and political systems that Spanish and Antillean abolitionists, like abolitionists in other corners of the Atlantic world, were seeking to transform.

Circum-Atlantic Currents

One approach focuses on movements across imperial and national boundaries manifested through the flow of information, peoples, and goods (Armitage 2009: 18–20). While focused on the early modern period, it is perhaps even more germane to the nineteenth century than to earlier periods of Atlantic history, because of the great increase in forced and voluntary trans-Atlantic migrations, the scale of commerce, and technological innovations that facilitated migration and commerce, including the steamship and the telegraph (Moya 2007). This perspective would help to explain how Spanish abolitionists tailored Atlantic antislavery rhetoric and strategies to local political conditions. The obvious shortcoming of this approach is that it says little about the actual object of abolitionists' efforts: the transformation of the colonial plantation economy through the dismantling of slavery.

The Problem of Slavery

Another line of attack, addressing the ideological and political problem of slavery, is derived from the influential work of David Brion Davis, Seymour Drescher, and David Eltis. Their studies of British antislavery in comparative perspective have systematically discounted economic explanations for the rise of abolitionism, emphasizing instead both the ideological functions of abolitionism and the movement's political and social foundations in the metropoles. I followed this approach in my study of the Spanish Abolitionist Society (Schmidt-Nowara 1999) because I consider it fundamental for understanding the metropolitan dynamics of abolitionism. However, the shortcoming of this way of framing the question is that it creates flatness in its depiction of New World slavery, especially of the plantation societies of the Caribbean. By casting antislavery as the historical exception that must be explained, these authors suggest that slavery itself is a historical constant. Yet it seems clear that the antislavery movement, not only in Britain but in France and Spain, was provoked by *plantation* slavery and the massive transatlantic slave traffic, phenomena with a fairly circumscribed history (Schwartz 2004; Larson 2007). The time between the rise of Barbados, Jamaica, and Saint Domingue and the first British and French criticisms of the violence of slave traffic and the plantation can be measured in decades rather than the millennia of Western culture. The transformation of Cuban slavery and the surge in the slave traffic in the late eighteenth and early nineteenth centuries similarly created new metropolitan views of slavery and demands for its reform or abolition.

The Second Slavery

Finally, from the perspective of the second slavery, I would suggest that the emergence of abolitionism in Spain represents ideological convergence among groups engaged in contentious politics within a connected Atlantic system. Spanish celebrations of Lincoln, translations and adaptations of *Uncle Tom's Cabin*, and the formation of the Spanish Abolitionist Society were not only borrowings and refinements of Anglo-American republicanism and abolitionism adapted to local repertoires of political contention, but also critical reflections on the slave society that had taken shape in Cuba during the nineteenth century. Unlike earlier Spanish critics of the budding slavery–slave trade complex, Spanish abolitionists now took as givens the plantation and the violence that took place on it. What enlightened Spaniards at the end of the eighteenth century considered a noxious innovation in the Spanish colonial system, abolitionists and republicans in the mid-nineteenth century had come to understand as the essential reality of New World slavery. Slavery in Cuba had its parallel in the plantations of the American South, as did the stock characters of abolitionism, including the cruel overseers, slave traders, and the long-suffering, docile slave.

The Spanish Abolitionist Society's attack on the use of stocks and shackles on the Cuban plantations epitomizes the metropolitan vision of colonial slavery by the mid- to later nineteenth century. One pamphlet condemned Cuban planters for the use of unmeasured violence against their slaves to extract labor from them. The abolitionists condemned "the harshness of the work" that took place "under the open sky in an extreme climate with a sun that burns like no other," producing often fatal injuries and sicknesses (Sociedad Abolicionista Española 1881). Published early in the 1880s, this work drew on a constant stream of abolitionist images that featured brutal masters and overseers and implements of punishment and torture, including the whipping post and the lash, all associated with the plantation. While this criticism might appear fairly generic at first reading, I believe it indicates the impact not only of the strategies and rhetoric of Anglo-American abolitionism but also of the second slavery in Cuba. Spain's colonial empire, once on the margins of the Atlantic slave complex, was now at its center.

Antislavery in Spain's War of Independence, 1808–1814

The first overt Spanish attacks on the emerging slave complex in Cuba took place during the War of Independence against France between 1808 and 1814 and showed the influence of British and French abolitionists. Critics such as Agustín de Argüelles, who proposed abolishing the slave trade in Spain's Cortes (constitutional assembly) in 1811, and Joseph Blanco White, an expatriate writing from London, engaged personally or by correspondence with British abolitionists such as William Wilberforce and Lord Holland. The geographer Isidoro de Antillón, who published the most brilliant analysis of slavery in the European empires, was read more widely among French abolitionists, including the Abbé Gregoire and Brissot de Warville. Yet in contemplating British and French antislavery, these Spanish abolitionists drew attention to how profoundly different the role of slavery was in the Spanish colonies. Unlike Jamaica and Saint Domingue, the unfettered slave trade to Cuba was a recent development, confirmed only in the 1790s, after decades of lobbying by Havana planters and colonial functionaries (Moreno Fraginals 2001; González-Ripoll and Álvarez Cuartero 2009; Delgado 2013). Until these reforms, the Spanish crown regulated and limited the flow of slaves to its American colonies through the mechanism of the *asiento*, a monopoly contract usually ceded to foreign slavers, most recently to the British in the first half of the eighteenth century. Unlike Britain, Portugal, France, or the Netherlands, Spain possessed no trading forts on the west coast of Africa, and its reliance on colonial plantation agriculture was relatively minor compared to its imperial rivals in the Caribbean and Brazil (Fradera and Schmidt-Nowara 2013). An important aspect of the Bourbon reforms carried out in the Caribbean in the aftermath of the Seven Years' War (1756–1763) was the stimulation of plantation economies, a process that eventually led to the first unbridled slave traffic to the Spanish colonies, which was increasingly controlled by Spaniards and Creoles.

The novelty of the burgeoning slave complex in Cuba was the target of the first Spanish antislavery writings. In attacking plantation slavery and demanding the suppression of the slave trade (but not of slavery altogether), Blanco and Antillón insisted that Spain's colonial empire had flourished over the centuries without slave trade. The lesson that Antillón drew from reading Brissot and others was that plantation slavery was inherently violent and unstable: the Saint Domingue revolution was the inevitable outcome of fully developed Caribbean plantations. France and Britain would have to abandon their Caribbean colonies and rely on free wage labor *in* Africa to provide for their imperial economies. Spain enjoyed a huge comparative advantage over its rivals because the mainland indigenous populations formed the core of its colonial workforce. Treated more in accord with the spirit of the Laws of the Indies, the indigenous workers of Mexico, Peru, and New Granada would allow Spain alone to retain a prosperous American empire.

Blanco White's *Bosquejo del comercio en esclavos* was meant to be a translation of Wilberforce's 1807 *Letter on the Abolition of the Slave Trade*, but he substantially rewrote it to reflect the differences between British and Spanish colonial societies (Schmidt-Nowara 2013). He was not as well versed in the workings of the colonial economy as Antillón, but he too signaled that the slave trade to Cuba marked a profound rupture in Spain's colonial history. "One must keep in mind that no other European nation has had fewer slaves, considering the extension of its colonies, nor has any other based less of its prosperity on the labor of those unhappy beings than the Spanish nation." Cuban planters' ambitions went against the grain of the history and structure of Spanish rule in the Americas: "in the political balance of Spain there is no interest that weighs against the reasons of humanity and against the morality opposed to the commerce in blacks other than the benefit and interests of the city of Havana" (Blanco White 1999: 152). In short, while engaging with British and French abolitionism, these Spanish critics of Cuban slavery and the Spanish slave trade were calling attention to a recent phenomenon, the deregulated slave trade. They demanded a return to older forms of Spanish colonial rule, which they depicted as more stable and humane than those practiced in the French and British colonies that the Bourbon reformers and Antillean planters sought to emulate and surpass.

Slavery Ascendant, 1814–1865

Though the resistance to French rule witnessed this significant surge in Spanish debate about the nature of the colonial system and the role of slavery and the plantation within it, the restoration of the Bourbon monarch Ferdinand VII marked the consolidation and defense of the shape of things in Cuba. Britain finally cajoled Ferdinand into agreeing to a treaty to suppress for the suppression of the slave trade to Cuba in 1817, but both Spanish and Cuban opinion and interests remained defiant. Indeed, soon after 1820, when the treaty was to take effect, Cuban advocates of the traffic were sounding a triumphalist note in public writings and debates in the metropole (O'Gavan 1821). The slave traffic surged to unprecedented heights in the 1820s and the 1830s in spite of British efforts to police and abolish it (Murray 1980; Berbel et al. 2010), as the Spanish state consolidated a model of colonial rule in the Caribbean with the plantation and the slave trade at its core (Fradera 2005).

Historians have long argued that this new colonial order remained intact until the outbreak of revolutionary movements in the colonies and the metropole in 1868, when the disruption of the political system led to the gradual dismantling of slavery. One aspect of the new order was the "law of silence" (Maluquer de Motes 1986: 322), which stifled debate about colonial slavery in the metropole. There were few expressions of antislavery after the war against the French because the dominant political and economic groups were complicit in various aspects of the colonial order: "in the most powerful sectors and currents, those that shared power, the law of silence ruled because they understood, with good reason, that slavery was the best ally of Spanish dominion" (1986: 314). Sovereignty was not the only concern; economic groups from throughout the peninsula were directly involved in the slave trade, and they protected commerce with the colonies, banking, and investment in sugar and other crops (Maluquer de Motes 1974; Piqueras and Sebastià Domingo 1991; Zeuske and García 2013; Rodrigo y Alharilla 2013). Cuban and Puerto Rican slavery, in other words, was very good for Spanish business.

While our knowledge of Spanish involvement in colonial slavery and the slave trade has become more nuanced and complex, confirming that there was widespread commitment in the peninsula, recent research has questioned the degree of silence about the colonial status quo. Historians and literary scholars have uncovered not only greater evidence of antislavery sentiment (Surwillo 2005, 2007; Boyd 2011; Almeida 2011: 105–50; Partzsch 2012; Garcia Balañà 2013; Schmidt-Nowara 2013), but a new understanding of *pro*slavery ideology (Tomich 2005; Berbel et al. 2010; Marquese and Parron 2011), which, far from being silent, was often quite obstreperously expressed.

Let me begin by discussing the crystallization and mutations of proslavery thought, both colonial and metropolitan. The new capacities for production and the demand for forced labor of the second slavery led to new ideas about slavery in the Hispanic world and deeply inflected the justifications for its persistence and transformation. Planters and publicists from Cuba, such as Francisco Arango y Parreño and the priest Juan Bernardo O'Gavan, consistently harped on the centrality of slavery to Cuban, and by extension Spanish, productivity and prosperity. To metropolitan officials and producers seeking to regroup after the calamities of the war against the French and the loss of the mainland American colonies, such warnings were grave indeed. But Arango and O'Gavan went further, insisting that slavery was not a necessary evil but actually a positive force that rescued Africans from a worse fate in their homelands and introduced them to the benefits of Christianity and Spanish laws. According to their justifications for the slave trade, voiced in opposition to both Spanish and British antislavery in the 1810s and 1820s, Spanish colonial laws and customs made slavery more humane than it was in the neighboring French and British sugar islands. There was no threat of uprisings like the revolution in Saint Domingue because, in Arango's words, "the French looked at the slaves as beasts, and the Spanish looked at them as men" (quoted in Tomich 2005: 74). This description of a benign Spanish colonial slavery, governed by wise laws, was far from original, having become commonplace in foreign commentators' accounts in the eighteenth century, Edmund Burke's for example, that contrasted the apparent harmony of Spanish colonies to the turmoil of the British and French colonies. Yet, as Antillón and Blanco White were acutely aware, the Havana proslavery advocates were consciously mystifying the emerging reality of Cuban plantation society, hearkening back to a pre-slave-trade era that was quickly being effaced.[1]

If Cuban advocates took the lead in mounting a robust defense of the slave trade and slavery in the early brush with Spanish and British antislavery, peninsular voices came to ring even louder thereafter. Part of the reason for the prominence of Spanish publicists was that after the 1820s, there were stirrings against the slave trade within the very Havana elite that had so effectively lobbied for its deregulation since the 1780s. While continuing to buy slaves, open *ingenios*, and invest in sophisticated transportation and productive technology, Creole planters also supported the first criticisms of the slave traffic, although they steadfastly opposed the abolition of slavery. José Antonio Saco and Domingo del Monte, connected to the richest Creole planting families in Cuba by marriage and patronage, were at the same time critics of the unbridled slave trade and of the growing influence of Spanish slavers and planters, who clustered around the office of the captain general, the supreme Spanish military and political commander whose powers the metropole greatly increased in the 1820s.

Thus, instead of planters and their protégés such as Arango and O'Gavan, the most vocal defenders of the slave trade came to be Spaniards such as Mariano Torrente, an office holder in Cuba and sometime spy for the Spanish government, and José Ferrer de Couto, a publicist and agent of the Spanish government based in New York City. There were several moments of crisis surrounding the legality and viability of the trade between the 1820s and the 1860s, largely because of the ineffectual 1817 Anglo-Spanish treaty and its successors (Corwin 1967; Murray 1980). When rumors circulated that the British navy would more aggressively persecute the traffic or that the Spanish government would capitulate, Torrente and Ferrer de Couto would take up their pens and publish fiery defenses of Spain, slave trafficking, and the colonial order in both Spanish and English. They sought to assuage pro-slave-trade opinion in Spain and Cuba, while also, apparently, trying to convince Americans and Britons of the humanity of Spanish slaving, though their views were so grotesque that it is difficult to gauge their impact beyond Spanish and Cuban proslavery circles.[2]

What distinguished the peninsular advocates from their Antillean predecessors was the violent assault on Africa and Africans, whose supposed barbarism fully justified the slave trade and enslavement in Cuba. Arango and O'Gavan also voiced such views, Arango arguing in 1811 that "in all of the centuries past and probably in all of the centuries to come, the benefits that the blacks receive by being left on their native soil are imaginary" (Arango y Parreño 1952: 167). But their emphasis really lay in the defense of Cuban, and Spanish, prosperity. Torrente and Ferrer de

Couto, in contrast, made pro-slave-trade propaganda into an anti-African diatribe.[3]

That the slave trade was more humane than abolition was a common theme in their works. Torrente recounted at length a tale told him by a Puerto Rican planter and slaver about the mass murders carried out on the African coast when abolitionists threatened to suppress the traffic. D. Francisco Soler claimed that he

> saw 4,190 prisoners murdered, when the chief, who was named the Duke of Old Calabar, became convinced that there was no chance of selling them; and being remonstrated with by the commander of an English vessel anchored in those waters for such an inhuman action, replied that he should do the same with all that might fall into his hands, because, being involved in endless wars with his neighbours, he could not keep his captives, nor could he, of course, release them; and that killing them was consequently his only recourse, since he was no longer at liberty to send them out of the country in any way. (Torrente 1853: 15)

Ferrer de Couto also depicted the slave trade as philanthropic, a form of rescue for those who would otherwise be butchered and eaten (Ferrer de Couto 1859). Cannibalism was a charge that he leveled against Africans to defend the Cuban complex in several of his writings. Like Torrente, he turned to anecdote to illustrate his argument: "The *Congos* and the *Carabalís* have the reputation in Cuba, among the negroes of milder customs, of being anthropophagi, or as they more naturally say, man-eaters. I questioned one of these miserable beings myself, in Havana, enquiring if it were true that they eat one another when at war, and on his answering me affirmatively with blood-shot eyes, as though he were on the point of luxuriating once more in so horrible a feast, I must confess I began to doubt the fact of our springing from the same origin" (Ferrer de Couto 1864: 28–29). He concluded this work with a chapter in which he argued for the resumption, not the abolition, of the slave traffic by the European powers as a way of rescuing and civilizing Africans.

What these seemingly unhinged writings by Torrente and Ferrer de Couto indicate is that the discussion of slavery and the slave trade was not as silent as historians once believed. Moreover, they show that the spatial dimensions of the debate went beyond the peninsula and were truly circum-Atlantic. It was not just Spanish cities such as Madrid, Barcelona, and Cádiz that were sites of publication and debate; so too were Havana, New York City, and London. The writings also show us that in defending the slave traffic to Cuba and the expanding plantation zone, Spanish advocates spoke in increasingly violent and racist terms. Why is that significant, or even surprising? Because this hyperbolic rhetoric shows that the scale of the Cuban traffic and plantation complex had forced an ideological mutation in Spain. Slavery was a venerable institution in Spain's overseas empire, but one regulated by laws and customs and justified by supposedly humane treatment that set Spain apart from Britain and other slaveholding powers, largely because it abstained from direct participation in the transatlantic slave trade. Slavery was a necessary but unfortunate element of colonial society. Blanco White, Antillón, and even the proslavery advocates Arango and O'Gavan had couched their debate in this rhetorical and historical framework, although the abolitionists insisted on the anomaly of the deregulated traffic and the eclipse of traditional colonial society. But Torrente and Ferrer de Couto shifted the terms of debate in response to the scale of the second slavery in Cuba, the persistence of the slave trade, and the challenge by the British against slavery. They no longer viewed slavery, and trafficking, as a temporary and necessary evil but as a positive good that rescued African captives from war, cannibalism, and murder and delivered them to a society that would protect them from their own barbarism. Indeed, Torrente, perhaps echoing the strident proslavery advocates of the United States or critics of emancipation in Britain (Hall 1989; Drescher 2002; Rugemer 2008), held that the condition of the slave in Cuba was far more comfortable and secure than that of the proletarians in Europe. Given Torrente and Ferrer de Couto's vehement and noisy polemics, it is small wonder that when Spain occupied Santo Domingo between 1861 and 1865, the insurgency against Spanish rule that broke out in 1863 was fueled by rumors that part of the occupation plan was the restoration of slavery (Eller 2012).[4]

When we turn to Spanish antislavery, we find quite different assumptions. For one, in the foundational moments of the debates over slavery and the traffic,

Blanco White and Antillón insisted on the essential equality of all peoples. As Blanco affirmed in his *Bosquejo*, "in the so-called state of nature every individual is *free*; that is to say, the absolute owner of his person, and therefore of the fruit of his personal labor" (Blanco White 1999: 139, emphasis in the original). Blanco also targeted the anti-African jibes in Arango's 1811 *Representación*. To Arango's charge that, left in their homeland, Africans would invariably sink into barbarism, Blanco responded that it was the slavers and the would-be colonizers who degraded Africans by stirring up constant wars and by raiding parties; he argued that if undisturbed by Arango and his ilk, the European and Creole merchants, slavers, and ship captains who flocked to African shores, the people of Africa would thrive and live in peace (1999: 93).

As we know, however, Blanco White and other early abolitionists lost out to slavery's many defenders and beneficiaries. But antislavery sentiment never completely disappeared, and, while often muted and allusive, it was not silent. In Barcelona between the 1820s and the 1840s, radical liberal, republican, and Protestant circles kept alive the antislavery sentiment of the Cortes of Cádiz era, sending participants to international antislavery congresses. They also published works critical of the slave trade, such as the 1825 translation of Thomas Clarkson's *The Cries of Africa*, replete with the famous images of the slave ship *Brookes*. The city remained a hotbed of conflict over the colonial order because the dominant economic groups were so heavily implicated in the slave traffic and colonial commerce (Maluquer de Motes 1974; Fradera 1984; Garcia Balañà 2013; Rodrigo y Alharilla 2013).

Receptions, glosses, and reworkings of Harriet Beecher Stowe's *Uncle Tom's Cabin*, as well as her *Key to Uncle Tom's Cabin*, show that familiarity with foreign abolitionism persisted and that Spaniards found it directly relevant to understanding and debating colonial slavery and the Cuban slave traffic. As Lisa Surwillo (2005: 769–70) has shown, the novel exploded onto the Spanish scene shortly after its publication in the United States in 1852; it was translated in various editions, serialized in the major newspapers of the day, and rewritten for theatrical productions. One version staged in the port city of Cádiz in 1853, a play called *Haley, o, el traficante de negros*, picked up on the theme of the slave trade in Stowe's novel and adapted it to the Spanish setting to explore how defense of the traffic imperiled Spanish sovereignty in Cuba by inciting possible interventions by the United States and Britain. The implicit message of the work was that to preserve Cuba and its plantation economy, Spain must abolish the slave trade, if not slavery.

Other versions of the novel spelled out different lessons. The most unequivocally abolitionist reading came from the well-known novelist, translator, and publisher Wenceslao Ayguals de Izco, who introduced his translation by reminding the readers of his longstanding views in favor of abolishing slavery. He called attention to his play *Los Negros* (set in Jamaica, rather than Cuba or Puerto Rico), staged in Valencia in 1836, in which he attacked the cruelty and injustice of colonial slavery to much fanfare and support: "I will say that I was grateful for the public's applause for the morality of my work, its humanitarian tendencies, its faithful rendering of the horrors of slavery, and the condemnations that rang from all of its lines against the abominable traffic in blacks" (Ayguals de Izco 1853: 3).

The emphasis on the horrors of slavery, such as separation from family and extreme physical punishment, were important themes in Stowe's follow-up work, *A Key to Uncle Tom's Cabin* (1853), in which the author recounted the real episodes on which she based her novel, to demonstrate its veracity. As with the novel, a translation soon followed, *La llave de la cabaña del tío Tom* in 1855, though with an important addition: the Spanish edition was vividly illustrated by Vicente Urrabieta y Ortiz to dramatize several of the anecdotes. Among them was a punishment scene in which a black man was tied to a whipping post and beaten with a rod by a man who would fit the visual description of an overseer that later appeared in Spanish abolitionist publications (broad-brimmed hat and glowering expression). In the background, slaves labored in a field, while a fat, well-dressed white man, presumably the planter, shaded himself with a parasol as he watched the punishment being meted out (Stowe 1855: 14). Other illustrations depicted a shackled woman cleaning the street in a city, a black man hanged by a mob, another beheaded aboard a ship, and a mob in St. Louis attacking and burning the offices of a newspaper that had defied public opinion. The Spanish version of the *Key* thus not only related the events that Stowe transmuted into her fictional account of slavery and trafficking, but also provided striking images of slavery, slave ownership, corporal punishment, and mob violence in defense of slavery that might provide relevant parallels to the Spanish colonies and the political defense of the status quo.

However, the meaning of Stowe's work did not go unchallenged in Spain. While several versions, and the translated and illustrated *Key*, advocated the suppression of the slave trade and condemned the violence of plantation slavery, there were also proslavery glosses that spoke very much in the aggressively racist tones of Torrente and Ferrer de Couto. An anonymously translated edition of the novel introduced the story with a biography and study that questioned and mocked Stowe's abolitionism, arguing that she distorted the reality of slavery in the United States: "the author knows as well as anyone that she has depicted the *exception* and not the *rule*" because the slaves' condition was "twenty times more preferable to that of the majority of the free workers in the English and American factories" (B*** 1853: vi, emphasis in the original). Moreover, Africans and their descendants in the Americas had shown themselves to be resistant to civilization and thus unprepared for emancipation. Slavery benefitted them by putting them in a better position than both free white workers and the Africans who remained in Africa: "Mistress Stowe's enchanting blacks, . . . if they had not been brought from Congo or Guinea by the philanthropic slavers are unaware that instead of piously reading the Bible they would be dancing a horrifying dance around a bonfire roasting the cadavers of their enemies" (1853: vi).

Abolitionism, Moderate and Radical, 1865–1868

Though abolitionist works and images circulated through Spain, an abolitionist movement did not take shape until the end of the Civil War and the abolition of slavery in the United States, events much commented upon in the press and actively discussed in semiofficial circles (Cortada 1980; Surwillo 2007; Boyd 2011). Together with a new British-U.S. alliance to pursue the slave trade to Cuba, these profound changes urged Cuban planters and the Spanish government to consider transitions toward new kinds of labor, though they were hesitant to end slavery. Since the late 1850's, the global price of sugar had spiked and in response, so did the price of slaves and the traffic to the island. Planters were also modernizing production by investing heavily in railroads and industrial sugar-processing technology. The crisis of the second slavery occasioned by war and abolition in the United States thus coincided with a new phase of expansion and investment in Cuba's slave-worked plantations (Bergad et al. 1995).

Nonetheless, the emerging geopolitical realities were undeniable, so the Spanish government sought to open discussion of a controlled and protracted abolition process that included the definitive suppression of the slave trade in 1867. Among the changes wrought by the changing political conditions was greater public debate in Spain, and to a lesser degree in the colonies, concerning the ways to abolish slavery and reform the colonial order. In this atmosphere, Spanish and Antillean, chiefly Puerto Rican, reformers founded the Spanish Abolitionist Society in Madrid in 1865.

Abolitionism did not appear ex nihilo. As we have seen, Spanish criticisms of the slave trade and colonial slavery had emerged in tandem with slavery's advocates and the profound transformations taking place in Cuba since the late eighteenth century. However, the situation at midcentury was significantly different. By that time, the colonial dystopia feared by Antillón and Blanco White had become reality as the illegal slave trade continued to flow to the island, planters invested in enslaved workers and cutting-edge technology, and proslavery advocates assumed more prominent and brazen positions. Cuban slavery had changed dramatically over the decades, driven by the vast demand for its products and new production and transportation capacities that delivered them ever more effectively (Tomich 2004).

Antislavery had also changed, encouraged not only by the circulation of foreign abolitionist works and debate over the U.S. Civil War, but by the associational culture that had grown in the Spanish capital through the 1850s and 1860s and that provided the repertoires for an active abolitionist movement. Associations dedicated to the education of women and workers, legal reform, religious freedom, broader political rights, and the promotion of free trade had forged a tenuous public sphere of political and propagandistic action (Corwin 1967: 153–214; Gil Novales 1968; Schmidt-Nowara 1999: 51–125). Their repertoires included public meetings held in theaters, lecture series held in clubs and academies, poetry and essay contests, banquets, and an extensive presence in print, including books and pamphlets and numerous dedicated periodicals. These included *El Economista*, a paper committed to free trade and economic liberalism; *La Revista Hispano-Americana*, which reported on Spain's relations with the Americas; and *La Violeta*, a women's paper edited by the writer Faustina Saez de Melgar that helped to forge a role for women in Madrid's political and reformist circles. Indeed, one of the more controversial and novel aspects of abolitionism proved to be the significant presence of women, not only in print but also in public meetings, a presence trumpeted by reformers and reviled by conservatives (Surwillo 2007; Partzsch 2012).

At first, the proposals of Spanish and Antillean abolitionists were moderate: abolition of the slave trade and a gradual, controlled, and compensated abolition of slavery, more or less the aims of the Spanish government. However, tensions soon emerged because of the distinctive nature of slavery and the plantation economy in Puerto Rico and Cuba. Among the founders of the Spanish Abolitionist Society were the Puerto Rican Julio de Vizcarrondo and his wife, Harriet Brewster de Vizcarrondo. They came to the capital from a colony where the slave trade had come to an effective end by 1850, more from economic than from political causes. The slave population had been in decline, and sugar was being challenged by coffee as the main export crop, coffee being worked largely by proletarians rather than slaves (Picó 1979; Curet 1980; Bergad 1983; Cubano-Iguina 1990). Puerto Rican goals and interests, while far from being uniform because proslavery advocates remained alive and well (Cubano-Iguina 2011), were more far-reaching than those of their Spanish and Cuban counterparts. Vizcarrondo and others were in favor of the immediate abolition of slavery on the island, and while they insisted that they did not speak of Cuba, Cuban opinion perceived their demands as an immediate threat to the neighboring colony's security and prosperity.

Events in both the metropole and the colonies in 1868 radicalized abolitionism: anticolonial rebellions in Puerto Rico and Cuba and the overthrow of the Bourbon monarchy in Spain. On the one hand, the resilience of the rebellion in Cuba (the Puerto Rican uprising was short-lived) put the question of abolition front and center. Rebel leaders had to respond to the reality of slaves fleeing from slavery (Scott 1985; Robert 1992; Ferrer 1999), while in the metropole, abolitionists came to argue that only immediate abolition would quell the rebellion, by ensuring the gratitude and loyalty of slaves emancipated by Spain (Schmidt-Nowara 1999: 139–60). On the other hand, the new regime in the metropole was democratic and introduced broad freedoms of the press and association, greatly increasing the space for abolitionist agitation and propaganda. Demands for abolition were no longer allusive, but had become direct and persistent. To the repertoire of political contention that had taken shape in the 1850s and 1860s, abolitionists added marches through cities such as Madrid and Seville; petition campaigns to the government that involved associations, parties, and municipalities from throughout the peninsula requesting action against slavery; and for the first time since the Cortes of Cádiz, open parliamentary debate about slavery and abolition, as abolitionists took on positions of power in both the legislative and executive branches of government.[5] In turn, the powerful vested interests in Spain and Cuba that sought to defend slavery, or at least to delay its abolition, organized their own associations, periodicals, demonstrations, and petition campaigns as the politics of the second slavery played out in the streets, theaters, and meeting rooms of the metropole (Maluquer de Motes 1974; Schmidt-Nowara 1999: 126–60; Rodrigo y Alharilla 2013).

Conclusion: Atlantic Slavery and Local Repertoires

The struggle to defend or to abolish slavery had changed significantly since the first polemics of the early nineteenth century. During the war against the French, antislavery politicians and writers such as Agustín de Argüelles and Joseph Blanco White had focused principally on suppressing the slave trade, which they viewed as a dangerous innovation to Spain's overseas empire. The range of debate was limited to the Cortes of Cádiz, where it was debated very briefly, and to occasional pamphlets. There was no widespread metropolitan mobilization behind the cause.[6] To the contrary, proslavery forces were predominant in both Spain and its major plantation colony, Cuba. After the restoration of Ferdinand VII and the debacle of the Spanish-American revolutions, the commitment to slavery only grew: the loudest voices in debates over slavery were its advocates, though, as we have recently learned, criticisms of the slave trade and slavery never disappeared; the circum-Atlantic nature of antislavery and abolitionist ideas, images, and political strategies helped to keep it alive under shifting economic and political circumstances. While borrowing from British and U.S. abolitionism, the peninsular and colonial reformers gathered in the Spanish Abolitionist Society drew on local repertoires, consolidated at midcentury around a variety of social, economic, and political causes tangential at best to colonial slavery. But as in other metropolitan societies (Davis 1975; Drescher 1987; Alonso 2012), abolitionists confronted the problem of slavery through particular modes of organization and ideological preoccupations that permitted them to take action and to elaborate arguments about colonial slavery and freedom. Spanish and Antillean abolitionists could partake of Atlantic antislavery currents because they found themselves enmeshed in an Atlantic system of slavery and slave-trafficking consolidated in the aftermath of significant moments of abolition, the Haitian Revolution, and the suppression of the British slave trade, of which Cuba was one of the main nodes (Tomich 2004). The hectic growth of the plantations, the persistent slave trade, and the large-scale investment in technologies by planters and merchants forged a slave colony unlike any other in Spain's long history of overseas rule. While abolitionists and proslavery advocates might signal Spain's differences from other colonial empires during the expansion of the Cuban slave trade and plantation economy, by the middle of the nineteenth century, Cuba no longer appeared as distinct from the U.S. South, the Paraíba Valley in Brazil, or Caribbean predecessors such as Jamaica and Saint Domingue. Foreign abolitionism acquired new relevance and meaning to the Spanish Abolitionist Society because its members, like abolitionists in other Atlantic societies, were engaged in challenges to one of the fundamental aspects of the Atlantic-world economy in the nineteenth century.

Notes

1. This disjuncture was at the heart of the well-known polemic between the Creole publicist José Antonio Saco and the Spanish functionary Vicente Vázquez Queipo in the 1840s over the need to encourage European immigration to the colony. Vázquez Queipo, who downplayed the need for immigration, argued that Cuban slave society was fundamentally different from its British and French Caribbean predecessors because of the large free population, black and white, making it more stable and secure. In contrast, Saco, who had demanded increased European immigration since the 1820s, insisted that the illegal slave trade, which was actually slowing in the 1840s before rebounding significantly in the 1850s and 1860s, was driving the island toward the kinds of revolutionary violence that had shaken neighboring sugar islands because of the majority slave and free black population; see Vázquez Queipo (1847) and Saco (1847), and also Saco (1845). On the controversies over slavery and the colonial order in Cuba at midcentury, see Opatrny (1986).

2. Rafael Marquese and Tâmis Parron's research on the "proslavery international" will give us a better sense of the readerships for such works; see Marquese and Parron (2011).

3. Cf. Maluquer de Motes, who argues that "in general, defense of the trade and of slavery was couched in terms of economic necessity and/or political expediency but never, or almost never, as an intrinsic defense of the system" (1986: 321).

4. There was some link between proslavery and annexationist advocates. Torrente not only wrote in defense of the slave trade but penned a public report, and a more aggressive secret report, for the Spanish government in which he recommended that Spain combine with France to reoccupy Hispaniola jointly. He had carried out a spying mission for the government in both Haiti and Santo Domingo in 1852. The public account and recommendations on diplomacy in the region can be found in Torrente (1854). The secret recommendations about invasion and annexation are in Mariano Torrente, "Segunda memoria sobre el Imperio de Haití," Havana, January 14, 1853. Archivo del Ministerio de Asuntos Exteriores, Política, Política Exterior, Haití, 1822/1867, legajo 2523. His idea was to stir up political conflict in Haiti by encouraging divisions between blacks and mulattoes, setting the stage for a French and Spanish intervention to restore order, and colonialism.

5. Moreover, in Puerto Rico, abolitionists not only represented the colony in the metropolitan Cortes, but assumed important local offices that allowed them to intervene directly on behalf of slaves against masters as they sought to exercise the new freedoms created by

legislation, including the gradualist Moret Law (1870) and the abolition of slavery on the island (1873); see Cubano-Iguina (2011).

6. In the colonies fighting for independence, of course, there was broad conflict over slavery, as both the loyalist and independence forces sought to attract slaves to their armies. The end result of such mobilization was the weakening of the slave systems and the passing of gradual abolition laws in the independent republics; see Andrews (2004: 53–115); Blanchard (2008); and Schmidt-Nowara (2011: 90–119).

Works Cited

Almeida, Joselyn B. 2011. *Re-Imagining the Transatlantic, 1780–1890*. Burlington, VT: Ashgate.

Alonso, Angela. 2012. "Repetório, segundo Charles Tilly: história de um conceito." *Sociología & Antropología* 2 (3): 21–41.

Andrews, George Reid. 2004. *Afro-Latin America, 1800–2000*. New York: Oxford University Press.

Antillón, Isidoro de. 1811. *Disertación sobre el origen de la esclavitud de los negros, motivos que la han perpetuado, ventajas que se le atribuyen y medios que podrían adoptarse para hacer prosperar nuestras colonias sin la esclavitud de los negros*. Mallorca: Imprenta de Manuel Domingo.

Arango y Parreño, Francisco de. 1952. "Representación de la Ciudad de la Habana a las Cortes, el 20 de julio de 1811, con motivo de las proposiciónes hechas por D. José Miguel Guridi Alcocer y D. Agustín de Argüelles, sobre el tráfico y esclavitud de los negros; extendida por el Alferez Mayor de la Ciudad, D. Francisco de Arango, por encargo del Ayuntamiento, Consulado y Sociedad Patriótica de la Habana." *Obras*. Vol. 2. Havana: Dirección de Cultura, Ministerio de Educación, 145–237.

Armitage, David. 2009. "Three Concepts of Atlantic History." In *The British Atlantic World, 1500–1800*, 2nd ed., edited by David Armitage and Michael J. Braddick. New York: Palgrave Macmillan: 13–29.

Ayguals de Izco, Wenceslao. 1853. "Advertencia preliminar." In *La choza de Tom, o sea vida de los negros en el sur de los Estados Unidos, novela escrita en ingles por Enriqueta Beecher Stowe*, 2nd ed., translated by Wenceslao Ayguals de Izco. Madrid: Imprenta de Ayguals de Izco Hermanos, 3–4.

B***. 1853. "Biografía." In *La Choza del negro Tomás*, by Harriet Beecher Stowe (Spanish translation). Madrid and Paris: Mellado: iii–vii.

Berbel, Márcia, Rafael Marquese, and Tâmis Parron. 2010. *Escravidão e política: Brasil e Cuba, 1790–1850*. São Paulo: Ed. Hucitec.

Bergad, Laird. 1983. *Coffee and the Growth of Agrarian Capitalism in Nineteenth-Century Puerto Rico*. Princeton, NJ: Princeton University Press.

Bergad, Laird, Fe Iglesias García, and María del Carmen Barcia. 1995. *The Cuban Slave Market, 1790–1880*. New York: Cambridge University Press.

Blanchard, Peter. 2008. *Under the Flags of Freedom: Slave Soldiers and the War of Independence in Spanish South America*. Pittsburgh, PA: University of Pittsburgh Press.

Blanco White, Joseph. 1999. *Bosquejo del comercio en esclavos y reflexiónes sobre este tráfico considerado moral, política y cristianamente*, edited by Manuel Moreno Alonso. Seville, Spain: Ed. Alfar.

Boyd, Carolyn. 2011. "A Man for All Seasons: Lincoln in Spain." In *The Global Lincoln*, edited by Richard Carwardine and Jay Sexton. Oxford, UK: Oxford University Press, 189–205.

Clarkson, Thomas. 1825. *Grito de los africanos contra los europeos, sus opresores, o sea rápida ojeada sobre el comercio homicida llamado Tráfico de Negros*, translated by Agustín de Gimbernat. Barcelona: Imprenta de José Torner.

Cortada, James W. 1980. *Spain and the American Civil War: Relations at Mid-Century, 1855–1868*. Vol. 4. Philadelphia: Transactions of the American Philosophical Society.

Corwin, Arthur F. 1967. *Spain and the Abolition of Slavery in Cuba, 1817–1886*. Austin: University of Texas Press.

Cubano-Iguina, Astrid. 1990. *El hilo en el laberinto: claves de la lucha política en Puerto Rico (siglo XIX)*. Río Piedras, Puerto Rico: Ed. Huracán.

———. 2011. "Freedom in the Making: The Slaves of Hacienda La Esperanza, Manatí, Puerto Rico, on the Eve of Abolition, 1868–76." *Social History* 36: 280–93.

Curet, José. 1980. "From Slave to 'Liberto': A Study on Slavery and Its Abolition in Puerto Rico, 1840–1880." Unpublished PhD diss., Columbia University.

Davis, David Brion. 1975. *The Problem of Slavery in the Age of Revolution, 1770–1823*. Ithaca, NY: Cornell University Press.

Delgado, Josep M. 2013. "The Slave Trade in the Spanish Empire (1501–1808): The Shift from Periphery to Center." In *Slavery and Antislavery in Spain's Atlantic Empire*, edited by Josep M. Fradera and Chr. Schmidt-Nowara. New York: Berghahn, 13–42.

Drescher, Seymour. 1987. *Capitalism and Antislavery: British Mobilization in Comparative Perspective*. New York: Oxford University Press.

———. 2002. *The Mighty Experiment: Free Labor versus Slavery in British Emancipation*. New York: Oxford University Press.

Eller, Anne. 2012. " 'La audacia de unos pocos': Spanish Annexation and Popular Discontent on Hispaniola (1861–1865)." Unpublished paper presented to the annual meeting of the Society for Spanish & Portuguese Historical Studies, Tufts University; cited with permission of the author.

Eltis, David. 1987. *Economic Growth and the Ending of the Transatlantic Slave Trade*. New York: Oxford University Press.

Ferrer, Ada. 1999. *Insurgent Cuba: Race, Nation, and Revolution, 1868–1898*. Chapel Hill: University of North Carolina Press.

Ferrer de Couto, José. 1859. *América y España consideradas en sus intereses de raza ante la república de los Estados Unidos del Norte*. Cádiz: Imprenta de la Revista Médica.

———. 1864. *Enough of War! The Question of Slavery Conclusively and Satisfactorily Resolved as regards Humanity at large and the Permanent Interests of Present Owners*. New York: S. Hallet.

Fradera, Josep M. 1984. "La participació catalana en el tràfic d'esclaus." *Recerques* no. 16: 118–39.

———. 2005. *Colonias para después de un imperio*. Barcelona: Edicions Bellatera.

Fradera, Josep M., and Christopher Schmidt-Nowara. 2013. "Introduction: Colonial Pioneer and Plantation Latecomer." In *Slavery and Antislavery in Spain's Atlantic Empire*, edited by J. M. Fradera and Chr. Schmidt-Nowara. New York: Berghahn, 1–12.

Garcia Balañà, Albert. 2008. " 'El comercio español en África' en la Barcelona de 1858, entre el Caribe y el Mar de China, entre Londres y París." *Illes i Imperis* nos. 10 and 11: 167–86.

———. 2013. "Antislavery before Abolitionism: Networks and Motives in Early Liberal Barcelona, 1833–1844." In *Slavery and Antislavery in Spain's Atlantic Empire*, edited by Josep M. Fradera and Chr. Schmidt-Nowara. New York: Berghahn, 229–55.

Gil Novales, Alberto. 1968. "Abolicionismo y librecabmio." *Revista de Occidente* no. 59: 154–81.

González-Ripoll, Ma. Dolores, and Izaskun Álvarez Cuartero, eds. 2009. *Francisco Arango y la invención de la Cuba azucarera*. Salamanca: Ed. Universidad de Salamanca.

Gould, Eliga. 2007. "Entangled Histories, Entangled Worlds: The English-Speaking Atlantic as a Spanish Periphery." *American Historical Review* 112 (3): 764–86.

Hall, Catherine. 1989. "The Economy of Intellectual Prestige: Thomas Carlyle, John Stuart Mill, and the Case of Governor Eyre." *Cultural Critique* no. 12 (Spring): 167–96.

Jacobson, Stephen. 2012. "Imperial Ambitions in an Era of Decline: Micromilitarism and the Eclipse of the Spanish Empire, 1858–1923." In *Endless Empire: Spain's Retreat, Europe's Eclipse, America's Decline*, edited by Alfred W. McCoy, Josep M. Fradera, and Stephen Jacobson. Madison: University of Wisconsin Press, 74–91.

Larson, Piers. 2007. "African Diasporas and the Atlantic." In *The Atlantic in Global History, 1500–2000*, edited by Jorge Cañizares-Esguerra and Erik Seeman. Upper Saddle River, NJ: Pearson, 129–47.

Maluquer de Motes, Jordi. 1974. "La burgesia catalane i l'esclavitud colonial: modes de producció i pràctica política." *Recerques* no. 3: 83–136.

———. 1986. "Abolicionismo y resistencia a la abolición en la España del siglo XIX." *Anuario de Estudios Americanos* no. 43: 311–31.

Marquese, Rafael, and Tâmis Peixoto Parron. 2011. "Internacional escravista: A política da Segunda Escravidão." *Topoi* no. 23 (12): 97–117.

Moreno Fraginals, Manuel. 2001. *El ingenio: Complejo económico social cubano del azúcar.* Barcelona, Spain: Crítica.

Moya, José. 2007. "Modernization, Modernity, and the Trans/formation of the Atlantic World in the Nineteenth Century." In *The Atlantic in Global History, 1500–2000*, edited by Jorge Cañizares-Esguerra and Erik Seeman. Upper Saddle River, NJ: Pearson, 179–97.

Murray, David. 1980. *Odious Commerce: Britain, Spain and the Abolition of the Cuban Slave Trade.* Cambridge, UK: Cambridge University Press.

O'Gavan, Juan Bernardo. 1821. *Observaciónes sobre la suerte del los negros del África.* Madrid: Imprenta Universal.

Opatrny, Josef. 1986. *Antecedentes históricos de la formación de la nación cubana.* Prague: Charles University.

Partzsch, Henriette. 2012. "Violets and Abolition: The Discourse on Slavery in Faustina Sáez de Melgar's Magazine *La Violeta* (Madrid, 1862–1866)." *Bulletin of Spanish Studies* 89 (6): 859–75.

Picó, Fernando. 1979. *Libertad y servidumbre en el Puerto Rico del siglo XIX.* Río Piedras, Puerto Rico: Ediciones Huracán.

Piqueras, José A., and Enric Sebastiá Domingo. 1991. *Agiotistas, negreros y partisanos: dialéctica social en vísperas de la Revolución Gloriosa*. Valencia: Alfons el Magnànim.

Robert, Karen. 1992. "Slavery and Freedom in the Ten Years' War, Cuba, 1868–1878." *Slavery and Abolition* 13 (3): 181–200.

Rodrigo y Alharilla, Martin. 2013. "Spanish Merchants and the Slave Trade: From Legality to Illegality, 1814–1870." In *Slavery and Antislavery in Spain's Atlantic Empire*, edited by Josep M. Fradera and Chr. Schmidt-Nowara. New York: Berghahn, 176–99.

Rugemer, Edward Bartlett. 2008. *The Problem of Emancipation: The Caribbean Roots of the American Civil War*. Baton Rouge: Louisiana State University Press.

Saco, José Antonio. 1845. *La supresión del tráfico de esclavos africanos en la isla de Cuba examinada con relación a su agricultura y a su seguridad*. Paris: Imprenta de Panckoucke.

———. 1847. *Réplica de D. José Antonio Saco a la contestación del señor fiscal de la Real Hacienda de la Habana, D. Vicente Vázque Queipo; en el exámen del informe sobre el fomento de la población blanca etc., en la isla de Cuba*. Madrid: Imprenta de La Publicidad.

Schmidt-Nowara, Christopher. 1999. *Empire and Antislavery: Spain, Cuba, and Puerto Rico, 1833–1874*. Pittsburgh, PA: University of Pittsburgh Press.

———. 2011. *Slavery, Freedom, and Abolition in Latin America and the Atlantic World*. Albuquerque: University of New Mexico Press.

———. 2013. "Wilberforce Spanished: Joseph Blanco White and Spanish Antislavery, 1808–1814." In *Slavery and Antislavery in Spain's Atlantic Empire*, edited by Josep M. Fradera and Chr. Schmidt-Nowara. New York: Berghahn, 158–75.

Schwartz, Stuart B., ed. 2004. *Tropical Babylons: Sugar and the Making of the Atlantic World, 1450–1680*. Chapel Hill: University of North Carolina Press.

Scott, Rebecca J. 1985. *Slave Emancipation in Cuba: The Transition to Free Labor, 1860–1899*. Princeton, NJ: Princeton University Press.

Sociedad Abolicionista Española. 1881. *El Cepo y el grillete (La esclavitud en Cuba)*. Madrid: Sociedad Abolicionista.

Stowe, Harriet Beecher. 1855. *La llave de la cabaña del tío Tom. Segunda parte de la celebre novela de Mistress Enriqueta Beecher Stowe, la cabaña del tío Tom, que contiene los hechos y documentos originales en que se funda la novela, con las piezas justificativas*, translated by G. A. Larrosa. Barcelona: Imprenta Hispana de V. Castaños.

Surwillo, Lisa. 2005. "Representing the Slave Trader: *Haley* and the Slave Ship; or, Spain's *Uncle Tom's Cabin*." *PMLA* 120 (3): 768–82.

―――. 2007. "Poetic Diplomacy: Carolina Coronado and the American Civil War." *Comparative American Studies* 5 (4): 409–22.

Tomich, Dale. 2004. *Through the Prism of Slavery: Labor, Capital, and World Economy.* Lanham, MD: Rowman & Littlefield.

―――. 2005. "The Wealth of Empire: Francisco Arango y Parreño, Political Economy, and the Second Slavery in Cuba." In *Interpreting Spanish Colonialism: Empires, Nations, and Legends,* edited by Christopher Schmidt-Nowara and John Nieto-Phillips. Albuquerque: University of New Mexico Press, 55–85.

Torrente, Mariano. 1853. *Slavery in the Island of Cuba.* London: H. Baillere.

―――. 1854. *Política ultramarina: que abraza todos los puntos referentes a las relaciónes de España con los Estados Unidos, con la Inglaterra y las Antillas, y señaladamente con la isla de Santo Domingo.* Madrid: D. A. Avrial.

Vázquez de Queipo, Vicente de. 1847. *Contestación a la carta de un cubano suscrita por Don José Antonio Saco, en la que se impugnan algunas de las ideas emitidas en el informe fiscal sobre el fomento de la población blanca en la isla de Cuba.* Madrid: Imprenta de J. Martín Alegría.

Wilberforce, William. 1807. *A Letter on the Abolition of the Slave Trade: Addressed to the Freeholders and Other Inhabitants of Yorkshire.* London: T. Cadell and W. Davies.

Zeuske, Michael, and Orlando García Martínez. 2013. "La Amistad: Ramón Ferrer in Cuba and the Transatlantic Dimensions of Slaving and Contraband Trade." In *Slavery and Antislavery in Spain's Atlantic Empire,* edited by Josep M. Fradera and Schmidt-Nowara. New York: Berghahn, 200–28.1. Notes, 200–28.

The Return to the *casa de vivienda* and the *barracón*

The Terms of Social Action in Slave Plantations[1]

José Antonio Piqueras

The writing of the history of modern slavery in the Americas began as one aspect of the study of economic activities, and to a large extent it remains so still. The historical origins and evolution of slavery were linked to the demand for subservient labor to work in mines, plantations, and jobs in cities involving the haulage and shipment of goods, official building work, jobs in certain trades, and from the very beginning, domestic service, which can hardly be limited to domestic tasks unrelated to the productive economic context of the colonies. Yet the institution developed to the greatest extent on plantations engaged in commercial agriculture, that is, in large-scale production units with a large number of workers based on an extensive cultivation model and the intensive use of labor. Its legacy has influenced the existence of an ethnic, cultural, and demographic model (Klein 1967; Andrews 2003). For a long time it shaped society, and among its legacies was the prolonged persistence of colonial enclaves in the Caribbean (Williams 1970; Knight 1990, 1997; Moya Pons 2007).

It is true that until almost the second third of the nineteenth century, in numerous regions of the American continent the average number of slaves used in each productive unit was modest compared to Caribbean plantations and the new regions where cotton plantations had been established. The proportion of urban slaves registered in the category of domestic servants was extraordinary in the main towns of the Spanish Caribbean and Latin America. Owning slave servants was a mark of distinction, and it was a fundamental aspect of social capital. Moreover, they often did work that was a mixture of domestic tasks (of unquestionable value) and specifically economic tasks, since they often performed jobs related to the storage and commercialization of plantation produce. Some domestic servants, as we know, were *hired out to earn*; in other words, they were forced to seek work in the labor market and carry out a wide range of trades and activities. Cases of slaves being hired out were more common among landowners who were in a precarious position, who owned few slaves and used them to obtain external income (Bernand 2001; Graham 1988; Varella 2010).

Slave labor tended to be concentrated in rural areas. In the places where it remained the longest, slave labor passed from the less efficient farms to larger, more productive units, a fact that reveals the intimate relationship between this type of economy and the use of forced labor, regardless of the degree of technical development reached in some of its phases and indeed, at times, due precisely to such technological development.

Observing Slavery and the Options Open to Observers

The study of plantations became one of the main subjects of economic and social history. However, it must be remembered that at the beginning of the twentieth century, modern slavery started out as an object of study somewhere between ethnography, anthropology, and sociology. There was, however, one prominent exception: the influential and controversial work of the historian Ulrich B. Phillips, *American Negro Slavery* (1966), a book first published in 1918, which to a large extent laid the foundations for modern studies on the subject. This was not so much due to its interpretation (basically pro-South and categorically racist), but rather because it looked at the subject on three levels: economy, race, and the mutual relationship between master and slave. His theses on the motives of the white population of the South—the kind-hearted treatment of slaves, the civilizing function of the institution, and the diminishing profitability and decline of the plantation (which meant that the Civil War was unnecessary)—reflect the prejudices of a particular class and a particular era, four decades after the abolition of slavery. It also illustrates the consequences that the racial question and civil and political segregation were starting to have on life in the United States toward the end of the Progressive Era. However, Phillips's work established some of the main issues that would constitute subsequent research into slavery. Eugene Genovese highlighted this in his first works when he put forward a different interpretation of Phillips's work (which to a certain extent went against the grain of the author) when reflecting on the relationships between master and servant, the establishment of white dominance, and the creation of a culture in response to white domination (one that was *created by slaves*), and when examining the characteristics of the plantation and the modern system of slavery. With regard to this system, Genovese made use of Phillips's opinions on the patriarchal nature of slavery in the South and the absence of capitalist rationality when it came to making everyday economic decisions. These decisions can, however, be considered socially rational and necessary to maintain production with slaves and preserve the role of the ruling classes (Genovese 1990b: 203–6; also 1990a: 113–28; on the critical recovery of Phillips in the 1960s, see Smith 1992: 20).

The concerns that oriented the work of the three most important authors of the first half of the twentieth century (apart from Phillips) involved in the study of African slavery in America were closely related to the multiracial postslavery society. Fernando Ortiz in Cuba, Gilberto Freyre in Brazil, and Frank Tannenbaum in the United States offered different responses to the issue of blacks' integration or lack of integration in present-day societies and analyzed slave regimes to explain this. The quality of the results varied, and nowadays they are of more interest to the history of historiography and to debates among historians than for the information they provide. Fernando Ortiz's book *Los negros esclavos*, written in 1916, claimed to have a sociological aim: to explain the "environment" of slaves that prolonged the moral and intellectual inequality of Africans (a lack of civilization, he claimed) with regard to whites. This was to become one of the main difficulties of the young republic, because, Ortiz maintained, an *entire race began to lead a bad life* and entered the criminal underworld. The author based this perception on his training (and occupational distortion) in law and criminology, but he was still a long way from the valuable anthropological papers he subsequently wrote (Ortiz [1916] 1988: 28–29). When he wrote the book, the author was seduced by the theories of Enrico Ferri and Cesare Lombroso on the biological basis of criminality. When applied to societies in which, due to poverty and exclusion, Afro-Cubans (former slaves and their descendants) were prominent in crime statistics, the theory was charged with racist content veiled in pseudoscientific criteria (Naranjo Orovio 2005: 137–78). Aside from the aims set out in the introduction to the book, Ortiz's contribution in *Los negros esclavos* is limited to the compilation of the printed material available and its presentation in a balanced, descriptive volume that is not without compassion. To a considerable extent, the work owes its reputation to the fact that it was a forerunner, and to the scholarly slant that a patient compilation acquired among studies on the subject at a time when in Cuba practically the only materials that existed were half-finished works by José Antonio Saco in his *Historia de la esclavitud* and Aimes's text, to which reference is made below.

Gilberto Freyre's approach in *Casa-Grande e senzala*, written in 1933, was very different. It was a brilliant narrative essay aimed at demonstrating the influence of colonial estates as *colonizing units* in the formation of Brazilian society. Despite acknowledgment that (manorial) estates constituted an economic, social, and political system that included production, work, religion, and family, the author rejected the perspective of studying the economy (material life, whose explicative interest conforms to a Marxist obsession) and adopted an ethnographical point of view centered on the domestic life of what he called *slavocratic patriarchalism*, which would help to reveal the detailed history of Brazilians, the formation of the social community, and the national character (Freyre [1933] 2002: 10–12, 22). Where other authors encountered conflict, Freyre discovered astonishing harmony, which actually helped to conceal the dramatic past of forced servitude with updated paternalism.

In *Slave and Citizen*, published in 1946, the sociologist and criminologist Frank Tannenbaum turned back to slavery to understand the problem of race relations. He used a comparative perspective to explain how the abyss that appeared to exist between communities in the United States did not seem to exist in Latin America (Tannenbaum 1946). Just as Humboldt observed at the beginning of the nineteenth century and as the anthropologist Hubert Aimes wrote in 1907 when studying the case of Cuba (Aimes 1907), Tannenbaum subscribed to the theory that slavery as practiced by the Spanish and Portuguese treated slaves more humanely than slavery in countries populated from northern Europe, in the Caribbean, and in Anglo-American territories, and that those northern European attitudes later continued in the United States. Religion and juridical practices formed the basis of the difference that not only granted or denied slaves juridical and moral status, but also hindered or facilitated social mobility.

While historians have debated Tannenbaum's analyses and conclusions and have even updated them (De la Fuente 2004), they have generally overlooked his methodological presuppositions. Following the theory of *social reaction*, which was fashionable in the 1930s in the Chicago School, Tannenbaum considered that stereotypes conditioned behavior and identity in the same way that the social frames of reference in which individuals act (the various different slave regimes) were decisive in explaining collective behavior. Thus, Tannenbaum extended the microsocial theoretical model in which *interactionism* began to take effect and that soon became symbolic interactionism. Charged with functionalism ("any change which is verified in any part of the social structure affects the whole of society. . . . All influences are vertical . . . , they all tend to affect the social structure"), he interpreted slavery as the system that created a society and gave it its characteristics and customs, including, of course, its upper caste. Influenced by interactionism, following the postulates of this latest tendency on the "loans" of all human action, in particular those articulated by means of socialization and culture (from language to symbols), he laid the foundations for explanations of the creative impact slaves had on the various different contexts, either repressive or tolerant, in which they acted: "Despite all the efforts to define the role of the negro in order to turn him into an object or a real estate property in legal terms, he continued to be a human being," he said. And he added, "Because of his presence, he modified the format of the State, the nature of property, the legal system, the organization of labor, the role of the Church, in addition to its character, the concept of justice, ethics, ideas of what is just and what is unjust." In short, slavery had an influence on "the whole group," on whites and blacks, men and women, young and old (Tannenbaum 1946; the quotations are translated from the Spanish version: Tannenbaum 1968: 111–12). It is worth highlighting the terms by which slavery "contaminated," by which it had a bearing on the whole social structure and even conditioned the white ruling classes: *because of its presence*, in other words because of its existence, which may be passive (thus reducing the topicality of the author's approaches in an era governed by the *agency* of individuals, which we will refer to below). Yet for Tannenbaum, this presence was strong enough to *modify*.

In 1944 Eric Williams, a historian from Trinidad who was educated at Oxford, began to study slavery from a completely new perspective. In *Capitalism and Slavery*, he ignored the life of slaves in the plantation and directed his attention to the role that the trade in Africans and the plantation system had in the formation of English capitalism. Aside from his conclusions, which continue to divide readers, the most lasting aspect of the work is that he situated the colonial productive regime in a wider economic system, at least that of the metropolis and more specifically that of the most advanced economic region in terms of the supply of capital, consumer markets, labor force, and products manufactured in highly competitive conditions (Williams 1944). In short, slavery could be explained through economics.

Not until the 1960s was there a considerable increase in the number and quality of studies on slavery. The historiography of the United States contributed the most studies and the majority of new perspectives, which began to focus attention on the Caribbean with works by Sidney Mintz, Herbert Klein, and Franklin Knight. At the same time, a specific Caribbean historiography was created by the Cuban historian Moreno Fraginals.

Before turning his attention once again to Puerto Rico, the anthropologist Sidney Mintz, who was concerned with relations between the peasantry and the plantation system, began researching the formation of the protopeasantry under slave conditions in Jamaica, when the concession of land to slaves for subsistence made marginal agriculture possible and enabled a series of products to be introduced into the local market (Mintz 2007: especially 193, 197–98). Mintz's work drew attention to the existence of slaves' own space and their ability to go beyond the limits imposed by their condition and become part of society.

In two outstanding books which appeared in 1969 and 1974, Eugene Genovese shifted the emphasis onto the construction of culture by slaves themselves, inspired by the Gramscian notion of the construction of an alternative hegemony by the subordinate classes (Genovese 1969, 1974). Genovese paid attention to the ways of everyday life, to qualitative elements as opposed to the quantitative emphasis of economic history. It should be pointed out that quantitative history was just beginning to bear fruit on the subject of slavery and was still a long way from determining essential issues, such as the number of Africans transported, the vegetative growth of slave populations, the demographic structure of the group, the number of workers in the productive units and their relation to the volume of goods produced, and related matters—in other words, a considerable proportion of the information required to assess the slave regime in its entirety and the social structure to which it gave rise. The publication of Robert Fogel's *Time on the Cross*, the greatest example of what Genovese called "abstract empiricism," coincided with the publication of the second of Genovese's books in 1974.

In *The World the Slaveholders Made* and in particular in *Roll, Jordan, Roll*, Genovese took an interest in the action of individuals and attempted to liberate this from the conditioning of structures, in an approach similar to the one put forward by Edward P. Thompson to study the formation of the working class (1963). However, the social relations and the societies in which free craftsmen worked in England in the eighteenth century and slaves worked in Carolina, Virginia, or Georgia in the nineteenth century were radically different from one another. Let us stop here for an instant to draw some methodological conclusions that have gone unnoticed.

For Thompson, class culture was the mainstay of the social identity (an identity that presupposes certain specific relations of production) in which it is formed, despite not being determined by these relations (*determine* is the key concept here, in two senses: the direct and inevitable correlation between infrastructure and superstructure, and the conditioning of social being based on social consciousness). Secondly, the formation of a class required collective action, *action* in terms defined by Max Weber but also, although it is not usually mentioned, by Marx (1985: 349–50; Marx and Engels 1974: 60–61). The differences with Thompson, which did not prevent his work from having an enormous influence on historians and sociologists, arose from various perspectives. Aside from ideological discussions, the most cutting criticism questioned the process by which a social group generated a distinguishing culture, since according to his detractors, that was the weak point of *The Making of the English Working Class* (Wood 1990: 125–52).

Transferring the propositions put forward by Thompson to a slave society presented some major problems. The first was that the capacity for social action in slave societies was severely limited, and not only because of the legislation governing the freedom of association or opinion. In slave societies the actors did not own the property rights to their own persons, and the social regime in which they found themselves went to considerable lengths to keep them under control. The system not only compelled them to work, but also attempted to regulate most of their actions. As a result, if action could not take the form of open protest, mobilization, or revolt (which under conditions of slavery were very rare), and it could not take the form of association (which was typical of the world of free labor), action had to take the form of resistance, to which little attention had yet been paid in the 1960s and 1970s, especially if the intensity of the resistance was low. Genovese chose to focus attention on culture and on amplifying its importance, analyzing the two ways slaves used to identify and reassert themselves. These involved the preservation of African traditions (to which limited attention was paid, unlike the situation during the first decade of the twenty-first century), and in particular, in the reception and reinterpretation of influences received from the white world of their masters (and of poor white people). These influences are endowed with meanings different from those attributed to them by whites, in an exercise that not only led to the recognition and formation of a class, but also to the political expression of class struggle. After rejecting the notion of acculturation and ignoring the notion of transculturation (which was defined by Fernando Ortiz and praised by Malinowski), Genovese drew attention to the process by which slaves reassigned meaning to the culture received and converted it into their own culture, guided by the values that they were creating (particularly through religion) and that helped them to bear the moral and psychological aggression of slave regimes (Genovese 1974: 658–60). In short, *the world the slaves made* acquired a specific character and gave black slaves the qualities required to construct a particular social identity and condition. The context was provided by the paternalism of slave relations. If, on the one hand, paternalism provided the planters with the ideology on which they based their hegemony (the notion of mutual obligations) and on the basis of which it was possible to reduce coercion, on the other hand, the sense of reciprocity implied recognizing the slaves' condition as human beings and allowed slaves to make use of paternalism for their own interests.[2]

Genovese's work put forward the dilemma between the history of slavery viewed from an economic history perspective and the history of slavery viewed from a social history perspective. In the case of social history, based preferentially on culture, this opened the doors to dialogue between social history and anthropology, after certain anthropologists (Aimes, Ortiz) or social scientists with an anthropological perspective (Tannenbaum) had broached the subject of history. It was, and still is, I believe, a false dilemma. Sidney Mintz highlighted this in 1961 in a brief, forceful text, which is misleading insofar as it appears as a bibliographical comment:

The economic arrangements which bound slave and master postulated that the master had the right to appropriate something which was the slave's—his time, or the products of his labor, his skill, often his children, perhaps his life. All definitions of the slave condition contain as a nucleus the idea of the property rights of one person in another. In certain circumstances, such rights take the form of capital. For the anthropologist, whether or not the slave is a capital good, a source of capital accumulation, a commodity, or something else and beyond these, is very relevant. . . . As for capital, it may be viewed concretely, as some store used to undertake fresh production, or as a social aspect of the productive process. (1961: 579)

Quoting a passage from *Das Kapital*, Mintz recalled that for Marx, "capital is not a thing, but a social relation between persons, established through the instrumentality of things" (Marx 1939, 1: 791). And he referred to an important note: "A negro is a negro. In certain circumstances he becomes a slave. A mule is a machine for spinning cotton. Only under certain circumstances does it become capital. Outside these circumstances it is no more capital than gold is intrinsically money, or sugar the price of sugar. . . . Capital is a social relation of production" (Marx 1939, 1: 791). This passage is the one that allowed Thompson to redefine the concept of class in relation to the formation of the industrial worker by removing him from his structural reification to give him back the dimension of relations between people (social relations) during the production process (and, naturally, from the relations created from the former, outside and beyond the area of production).

Insofar as he was describing something related to human behavior (which, let us remember, originated during the course of a material activity), Mintz highlighted the importance of slavery for anthropology. "Especially important is the degree to which a particular mode of slavery is primarily economic, or embedded within a code of behaviour such that the economic rationale is submerged or secondary. All slavery may be slavery, but not all slaveries are the same, economically or culturally," he added (1961: 580). He thus refers us to the issue of more or less patriarchal slavery and plantation slavery. He avoided using these terms, because under no circumstances did he forget the level of domination implicit in the slave relation, despite understanding that the decreased presence of economic rationality influenced not only the capacity to appropriate labor and goods, but also behavior in general. Mintz preferred to concentrate on the varying degree to which part of the product of others was appropriated, which depended on the social and technical organization *of the institutional system that accompanied it, including the economic system*, to determine whether slavery was aimed at maximizing profits or not. In contrast to Tannenbaum's argument, one type of slavery or another does not depend on issues such as "race, civil liberties, protection of the rights of individuals slave and free, or the presence or absence of one or several religious codes," but rather "as resulting from different ecologies, differential maturation of metropolitan markets and industries, and different political relationships between Creole governing bodies and the metropolitan authorities" (Mintz 1961: 579–87).

In short, economic, social, cultural, political, and historical aspects cannot be separated in order to understand the phenomenon of slavery, no matter how important a subject slavery is for anthropology; also in the tradition of cultural studies, culture tends to become the matrix of behavior. But as Mintz highlighted, for the anthropologist it is also very important to know whether the slave "is a capital good, a source of capital accumulation, a commodity, or something else and beyond these" (1961: 579), given that there is also a material perspective to anthropology.

Many of these proposals and debates, which appear to be anchored in a different age, have an enormous influence on the evolution of approaches to the history of modern slavery.

This section would not be complete without mentioning Manuel Moreno Fraginals' work *El Ingenio*, the first part of which was published in 1964 (the complete edition was published in 1978). It is a unique, brilliant work that still represents a benchmark in historical studies(whether one accepts his conclusions or debates them), to the extent that some authors have devoted all their efforts to demonstrating that the work contains certain inaccuracies. *El Ingenio* has proved to be a source of inspiration for new research and is still of exceptional worth more than half a century after it was published, due to the issues it deals with, the way in which it addresses them, and the conclusions it reaches. It is a good model for study regarding the possibility of history imbricating economic and social issues, technology, attention to natural resources, individual history (of one particular crop or one particular country), and international perspective. As a starting point and the main theme, Moreno took the production of sugar and created a vision of history in which the labor market and the slave condition occupied almost half the work, but in which slavery was a constant feature throughout.

From Enormous Magnitudes, Theoretical Frameworks, and Empathy to the Major Human Lessons of Minor Histories

During the 1960s and 1970s (and with some significant contributions still to come in the 1980s), academic studies on slave plantations were guided by three dominant lines. First, there was the quantitative aspect: production, commercialization, the number of workers employed, and their supply by means of the slave trade. Demographic aspects played a central role: the extent of the slave trade, the geographical and ethnic origins of slaves, the age pyramid, the gender ratio, the mortality and birth rates. It was also important to establish the property structure regarding slaves and their price, together with the territorial structure, volume of production, productivity indexes, and similar matters. The history of slavery in the Americas presented itself as one of the most fertile grounds for the development of academic history that made headway after World War II, when proposals put forward by the second generation of *Annales* represented by Fernand Braudel were assimilated, focusing studies on structures and the long-term perspective, in addition to theories regarding systems. It was also the time that witnessed the historiographical development of a branch of Marxism that Perry Anderson referred to as "western Marxism," which provided new categories of analysis and claimed to be more deductive than inductive. History benefited from the strong expansion of social sciences and its methods of processing information.

Second, there was an attempt to categorize the knowledge acquired by means of theoretical frameworks, allowing it to be placed within the systems or structures in which the plantation operated. One of its derivatives was the debate surrounding the location of the slave production regime in the international context. This debate started out as an acid test of the classic models of Marxism and constituted a theoretical challenge that urged the construction of specific models or their insertion in the world-system. For some it was the expression of a colonial mode of production, or modern slavery; others classified it within capitalism, which in America had developed prematurely since the sixteenth century, subordinated to centers that, under close analysis, were still transforming, thus only representing a capitalist subsystem destined to be peripheral and the origin of the development of underdevelopment. The most problematic aspect consisted of fitting reality, in its social and temporal dimension, into a highly abstract theoretical category, the *mode of production*. The proposals were extensive and aspired to a degree of originality that was not always achieved. The theoretical debates were particularly heated within Latin American historiography (Assadourian 1984; Gorender 1978; Lapa 1980; Cardoso 1988; Figueiredo 2004; Barcia 1988: 96–116).

The historically existing society is always more complex and displays a weave of social relations that coexist together with those that are predominant and that articulate society. The special characteristic of modern slavery, which coexisted with fully capitalist, industrial societies, is that in its dominions it continued to play a decisive role in social articulation with all of its consequences, while creating close ties with the markets (and the result was a marked effect on mercantile capital and its reinvestment in the plantation) and with all the elements referred to previously when characterizing *second slavery* (Tomich 2004; the original text in Tomich 1988: 103–17).

Third, the study of slavery was the perfect field to allow social history to address the most exploited of subalterns, along similar lines to studies on industrial workers. The control exerted by plantation owners, revolts, runaway slaves, and culture were the subjects that completed the panorama. The history of the slave trade and slavery was the other side of the prosperity of the metropolises. It was a reminder of the abuses on which the *great transformation* had been based (in the sense in which Karl Polanyi used the expression), that is, the birth of capitalism. And just as Eric Williams reminded us, slavery in America was inseparable from this incipient capitalism, whatever degree of reciprocity we are prepared to acknowledge. Social history also showed us the worst face of colonialism and its lasting effects on the African countries that supplied the labor force (and as a result, with other functions, an integral part of the same system) and on the countries in America that received the workers.

In accordance with the analytical perspective that was adopted, close to the subaltern classes and based on an attitude committed to the historical denunciation of the tragedy that this colonial and postcolonial form of production represented, the history of slavery that was being written was less and less related to economic activities that required coercive labor. Capitalism, which was entirely comprehensive, had become a premise that did not need to be demonstrated; human greed, a failure to act according to moral principles, and the existence of morals historically adapted to the ruling colonial societies were the ultimate reasons (which did not require further attention) for such reprehensible practices. The process of producing sugar, cotton, tobacco, coffee, and other products was secondary to the analysis of social relations and, more specifically (and apparently more importantly), human conditions, toward which attention was being focused.

The history of slaves, to a large extent separated from slavery as if human beings could be separated from the system in which they act, gradually "became more human." This trend of historiography should not necessarily be considered negative. How could it be, if the essence of slavery was the appropriation of certain human beings by other human beings! However, when suggesting that studies became more human, I wish to highlight that by removing slaves from the social regime in which they work, there is a certain risk of converting their history into a permanent assessment of the human condition instead of offering historical explanations, which is still the task of the historian (who otherwise simply becomes a lay moralist). By emphasizing the moral order of dignity, in addition to offering lessons for posterity and historical examples for preachers' Sunday sermons, we run the risk of including everyday conflicts and less frequent and more important conflicts in a similarly moral sphere, of considering what is just and what is unjust, what is good and what is bad, what is correct and what is unacceptable, virtue and sin, the desire to better oneself to beat the enemy, and the spirit of resignation.

The imputation of adopting a *humanist* perspective, to differentiate it from a scientific perspective, gave rise to two simultaneous controversies in the late 1970s. On the one hand, Althusserian Marxism, which during the 1970s and early 1980s had a significant influence on the British academic Left (among sociologists and critical historians), used Edward Thompson and Eugene Genovese as the scapegoats of their theoretical essays in order, as Thompson writes, to see who could best interpret Marxism or to demonstrate that the two historians were not "true Marxists." Althusserian structuralism, represented by, among others, the social theoreticians Barry Hindess and Paul Hirst, the sociologists Perry Anderson, Stuart Hall, and Simon Clarke, and the historian Richard Johnson, whose positions and criticisms did not fully coincide with each other, assimilated Thompson and Genovese's methodological premises; according to their opponents, the two historians had been carried away by the subjectivity of the individuals under study and by the importance given to the combination of experience and culture in the formation of social classes (Johnson 1978: 79–100). The two terms used by their opponents to define (and discredit) them were "humanist" (because they abandoned economic relations in favor of experience, and because of the historical abstraction with which human values were presented) and "culturalist."[3] Thompson retorted by explaining his approaches as follows: There was *lived experience* and *perceived experience*; Marx referred to the latter as social conscience. Lived experience, he continued, was the result of repeated everyday events *inside* the "social being," *which are often the result of material causes that usually occur behind consciousness or intention*; lived experience is not directly transferred or reflected in consciousness, but neither is it diverted or indefinitely falsified by ideology. Instead, it is subjected to constant friction. Culture provides the link between lived and perceived experiences, but that, he argued, did not mean he could be classed as "culturalist," if that meant that attitudes were explained through culture (Thompson 1981).

The second controversy took place in North America and involved Genovese and one of the main authors of the so-called *new labor history*, Herbert Gutman. Gutman's concerns were also similar to those of Thompson, although his responses within the framework of critical historiography distanced him from the English historian's flexible Marxism. Gutman criticized the notion of paternalistic relations, which according to Genovese articulated the masters' domination and the slaves' resistance. For Gutman, the world the slaves made was a reality created in opposition to their domination, while at the same time it was beyond the masters' influence; the slave family was an irrefutable demonstration of the desire to form strong, lasting bonds by means of which their own values were developed and the history of the group was transmitted (Gutman 1976; see also Fredrickson 1988: 116–24). If structuralists criticized Genovese because his humanism was not Marxist enough, Genovese replied to Gutman that the latter's humanism was liberal and idealist, as it disregarded reciprocal relations, dialectical relations, the experience of work, and the incipient violence involved in the political forms of the context and of the actors themselves, reduced to the sphere of private life and to their ability to miraculously create an *autonomous culture* (Fox-Genovese and Genovese 1983: 179–212).

Looking at the subject in perspective, if Genovese's work on the reassessment of slave culture was of outstanding importance, Gutman's approach eventually had a greater and longer-lasting influence, even though it was not necessarily built on firmer foundations. Pondering the reason for the latter's success is tantamount to reflecting on the recent development of social history, and in particular, on the exaltation of the concept of actors' *agency*, detached from social relations. This aspect is analyzed below, but prior to that, we shall introduce the reflections of an author who was an expert on slavery in the classical world.

In a text that should be obligatory reading for anyone interested in the history of slavery and historiography in general, *Ancient Slavery and Modern Ideology*, Moses Finley highlighted the separation that usually accompanies studies on the subject, some of which favor an ethical-spiritual approach and others the economic approach (1980). Referring to the authoritative opinion of David Brion Davis (1966; 1975), Finlay reminds us of two circumstances that are worth keeping in mind: First, the influence of the era has led to a situation in which each new interpretation of slavery claims to be more antiracist than the previous one, and second, the Enlightenment (with the consequent influence it exerted on the creation of historical science) took history to be a source of paradigms. Instead of taking an interest in promoting a subject of knowledge, history offered examples, models, and in the case of slavery, a paradigm that denied freedom and reduced human beings to subhuman status. In eighteenth-century French and British historical, economic, and moral literature, servitude in Europe and slavery in the New World were treated as if they were identical, or formal distinctions based on Roman law were made between real slavery (associated with the land) and personal (domestic) slavery (Finley 1982: 11, 22–23). Despite the existence of a wide variety of types of compulsory labor, only during the second half of the eighteenth century and the first half of the nineteenth could free and slave labor be assimilated as variants of the same dependence or of a dual phase of economic development, precisely by those who defended the advantages of free, paid labor for reasons of efficiency (Adam Smith, Karl Marx) or demography (David Hume), and for civil reasons (Benjamin Franklin).

The persistence of the past as a paradigm—*historia magistra vitae*—was reedited in successive approaches to the subject of slavery from a human perspective. This happened in Genovese's work, and it is also the case in the era of postmodernism and cultural history. The dominating perspective is that of microhistory, under-stood as a kind of history of private lives and individual experiences (the more individual and exemplary the better). This has led to a paradoxical situation, which has often seen the reversal of traditional ideographic history, with major figures being replaced by ordinary people. The casualty was the group picture, the shared backgrounds, the evidence that gives meaning to constitutive backgrounds of large groups, including social classes. And the result has been to confuse two principles of theoretical logic and historical experience: to confuse particularity and singularity.

The Social Framework of Slavery

During the last few decades, developments in scientific inquiry have been reflected in a change of perspective and in the choice of issues included as subjects of study.

Unquestionable progress has been made, which allows a better understanding of colonial and postcolonial societies through the study of human groups, in particular the actions and motivations of subaltern sectors, since hardly any attention has been paid to the other half of the equation, that is, to plantation owners. In contrast, macro analyses, dominated by the quantitative perspective, and micro analyses, converted into life histories, have tended to avoid the social framework in which such a long-lasting regime functioned and can be explained. In short, research into slaves and slavery has been affected by the recent (and radical) evolution of historical study. The methods used have become more sophisticated, more questions have been asked about the past, and the field of analysis has widened. Yet it is not certain that historians continue to search for an explanation for the social regime whose operation facilitated the actions of the subjected.

During the 1990s, historiography experienced the crisis of totalizing or systematic models, together with a reaction against economic determinism and the quantitativism of previous decades. That did not mean that quantitative studies subject to theoretical and methodological models disappeared. The vigor shown, for example, by one part of Brazilian historiography or by the foreign historiography about Brazil provided noteworthy results and reflects negatively on its virtual absence in the Hispanic Caribbean (see Bergad 2004; Luna and Klein 2005). But it is more often possible to find studies that refer to nondeterminism and methodological individualism as the reaction to earlier abuses: proposals of mechanist causation, cold economism, inflexible structural determinations—in short, different reductive approaches to social reality and, by extension, a more debatable reaction to any notion of structure. As a result, the interest of numerous historians has shifted toward the history of human beings who were slaves, whose lives were obviously not limited to working the fields, being whipped, or crawling through dismal bunkhouses. Men and women who lived as slaves were not a factor of production only, even though their status was defined through production, through their work.

After a long journey, it is worth looking back to see whether the path has led us to new objectives or whether we are walking round in circles without realizing it. Perhaps the time has come to ask ourselves, once again, about the possibilities and the limits of social history, which has perhaps become too anthropological, in a different sense from the one recommended by Mintz and other anthropologists who were heedful of material realities. We should ask ourselves how much more is offered by an analysis of human actions that is not propitiated or influenced by the relations of production, that is, by actions beyond the external norms affecting the actor, or at the disposal of those who occupied a superior position and who (undoubtedly) made up a particular social class, namely the slave-owning class.

Improving our knowledge of the "institution" has meant looking more deeply into issues such as the subjects' involvement in the system, the acceptance of responsibilities in exchange for rewards and incentives, and the independence enjoyed by some slaves at the heart of the plantation, which not only involved the possibility of planting and selling produce, but also bringing legal action, creating a family, and holding celebrations. We have discovered a detailed repertory of forms of passive resistance, along the lines suggested by James Scott (1986: 5–35; 1990) among free peasants in contemporary societies, which has revolutionized studies on social conflicts by paying attention to low-intensity, everyday conflicts that had been previously ignored. Yet Scott's work also questioned the Gramscian theory of hegemony and, supposedly, the mechanisms of passive (imposed) or active acculturation, in the style of Genovese's proposals. According to Scott, instead of constructing an alternative cultural hegemony, subaltern groups developed their own survival strategies without situating them in a perspective of social change, instead situating them in the limited scope of, perhaps, the group community and certainly the family and the individual.

Historical analysis has moved from macro analyses, which systematized cases and attempted to reduce them to their shared characteristics (while also simplifying social interaction and reducing its complexity), to microsocial studies concerned with the interests and motivations of human actions in severely adverse conditions, which provide lessons on dignity and survival strategies. What is more, we have greatly increased our knowledge of the processes by which ethnic and national identities are constructed. Without doubt, all the issues mentioned above are extremely important and I certainly do not underestimate their importance.

Acquiring more and better knowledge does not prevent us from reflecting on a method that implies certain risks. The first and most frequent is what could be referred to as a certain "humanization" of studies on slaves. Once again, we return to a debate that has been invoked several times from different perspectives: its persistence, or to be more exact, the fact that it has recurred periodically ever since studies were first carried out in the twentieth century, must be closely related to both the subject of study and the stance of the historian. In effect, we are studying human beings in extreme conditions of subservience, in a context that, unlike previous societies, has been presided over since the end of the eighteenth century by individual values and a widespread awareness of civil and political freedom. Therefore the contrast between the conditions of servitude and freedom in modern slavery is much greater than it was in the past.

Fortunately, the attitude of historians has changed since Phillips, Ortiz, and Freyre, among others, began their studies. The risk of a humanized perspective has been empathy toward suffering, toward the capacity for resistance used by slaves, toward strategies aimed at adapting and transforming adversity in ways through which the slave began to take ownership of part of his or her destiny.

Beyond examining the boundaries of such survival, attention has remained focused in particular on the process by which reciprocal advantages developed (for the slave and for the master) through mechanisms of negotiation that history had ignored. Genovese appears to be ahead of the game on this point. Insofar as negotiation strives to create autonomous spaces in which to house an exclusive culture, Gutman was victorious. Finding and documenting these areas of negotiation was a veritable sharp shock to the theory of absolute and complete domination of slaves' will, of the permanent and absolute negation of slaves' autonomy.

The extent to which such advantages were capable of changing the conditions of domination, and even domination itself, is the basis of a prolific line of study in recent years. Compared with classical works' reduction of slavery, often considered solely as work, as manpower, or as an object belonging to a master, studies undertaken during this latest stage have highlighted the slave's capacity to move within the limits of domination and expand these limits. The concept that sums up slaves' will and action is *agency*. It is a sociological derivation, generally individualized, of the Weberian concept of *action*. The agency of slaves appears to explain everything, to a large extent forgetting the agency of the owner and above all the power granted to the master to exercise his property rights over human beings, a power that regulates, restricts, or denies concessions. The exaltation of agency associated with will completes the "death of God," announced by Nietzsche, to situate the human being as the absolute master of his acts. Paradoxically, the quality is recognized in plantation slaves, the human beings with the least freedom of all.

It is worth remembering the report written by Juan de Erice and Nicolás Calvo for the Havana Royal Trade Consulate on July 8, 1795, on the subject of work. On this occasion they requested that owners be granted *total control* over slaves' lives.[4] By this they meant total control over their lives, as opposed to attempts at public regulation in the form of the Black Code, of regulations such as those that the Crown had passed around that time. In Cuban plantations, the margins of negotiation before the second half of the nineteenth century were relatively limited, so much so that it is perhaps worth asking if the concept of "negotiation" is appropriate when referring to what happened within the confines of the plantation.

Let us start with a question regarding methodology. Interactionist theories found a first-rate assistant in the legacy of contractual thinking, rooted in particular in the colonies of North America, where they had been founded or administered by companies that transferred company legal principles to civil life, a fact that would later have a considerable effect on political life. The development of commercial life in the Caribbean in the eighteenth and early nineteenth centuries could also have influenced Hispanic litigation culture, but under no circumstances should it be forgotten that a plantation was an enclosed space of domination and exploitation, a reality far removed from lawyers' offices. It is worth pondering the extent to which postslavery contractualism (the current system) affects historians' vision when they examine the past, and to what extent it conforms to national juridical traditions, which are disregarded when researching situations that took place in Cuba and Brazil in the eighteenth and nineteenth centuries.

On the other hand, the theory of negotiation taken to its conclusion brings up to date the controversies of thirty and forty years ago regarding the issue of consent in slavery. Forced into slavery by violent means and maintained in that condition through violence, the system was incapable of eradicating slaves' will to resist domination. I do not believe anyone would argue against that. From that point onward, the tension between resistance and domination could be resolved in many different ways. In Genovese's model, the resistance-struggle benefited from paternalistic ideology and from slaves' appropriation of outside values, which they transformed into their own values and incorporated into resistance. This model combines two competing cultural hegemonies within the framework of a conception based on limits enforced through violence (by the owners) and on redirecting the conflict to enable the creation of a particular social identity (by the slaves). In more recent models, slaves' autonomous agency promoted constant small-scale negotiation to increase their autonomy in exchange for reducing costs, which for the plantation owners implied exercising control over their workers (and who knows, although little emphasis is placed on this, ensuring production). In conditions of exploitation and domination such as those that exist in slavery, negotiation in pursuit of a new consensus could lead to the conclusion that slaves took responsibility for the system and were in some way responsible for the continued feasibility of the slave regime. Taken to its conclusion, history would justify Scarlett O'Hara's bewilderment when she was informed by her faithful housemaid that the slaves had abandoned the plantation when the Yankee army was approaching. She was unable to understand this, since she believed that the plantation had been a "home" for them all.

What are the limits to consensus? Here there is a total breakdown between Edward Thompson's proposals on the *moral economy of the crowd*, the reaction of free human beings whose interests were confronted at the end of the eighteenth century (which culminates in a formally restitutory consensus of changed conditions and which in actual fact supposed a new balance that was advantageous for the challengers), and the approaches to negotiation and consensus applied to a social regime as different as modern slavery in America.

The humanization of studies on slavery, with the risk of distortion that this carries, is undertaken through the analysis of the specific, through human beings taken individually. It refers us to "human nature," a timeless quality, an abstraction devoid of historical circumstances. It is the opposite of epistemological theories of neoclassical economy that take constant factors as premises and are concerned with their combination, disregarding the *historicity* (the historical quality) of social relations and their consequences in human beings.

In the end, slaves are presented as a representation of subjection and humiliation, people who *resist* and in a certain way change their destiny, improve their situation, recreate autonomous forms of social life, and exercise self-direction: family, procreation, religion, suicides, abortions, and other means that would imply a highly developed eugenic sensibility. Knowledge thus becomes an epic story of ordinary lives. The situation is reminiscent of the controversies that absorbed specialists in the social history of industrial labor during the mid-1980s. In particular, it recalls the recriminating text written by Lawrence T. McDonnell, "You Are Too Sentimental" (1984: 629–54). McDonnell proclaimed the existence of two (in his opinion disastrous) forms of worker-related sentimentalism in the United States that had ironically contaminated many of the best academics of the history of the working class. One case presented a harmonious vision based on fair treatment, and the other idealized the victories. Despite their good intentions, continued the critic, modern historians at times denied the hostility that existed between capital and labor, in particular when they observed the relations between individuals and celebrated the survival of those relations. In the other form, they exaggerated the coherence and resistance, underestimating their human costs and political subjugation. In both circumstances, historians appeared to be unaware of the sentimental conservatism of their positions and the concessions granted to behaviorist theories. A good many of these reflections can be applied to studies on slavery undertaken during the last two decades. Not for nothing were some of McDonnell's criticisms aimed at Gutman in his role as an industrial labor historian.

The enduring lines of what have come to be known as macro studies show a dedicated interest in issues such as economic growth, the comparative advantages that led to the explanation and exhaustion of the model, and to the study of factors presumed to be in equilibrium (land, labor and capital, perhaps also technology). In short, social factors have to a certain extent been reduced to interchangeable productive elements, in the manner in which they operate in modern industrial economies. The result, or the impression that we have, is that society appears to be slipping through our fingers. The same is true of micro models and micro analyses. The micro perspective, at one time adopted as the only hope amidst the shipwreck of scientific certainties, is essentially a means of approaching reality, a method of studying social problems. Yet society is not micro, and neither can it be understood by considering it as an aggregated network of individuals and families. It does not conform to a network in the style of a spider's web, radial and concentric at the same time, nor to a network in the style of human tissue, interconnected on a cellular base, however attractive the metaphor may be. It includes all this in addition to horizontal and vertical relations, the latter constructed on exploitation, dominance, and power.

Perhaps before we continue, it is worth stopping to reconsider some basic issues, such as: What is a plantation and how does it relate to and affect the natural environment? What meaning does the notion of master and slave have in the context of the plantation? The answers obtained will determine the position of many of the pieces we have been working with and enable us to put them together. I would like to draw attention, however, to some aspects that are in danger of disappearing from historians' interest and that once again link the social history of slavery to the economy.

Sidney Mintz was right when he warned that slavery was more than an economic issue and considerably more than a means of controlling the labor of others. It involved "a conception of the human condition, an ideology of society and a set of economic arrangements, in short, a cultural apparatus by which slaves and masters were related" (1961: 579). Yet it was the economic conditions that determined the relations of domination and justified the existence of a legal order that made one human being the property of another.

Master-slave relations are social relations of human dimensions, protected by legal considerations justified by means of economic criteria: the master is the owner of the external labor capacity to the maximum extent possible, since he owns the worker both as laborer and as the procreator of future workers, who can be used at any time as merchandise. The history of economic activities, as the name suggests, cannot be restricted to the history of the economy and its indicators: it also requires (for each moment) the analysis of the characteristics of these activities, of those who perform them, and of the conditions under which they are performed, and for what uses. Social history, for its part, cannot be restricted to the study of human behavior isolated from the conditions that created a particular use of labor and laborers, and an owner of ethnic people who were forced to make capital productive in the colonial world and subsequently. If the economic activities were not limited to agricultural production and to the production of goods, if the social relations were the result of a specific economic order, it is difficult to understand the category of *slaves* without the slave regime and all that constitutes it without aspiring to situate it in a particular economy. The intersection of structural conditions and individual and group responses in real history should guide the construction of models for study aimed at recounting such phenomena. Otherwise we shall perhaps continue to be occupied with periodic novelties that pass as genuine innovations.

Notes

1. This article was prepared as part of the research project HAR2009–07037, funded by Spain's Ministry of Science and Innovation; translated by Paul Edgar.

2. Genovese situated the social relations of slavery in a context about which he successively modified his opinion: if in his initial work he considered that this context was evidently capitalist (corrected or questioned by the slave workforce, the anomaly to which Marx referred), the author gradually moved toward a hybrid conception, in which he placed considerable importance on precapitalist social forms, in which paternalism played a central role (Genovese 1967, 1974; Fox-Genovese and Genovese 1983).

3. The assimilation between Thompson and Genovese, based on certain similarities when dealing with the subjects, the role both assigned to experience and their perception by the actors, the importance given to the mediating function of culture, the reinterpretation

of the traditions received, etc., concealed the differences that separated them (see Palmer 1981, in particular 79–80, 109 ff.).

4. Report by Pedro Juan de Erice and Nicolás Calvo proposing the order that the Consulate Government Board should follow in its work and projects. Presented to the board on July 8, 1795, and read during a sitting on July 15. Biblioteca Nacional José Martí, Colección Manuscritos, Morales, vol. 79, no. 31.

Works Cited

Aimes, Hubert H. S. 1907. *A History of Slavery in Cuba, 1511 to 1868*. New York: G. P. Putnam's Sons.

Andrews, George Reid. 2003. *Afro-Latin American 1800–2000*. London: Oxford University Press.

Assadourian, Carlos S., et al. 1984. *Modos de producción en América Latina*, 10th ed. Mexico, D. F.: Siglo XXI Editores.

Barcia, María del Carmen. 1988. "La esclavitud en las plantaciones: Una relación secundaria." In *Temas acerca de la esclavitud*, edited by Julio Le Riverend et al. Havana: Ciencias Sociales, 96–116.

Bergad, Laird. 2004. *Escravidão e história econômica: Demografía de Minas Gerais, 1720–1888*. Bauru, Brazil: Ed. Universidade do Sagrado Coração (EDUSC).

Bernand, Carmen. 2001. *Negros esclavos y libres en las ciudades hispanoamericanas*. Madrid: Fundación histórica Tavera.

Cardoso, Ciro Flamarion, ed. 1988. *Escravidão e abolição no Brasil: Novas perspectivas*. Rio de Janeiro: Jorge Zahar Ed.

Davis, David Brion. 1966. *The Problem of Slavery in Western Culture*. Ithaca, NY: Cornell University Press.

———. 1975. *The Problem of Slavery in the Age of Revolution, 1770–1823*. Ithaca, NY: Cornell University Press.

Figueiredo, José Ricardo. 2004. *Modos de ver a produção do Brasil*. São Paulo-Campinas, Brazil: Educ-Autores Asociados.

Finley, Moses I. 1980. *Ancient Slavery and Modern Ideology*. New York: Viking Press.

———. 1982. *Esclavitud antigua e ideología moderna*. Barcelona: Crítica.

Fox-Genovese, Elizabeth, and Eugene D. Genovese. 1983. *Fruits of Merchant Capital: Slavery and Bourgeois Property in the Rise and Expansion of Capitalism*. New York: Oxford University Press.

Freyre, Gilberto. 2002. *Casa-Grande & senzala* (orig. 1933). Nanterre, France: ALLCA XX; Conaculta-Fondo de Cultura Económica.

Fuente, Alejandro de la. 2008. *Havana and the Atlantic in the Sixteenth Century*. Chapel Hill: University of North Carolina Press.

Genovese, Eugene D. 1967. *The Political Economy of Slavery: Studies in the Economy and Society of the Slave South*. New York: Random House.

———. 1968. "Marxian Interpretations of the Slave South." In *Towards a New Past: Dissenting Essays in American History*, edited by Barton J. Bernstein. New York: Pantheon Books, 90–125.

———. 1969. *The World the Slaveholders Made: Two Essays in Interpretation*. New York: Pantheon.

———. 1974. *Roll, Jordan, Roll: The World the Slaves Made*. New York: Pantheon.

———. 1990a. "Race and Class in Southern History: An Appraisal of the Work of Ulrich Bonnell Phillips." In *Ulrich Bonnell Phillips: A Southern Historian and His Critics*, edited by John D. Smith and John C. Inscoe. New York: Greenwood Press, 113–28.

———. 1990b. "Ulrich Bonnell Phillips as an Economic Historian" (1968). In *Ulrich Bonnell Phillips: A Southern Historian and His Critics*, edited by J. D. Smith and J. C. Inscoe. New York: Greenwood Press, 203–06.

Gorender, Jacob. 1978. *O escravismo colonial*. São Paulo: Ática.

Graham, Sandra Lauderdale. 1988. *House and Street: The Domestic World of Servants and Masters in Nineteenth-Century Rio de Janeiro*. Cambridge, UK: Cambridge University Press.

Gutman, Herbert G. 1976. *The Black Family in Slavery and Freedom, 1750–1925*. New York: Pantheon.

Humboldt, Alexander von. 1998. *Ensayo político sobre la Isla de Cuba*, edited by Miguel Ángel Puig-Samper, Consuelo Naranjo Orovio, and Armando García González. Aranjuez: Doce Calles; Vallodid: Junta de Castilla y León.

Johnson, Richard. 1978. "Edward Thompson, Eugene Genovese, and Socialist-Humanist History." *History Workshop Journal* 6 (1): 79–100.

Klein, Herbert S. 1967. *Slavery in the Americas: A Comparative Study of Virginia and Cuba*. Chicago: University of Chicago Press.

Knight, Franklin W. 1990. *The Caribbean: The Genesis of a Fragmented Nationalism*, 2nd ed. New York: Oxford University Press.

Knight, Franklin W., ed. 1997. *General History of the Caribbean*, 3: *The Slave Societies of the Caribbean*. London: UNESCO Publishing.

Lapa, José Roberto do Amaral, ed. 1980. *Modos de produção e realidade brasileira*. Petrópolis, Brazil: Vozes.

Luna, Francisco Vidal, and Herbert S. Klein. 2005. *Evolução da sociedade e economia escravista de São Paulo, de 1750 a 1850*. São Paulo, Brazil: Editora da Universidade de São Paulo.

Marx, Karl. 1939. *Capital*. Vol. 1. New York: International Publishers.

———. 1978–1981. *El capital*, 2nd ed., Book I, Vol. 3; Book III, Vol. 8, translated by Pedro Scaron. Madrid: Siglo XXI.

———. 1985. *El dieciocho brumario de Luis Bonaparte* (18th bromaire of . . .). Madrid: Espasa-Calpe.

Marx, Karl, and Frederik Engel. 1974. *La ideología alemana*, 5th ed. Barcelona: Grijalbo; Montevideo, Uruguay: Pueblos Unidos.

McDonnell, Lawrence T. 1984. " 'You Are Too Sentimental': Problems and Suggestions for a New Labor History." *Journal of Social History* 17: 629–54.

Mintz, Sidney W. 1961. "*Slavery*, by Stanley M. Elkins." Book review in *American Anthropologist*, n.s., 63 (3): 579–87.

———. 2007. "The Origins of the Jamaican Internal Marketing System" (orig. 1960). In *Caribbean Transformations*. New York: Aldine, 180–214.

Moreno Fraginals, Manuel. 1964. *El Ingenio: Complejo económico social cubano del azúcar*, 1: *1760–1860*. Havana: Comisión Nacional Cubana de la UNESCO.

———. 1978. *El Ingenio: Complejo económico social cubano del azúcar*. 3 vols. Havana: Editora Ciencias Sociales.

Moya Pons, Frank. 2007. *History of the Caribbean: Plantations, Trade, and War in the Atlantic World*. Princeton, NJ: Markus Wiener.

Naranjo Orovio, Consuelo. 2005. "De la esclavitud a la criminalización de un grupo: La población de color en Cuba." *Op. Cit.: Revista del Centro de Investigaciones Historicas* (Río Piedras, Puerto Rico) 16: 137–78.

Ortiz, Fernando. 1988. *Los negros esclavos: Estudio sociológico y de derecho público* (orig. 1916). Havana: Ciencias Sociales.

Palmer, Bryan D. 1981. *The Making of E. P. Thompson: Marxism, Humanism, and History*. Toronto, Canada: New Hogtown Press.

Phillips, Ulrich Bonnell. 1966. *American Negro Slavery: A Survey of the Supply, Employment and Control of Negro Labor as Determined by the Plantation Regime* (orig. 1918). Baton Rouge: Louisiana State University Press.

Scott, James C. 1986. "Everyday Forms of Peasant Resistance." *The Journal of Peasant Studies* 13 (2): 5–35.

———. 1990. *Domination and the Arts of Resistance*. New Haven, CT: Yale University Press.

Smith, John David. 1992. "Introduction." In *Life and Labor in the Old South*, edited by Ulrich B. Phillips. Columbia: University of South Carolina, xvii–lv.

Tannenbaum, Frank. 1968. *El negro en las Américas: Esclavo y ciudadano* (orig. 1946, *Slave and Citizen: The Negro in the Americas*. New York: Random House), translated by R. Bixio. Buenos Aires: Paidós.

Thompson, Edward P. 1963. *The Making of the English Working Class*. London: Victor Gollancz.

———. 1981. "The Politics of Theory." In *People's History and Socialist Theory*, edited by Raphael Samuel. London: Routledge & Kegan Paul, 396–408.

———. 1984. "La política de la teoría." In *Historia popular y teoría socialista*, edited by Raphael Samuel, translated by Jordi Beltrán. Barcelona: Crítica, 301–17.

Tomich, Dale. 1988. "The 'Second Slavery': Bonded Labor and the Transformation of the Nineteenth-Century World Economy." In *Rethinking the Nineteenth Century: Movements and Contradictions*, edited by Francisco O. Ramirez. Westport, CT: Greenwood Press, 103–17.

———. 2004. *Through the Prism of Slavery: Labor, Capital, and World Economy*. Lanham, MD: Rowman & Littlefield.

Williams, Eric. 1970. *From Columbus to Castro: The History of the Caribbean, 1492–1969*. New York: Harper and Row.

———. 1994. *Capitalism and Slavery* (orig. 1944). Chapel Hill: University of North Carolina Press.

Wood, Ellen Meiksins. 1990. "Falling Through the Cracks: E. P. Thompson and the Debate on Base and Superstructure." In *E. P. Thompson: Critical perspectives*, edited by Harvey J. Kaye and Keith McClelland. Cambridge, UK: Polity Press, 125–52.

Archival Materials

Biblioteca Nacional José Martí (Havana, Cuba). Colección Manuscritos, Morales.

The Paths of Freedom

Autonomism and Abolitionism in Cuba, 1878–1886*

Luís Miguel García Mora

T he abolition of slavery is one of history's most complex phenomena. The number of players involved increases according to where we put the empha-sis. In principle, it is a dispute resolved between a master and a slave. When a slave becomes a free person, both have to redefine their status: owning a person is not the same as owning the work that person does. Masters, then, would seek to ensure that the conditions resulting from the transition to free work resembled the previous model. Slaves, on the other hand, would seek control over the work they did, plus access to land of their own. The end result was always going to be a compromise. In the case of Cuba, slaves were first patronized or sponsored, in a system that straddled a divide between slave and wage-earner, in which part of the stipend was used to compensate the person who had been their owner. In practice,

*The author would like to thank Marta Ruiz Jimenez for providing documents from the *Archivo Histórico Nacional* and the *Archivo del Congreso de los Diputados* used in this work, and María Dolores González-Ripoll for her helpful comments and analysis. Work funded by Project MNECO HAR2012-32510, Teoría y práctica de la representación colonial, 1868–1898.

then, former slaves partially bought their own freedom. Once such patronage was abolished, former slaves swelled the growing ranks of the agricultural proletariat (Klein and Engerman 1983: 41, 46–47).

Over and above the changes that took place in the social structure, abolition directly connected with the economic dimension and the social relations of production established between the owners of the means of production and the workers. In Cuba, more specifically, this meant relations in the sugar industry. As the nineteenth century moved forward, sugar production in the Greater Antilles faced two problems: the constant price reduction of this commodity and the fact that exports were focused on the North American market, problems compounded by competition from beet sugar. Deflation was an incentive to cut costs and avoid crisis, a cliché upheld in some Cuban economic historiography when it uncritically accepts the discourse of nineteenth-century landowners (García Mora and Santamaría 2002: 165–85).

Market reduction and the drop in prices spurred on the modernization of sugar mills, but the nature of this change was determined by the relative availability of production factors. In Cuba, land was more abundant, which meant that any growth strategy tended to replace it with labor or capital.

But to understand the technical and organizational changes that confronted the sugar industry in the second half of the nineteenth century, we need to take account of a third factor: the rising cost of slave labor and the certainty that slavery would soon become extinct. Although British pressure led the Spanish authorities to ban slavery on more than one occasion, slaving expeditions continued to reach the Cuban coast until the 1870s. Smuggling promoted increased prices, leading landowners to try their luck with other workers, such as Chinese coolies, Yucatec Indians, and even paid workers.[1]

Halfway through the century, the workforce and the mechanization of the Cuban sugar industry therefore underwent a period of reorganization, in which different kinds of work and an infinite number of technologies lived side by side. The Ten Years' War—with its consequences for the productive structure and, above all, its promotion of the abolitionist process—partially helped clarify this situation.

Sugar-cane farming was left in the hands of farmers with varying degrees of independence, settlers who sold their production to a sugar company, which obtained the end product. The sugar company reflected the efficiency of technological change and safeguarded the competitiveness of Cuba's sugar industry. Settlement was the perfect answer to the workforce problem in a postabolitionist society. White, mainly Spanish, emigrants were enticed into rural areas, their work compensating for part of the cost and risk involved in the business, because they were paid in sugar, but only for the part of the raw material that was actually sold, not for the full amount grown (Santamaría and García Mora 1998: 131–61). The statistics available, however, enable us to make certain assertions. In the first place, abolition in Cuba cannot be explained by microeconomic causes. Second, developments in the sugar industry show, in any case, that slaves were not replaced by paid workers, or at least not immediately. The mills embarked on a complex process of technological and organizational transformation, which centralized sugar production in a small number of plants at the same time that sugar cane production increased with settlement, saving on labor and optimizing the yield obtained from the raw material. Third, the direction taken by change can be explained by the relative availability of resources: land and capital were used to save on labor, the factor in shortest supply. However, labor continued to be essential to sugar manufacture, and our econometric analysis shows that, while it was still feasible, slaves remained the preferred source of labor among landowners; however, in the mid-nineteenth century, slavery was on the way out for reasons that had nothing to do with the economy (García Mora and Santamaría 2002).

This leads us to consider new perspectives and players that enable us to narrow our scope. Pioneering research has insisted on the role of the different Cuban notables in abolition, a process that began with the opposition to trafficking. Others have emphasized the links with Spanish colonial policy and international relations, and have even proffered explanations of a political-ideological nature, such as the Enlightenment, the Atlantic Revolution, and the Ten Years' War (Entralgo 1953; Corwin 1967: xii–xiii; Klein 1973: 307–18, quotation 315). This is the view favored by Laird Bergad, who in a recent book, acknowledges the importance of

British pressure to abolish trafficking and other sociocultural factors, including fear of black people, while rejecting other elements, such as the Catholic Church and the advance of democracy (Cuba did not have universal male suffrage until 1898), to show that abolition was always an argument against the colonial model (Bergad 2007: 272–82).

Throughout the nineteenth century, abolitionism and anticolonialism went hand in hand. Even in the 1820s, Félix Varela exclaimed "There is no love of Cuba here: only a love of boxes of sugar and sacks of coffee" (1824, quoted in Piqueras 2007: 108, trans. by LMGM). Years later, José Antonio Saco added to his criticism of colonialism the need to reduce the island's nonwhite population. In both cases, however, these were minority views, voiced from exile and dependent on the economic support of Creole landowners who, although in favor of changing the colonial order, were nevertheless *prisoners* of their slaves. The continued support of slavery became a guarantee of Creole loyalty to the metropolis, against which the international situation was conspiring. In 1865, after victory of the North in the War of Secession, Cuba, Puerto Rico, and Brazil remained the only slave territories in the New World. From that moment on, if the Cuban Creoles wanted to have more influence over the island's future, they would have to come to terms with the end of slavery. This was something that Cuba's liberal reformists understood, and they looked favorably on the creation of the Spanish Abolitionist Society in Madrid in 1865.[2] Two years on, at the Overseas Informative Reform Board, they also called on the metropolis for the gradual abolition of slavery, accompanied by political and economic reforms.

The year 1868 was a key date. In September, democratic forces overthrew the monarchy of Isabella II. The leaders of the 1868 Revolution included prominent abolitionists who had been committed to ending slavery from the outset. Liberals by conviction, many were also members of the Association for the Reform of Customs Duties, which advocated free trade. Their abolitionist views were perhaps influenced by a feeling that capitalism could not be consolidated in a state that used slave labor.[3] On October 17, 1868, the Revolutionary Board of Madrid called on the government to declare free any child born of a slave mother as of

September 17, the date of the democratic uprising in Cádiz, in what was a direct precedent of the Moret Law of July 4, 1870. These abolitionist yearnings preceded the outbreak of revolution in Cuba. Carlos Manuel de Céspedes rebelled on October 10, 1868, but it is highly unlikely that Madrid's democrats—who called for a freedom-of-wombs act just seven days later—would have done so purely to counter the Cuban rebels, whose uprising was probably unknown to them, for until that time, their attitude toward abolition had only been tentative. It is clear that, during the conflict, both sides played the abolitionism card, but to qualify the most consolidated historiographic interpretation, abolition did not arrive solely as a result of the Ten Years' War. The leaders of the 1868 Revolution had their own program right from the outset, and abolition was one of its points. Like the duty of 1869 and abolition in Puerto Rico, in a peaceful Cuba, the end of slavery could also have been achieved.[4]

In short, as Captain-General Caballero de Rodas acknowledged in 1870, "slavery ha[s] died with this uprising" (quoted in Roldán 1989: 149, trans. by LMGM). Initially, support of abolitionism by the Mambise independence fighters was very hesitant. Céspedes manumitted his own slaves, which, as Cepero Bonilla asserts, although indeed consistent with slavery legislation, was certainly not revolutionary (it was, however, revolutionary to have them join the ranks of his army). The insurgents' intention was to spread the war to the west of the island, where the major mills and larger numbers of slaves were to be found. To gain the support of the western landowners, they advocated gradual abolitionism with, in principle, compensation; later, at the Guaímaro Constitutional Assembly, they declared that "all inhabitants of the Republic are entirely free," but the Chamber of Representatives passed a regulation on freed persons ordering forced labor. Only when they became aware that they would not obtain the support expected—and once popular sectors, many of whom were black and mulatto, joined the revolutionary leadership—did radical abolitionism triumph; and on Christmas Day, 1870, the forced labor regulation was repealed.[5]

The response of the colonial authorities was the Moret Law of July 4, 1870. This was a preparatory and provisional law on the freedom of wombs, which declared that all children born to slave mothers after its publication or as of September 17 (the proclamation of the 1868 Revolution) would become the property of the state. In turn, it freed those over the age of sixty, and those who had worked for the army or belonged to the state. The same law also ruled that freed persons would be made available to their mothers' owners up to the age of eighteen; they would then receive half-day pay until they reached age twenty-two, and from that point on would enjoy full rights. The articles also granted compensation to former owners: it was established in Article 21 that definitive legislation would apply once Cuban representatives took their seats in the Spanish Parliament, a situation that was incompatible with the war; this was the argument favored by slaveholders: first peace, then reforms. Thus, the slaveholders were, at most, prepared to concede to a preparatory law, like that of July 4, 1870. In March 1873, the First Republic proclaimed immediate abolition with compensation in Puerto Rico. The money freed up from Cuban slavery was quickly placed at the disposal of the Bourbon Restoration.

By 1878, with the war in its tenth year, no side had gained victory. In view of the situation, the metropolis mooted an agreement. The Mambises were committed to greater political control and the abolition of slavery. The colonial authorities promised more in the Zanjón Pact than they actually signed for, which, among other things, was to grant Cuba the same "political, organic and administrative [conditions] enjoyed by the island of Puerto Rico" and to give "freedom [to] the Asian settlers and slaves in rebel ranks today" (Estevez and Romero 1974, 1: 21–22). Most of the proindependence leaders subscribed to this agreement, although some black leaders, including Antonio Maceo, protested that neither Cuban independence nor total abolition had been recognized. Maceo's stance was echoed around the world, particularly in the antislavery leagues in Britain and the United States.[6]

Although total abolition did not emerge from Zanjón, the peace agreement did facilitate the creation of political parties. In August 1878, a group of middle-class professionals—some landowners (most of whom were Creoles), former Mambises, and other peace-loving citizens who had sympathized with independence, but had preferred to stay out of the conflict—called on the country to form the Cuban

Liberal Party, which would later become known as the Autonomist Party. It was a party created to test the extent to which Spain was willing to allow Cubans to participate in colonial affairs once councils, provincial governments, and Parliament opened up to political representation. In their program, they called for a series of things: the complete removal of the taxation and duties system, with a view to introducing free trade, particularly with the United States; equal rights with inhabitants on the peninsula; Cuban access to public positions; the separation and independence of civil and military power; and colonial autonomy, given that Article 89 of the Constitution called for, as the Cuban Liberal Party said, the greatest possible decentralization within the national unit. Finally, as far as slavery was concerned, their initial approach was moderate: they demanded abolition with compensation for owners, in compliance with Article 21 of the Moret Law of 1870, without setting a specific deadline, and called for the promotion of white and family-based immigration. This article set about resolving a problem at the same time that it specified the kind of immigrants that were desired for the post-abolitionist workforce. The aforesaid article gave the government the power to present an abolition plan when Cuban representatives were accepted in the Spanish legislative assembly, the Cortes; they were not in fact committing to anything: every path was left open, although the article did contemplate guarantees for slaves (such as a ban on physical punishment and on separation of families).[7]

Shortly after the Liberals assembled,[8] a group of major landowners, merchants, industrialists, and senior civil servants—who were ideologically centralist and mainly from the peninsula—issued a manifesto that could be summed up in the slogan: "Peace, fatherland and constitutional union!" (García Mora 2009: 307–8). This planted the seed of the Conservative Party, known as the Constitutional Union, and heir to the Spanish Party, which had been a bastion against proindependence during the war, but had adapted to the new situation of political freedom and parliamentary representation. In contrast to the Liberals, it defined itself in terms of assimilationist criteria, favoring "rational and feasible assimilation" with the rest of the state. In the economic sphere, it also sought tariff reform and the establishment of trade agreements with the United States, as well as calling for coasting trade with the peninsula—in other words, for the Antilles to be included in the same trading regime as the rest of the state, regardless of geographical location or the specificities of its main exports. In regard to slavery, the party appealed for full implementation of the Moret Law, that is, maintaining the gradual nature of the abolitionist process so that the institution could continue for another forty years.[9]

The programs of the two parties were not dissimilar, although, as shrewd observer of colonial affairs Juan Gualberto Gómez has remarked, it was slavery that distinguished them. Although both appealed to the Moret Law, the Conservatives stuck to it, whereas the Liberals used it as a point of departure from which to develop toward total abolition. As Gómez puts it, "from a shamefully oligarchic and pro-slavery position, the Liberal Party was able to form a truly democratic and ultimately abolitionist grouping" (1974: 196, trans. by LMGM). In 1903, in the colonial aftermath, Constitutional Union leader Arturo Amblard, who later founded the Reformist Party, considered both programs akin to one another, although he pointed out that the Liberals had a more radical stance on abolition and autonomy (1903). Inés Roldán states categorically: "The Cuban Liberal Party . . . was undoubtedly one of the driving forces behind post-war abolitionist endeavours, despite efforts to portray it as pro-slavery" (1989: 133, trans. by LMGM).

Autonomists covered the whole spectrum of traditional Cuban reformism. The intellectual heirs of José Antonio Saco, they were law-abiding citizens, concerned to keep the peace, who hoped to be able to consolidate Cuban self-government within the nineteenth-century Spanish state, thereby strengthening a liberal and democratic order. Rather than abrupt change, they aspired to incorporate earlier proindependence ideas into the new political legality and peaceful development within the colonial order. They were aware of the specificities of a Cuba, which, at the war's end, still had 200,000 slaves. In the liberal and democratic Cuba they longed for, they saw slavery as a thing of the past, hence their preference for white and family-based immigration. Their model of nation-state rejected slavery and integrated the colored and Chinese population in line with acculturation to the mores of the white population. They tended to caution, and repressed the demand for radical abolitionism, just as they concealed their Autonomist yearnings in the euphemism "greatest possible de-centralisation within the national unit." This is of the utmost significance when assessing the role Autonomism played in the process. Another relevant consideration is that abolitionist legislation had to be passed in the metropolis, by the Spanish Parliament, where the party was represented by people who had always been in favor of radical abolitionism. The leadership of the Autonomist minority in the Cortes fell to Rafael María de Labra, who later became president of the Spanish Abolitionist Society. Between 1878 and 1886, it was virtually impossible to separate the activities of the Abolitionist Society from those of Autonomist parliamentarians.

Although the initial Autonomist position was a moderate one, a circular of August 2, 1879, declared unequivocal support for radical, simultaneous abolition, with no monetary compensation of any kind. What had happened in a year? There are different explanations. The Autonomists' initial moderation was due to the postwar climate in Cuba and their preference for the Moret Law, with an emphasis on Article 21, which meant that the final solution would be adopted once Cuban representatives had seats in the Spanish legislative assembly. On the other hand, in the days that followed the Zanjón Pact, there was total confidence in Miguel Martínez Campos, the governor general who achieved the peace and led the political reform initiative. This was not the time for the Creole party, made up of former Mambises, to get involved in a tug of war in which the rope might break, confounding a reformist project like that drawn up by Martínez Campos, who already had so many opponents both on and off the island (Beck 1976: 268–89; García Mora 1994: 197–212).

Autonomism also exhibited, at the outset, a certain ambiguity toward the abolition issue; although its advocates rejected slavery, there were interests at stake. It was not primarily a party of major landowners, although there were some in its ranks, but it was aware of Cuba's needs and wanted to make cautious decisions, both to defend its principles and to cater to the interests of Cuba's major industry, sugar. The party leadership was committed to the country's interests, although its militants were calling for a more radical stand, and the militants' demands eventually gained the upper hand.

Before the law reached the Cortes, Autonomists itemized their strategies regarding the social problem in their official press mouthpiece, *El Triunfo*, and the declarations of the Junta Central (senior party authority) Central Board.[10] Although its program backed labor regulation, just twenty-three days later it announced that it was preparing a broader plan and that it expected consensus could be reached. The self-same article started out launching ideas aimed at its militants, such as that it should be the slaves themselves who bought their freedom with the product of their labor, or that no definitive decision be taken until the problem reached the legislative assembly. Days later, the party advocated a solution for abolition that was to be agreed by consensus by all Cuba's political and social representatives (it expressly refers to the Landowners' Circle and the Economic Society of Friends of the Country), as the only effective mechanism for ensuring that private interests would not get in the way of the country's general welfare.[11]

In the meantime, the members of the Central Board were taking up differing positions. A more radical sector, represented by José Antonio Cortina and Enrique José Varona, was in favor of the immediate and simultaneous abolition of slavery. It was pressure from this sector, combined with the radical abolitionism of parliamentary representatives, that would lead to the program's amendment. Opposing them was a more moderate group, which was even willing to set aside their principles for the sake of an agreement that would suit everybody. The doctrinaire sector included the president of the board, José María Gálvez; Rafael Montoro, its main ideologue; Fernando Freyre; Francisco Gay; José María Zayas; and others, some of whom were mill owners and logically inclined to be more moderate.

Although other projects had previously been evaluated, the great debate on the subject took place on March 30, 1879, when Montoro presented the Central Board with an abolition plan, without compensation and with eight-year patronage.[12] In the end, this plan was rejected, and its exact text is unknown.

It may well be that Montoro did not write the plan himself, but simply read it out as spokesman of a committee that included Francisco Armas y Martínez and Antonio Govín, although the latter ultimately opposed the project.[13] The arguments of another member of the Central Board, José Manuel Pascual, are documented, however, and these were presented at the end of December 1878. Pascual, who was close to Cortina, with whom he worked at *Revista de Cuba*, sought to tone the project down. He proposed reducing patronage to six years from the signing of the Zanjón Pact and reducing the working day from twelve to eight hours. He also favored the freedom of sponsored workers, provided they could invoke a just cause against their patron.[14] At the board's debate, Varona and Cortina, the main challengers, managed to get the remainder to reject the committee's plan. They claimed there was no room for temporary arrangements. They must support immediate abolition without compensation or labor regulation, in line with what the militants were demanding.[15]

Gradually, the more radical sectors of Autonomism, for which *Revista Económica* was a key mouthpiece, steered the board toward categorical abolitionism. The leadership was repeatedly urged to provide a clearer stance. In April, Central Board member José María Zayas appeared to be in favor of abolition with compensation and labor regulation, in line "with the requirements of the age and circumstances of the country." Days later, this was publicly rectified in *El Triunfo*, with a declaration in favor of immediate abolition, freedom to hire, and civil and political rights for the colored population. Any kind of monetary compensation was renounced in favor of the implementation of economic reforms that would boost sugar exports. The mood was ripe for the disappearance from the program of any reference to compensation, labor regulation, and the moral or intellectual education of freed persons.[16]

With the move toward Autonomism, in addition to the pressure exerted by militants, the clarification of the political situation also played a role. In March, tired of struggling with the Cánovas government, which constantly hampered his reform projects, Martínez Campos, the guarantor of the promises made in Zanjón, left the metropolis to head the government, a situation that filled Autonomist ranks with trepidation.[17] Likewise, the April elections opened their eyes to the executive's attitude: temporary arrangements were to be put aside and the program had to be radicalized in keeping with the party's true line of thought. In May, it was announced to the Constitutional Union that a common policy could not be reached; in June, after analyzing the political program presented by the Martínez Campos government, it was asserted that "the Liberal Party defends immediate and simultaneous abolition without monetary compensation," although a party circular from the same month supported certain kinds of "transitory regulation of free work which in no way distorts the explicit recognition of absolutely sacred rights."[18] Despite this, on August 2, 1879, the new program openly declared its support for abolitionism: "In the social sense, there can be no other criterion but immediate and simultaneous abolition, with no monetary compensation. This is what is demanded by the purity of our principles and the proper interests of our country."[19] It was, as secretary Govín acknowledged at the meeting to commemorate the party's foundation, the moment when leadership and party were reunited: "The steering board calls for the immediate and simultaneous abolition of slavery, which is the desire of the Liberals" (Govin y Torres 1955: 37, trans. by LMGM).

Although we can see how Autonomism faced up to the issue of slavery in Havana, the picture cannot be complete without considering the attitude of its representatives in the Cortes, where abolitionist legislation was eventually passed. Between the 1879 legislature, when Cuban representatives returned to Parliament, and that of 1886, when definitive abolition was passed, the Autonomists chose thirteen deputies and five different senators, but in practice, their policy was both led and drawn up by Rafael María de Labra. Born in Cuba, he was a renowned republican, of strong democratic, Autonomist, and radical abolitionist convictions (García Mora 1992: 397–415).

The hallmark of Labra's political life was the solution of what was known at the time as the "overseas problem" (Labra 1901: 330).[20] In essence, it involved integrating overseas territories both socially and politically with the rest of the state, primarily by abolishing slavery. In other words, he sought the alignment of productive relations on both sides of the Atlantic, so that the colonial system could be modified, with the inhabitants of Cuba and Puerto Rico enjoying civil rights equal to those on the Spanish peninsula, and autonomy akin to that of the British colonies.

In 1864, Labra took part in a preparatory meeting to create the Spanish Abolitionist Society, held on the initiative of Puerto Rican Julio Vizcarrondo, although

he was not on the elected board. In 1866, Narváez's government suspended abolitionist propaganda, which only recommenced after victory in the Revolution of
1868. The new situation produced a change in abolitionist leaders. It was marked
by the takeover of Labra's generation, which was deeply democratic and more wont
to see the problem of slavery as part of a set of reforms needed both overseas and
in the Spanish state.[21]

By the time the new board was elected in 1868, Labra was a member. Two years
later, he chaired a newly created executive committee, and in 1876, he became
president of the Abolitionist Society, a position he held for as long as the institution existed. Labra advocated radical abolitionism, with no temporary arrangements
or casuistry, a position he defended unflinchingly, in his university lectures, at
political meetings, and from the pages of *El Abolicionista*, a publication he edited
and wrote virtually single-handed. However, once the solutions began to arrive
in Parliament, Labra—in a demonstration of pragmatism—accepted abolitionist
initiatives such as the Moret Law.

Labra attributed the relative ease with which slavery was abolished in Puerto
Rico to the democratic quality of Puerto Rican representatives and the facilities
offered by the Republic (Labra 1800, 1897: 34). In fact, it was undoubtedly due
to the minor importance of slavery on that island. After abolition in Puerto Rico,
Labra put all his energy into achieving the same for Cuba, an enterprise that was
thwarted by the advent of the Restoration and the Cuban war. These were difficult
times for abolitionists, whose activities were, in practice, virtually banned.[22] As
of 1878, with pacification, the situation changed. Labra obtained a certificate of
election for Cuba and ensured that the abolitionist cause was heard in Parliament.

With no further ado, in his very first parliamentary intervention on July 3,
1879, Labra asked to see the 1870 census of slaves and demanded that the overseas
minister provide details concerning the consequences of implementing the Moret
Law. He was supported in this by Bernardo Portuondo, the other Autonomist
representative in the Spanish legislative assembly, a Cuban military engineer, veteran
of the Ten Years' War and steadfast abolitionist. Just a few days later, on July 12,
Labra took advantage of the debate on the throne speech to communicate to the

government the Autonomist party's commitment to immediate and simultaneous abolition. Two days later, the first exhibition calling for an end to slavery opened in the Spanish city of Gijón.[23] Between 1879 and 1883, Autonomist representatives presented fifty-three antislavery manifestos from different Spanish cities and served as a sounding board for the Abolitionist Society in Parliament.

Although sessions in the Cortes were soon suspended, the Autonomists were still able to defend immediate and simultaneous abolition and denounce breaches of the law on the other side of the Atlantic. They began by asking for details of the Moret Law, the number of slaves on the census, and how many of them were African. They also called for information concerning agreements signed with the British government, with a view to demonstrating the discrepancies between the law and the real situation in Cuba. The only solution, as they saw it, was immediate and simultaneous abolition. This was the Autonomist answer. Deals—as conservative deputy Portuondo and future overseas minister Antonio María Fabié acknowledged—could be made, but principles could not be betrayed.[24]

With legislative assembly sessions suspended, Martínez Campos's government knew the reformist impetus could not be allowed to grind to a halt, and on August 15, an advisory committee was appointed on reforms in Cuba that the assembly was required to pass once sessions resumed. The slavery subcommittee was made up of four representatives of the Constitutional Union (Santos Guzmán, Bueno y Blanco, Vinent, and Sánchez Bustamante) and the Autonomist Portuondo. Three projects were presented by the subcommittee and a fourth was endorsed by Miguel Martínez Campos and Julio Apezteguía, both representatives of the Constitutional Union, the first of these the prime minister's brother and the second the owner of what was at the time Cuba's largest sugar mill.[25]

The Constitutional Union's abolitionist projects were characterized by conservatism. The senator for Santiago de Cuba, José Bueno y Blanco, presented a more advanced project, taking account of the specific circumstances of Eastern Cuba, which at the end of August found itself once again at war. He defended an agreement between slaves and masters, according to which the former would gain their freedom in four years, during which time they would receive wages and, once emancipated, would be obliged to work for their previous owner for three more years. Martínez Campos and Apezteguía advocated immediate abolition with patronage, from which former slaves would gradually be freed, starting with children and the elderly, namely, the least productive. The third project to be endorsed by Santos Guzman, Vinent, and Sanchez Bustamante was the one the committee eventually approved, and was the most conservative of all. It involved gradual abolition that would allow slaves to abandon slave status by age, starting first with those over fifty-five years. There would then be a further manumission every two years of those over age fifty, and so on in two-year increments, with the slaves' age reduced in each period by five years, so that abolition would not be complete until the 1890s. Moreover, masters could choose to release 2,000 slaves a year, for the sum of 350 pesos, which would be paid by the state. In short, it was an extremely conservative project designed to suit major owners, who would receive compensation for terminating their relationship with less productive workers and retain the more profitable ones until 1890 (Roldán 1989: 162–65).

Autonomist representative Bernardo Portuondo was against any kind of deferral, supporting instead immediate, simultaneous abolition without monetary compensation. He rejected the gradualist approach, which had already been tried by other nations (France, Britain, and the United States), and whose failure inevitably led to immediate abolition. He also recognized that, although gradualism might have been effective at an earlier stage, by 1879, in postwar Cuba, its implementation would entail reversing a right that had previously been recognized by the liberation of slaves who had joined the Mambise army, and by the Moret Law; gradualism also fostered corruption, as calculating slave ages was always difficult, particularly when most were not registered in the census, and many others had arrived in Cuba after trafficking had been abolished, so that, according to law they should in any case be totally free. Immediate abolition was needed to maintain the public order. Its only disadvantage was the problems it caused in the labor force, hence the request for the temporary regulation of the freed person's labor, at the same time guaranteeing the former master's obligation to hire that person. This phenomenon, in the eyes of the president of the slavery subcommittee, the Conservative Santos Guzmán, was tantamount to socialism.[26] As for compensation, this could not fall to the former slave, nor could the state provide any kind of funding. What it could do, however, was implement economic reforms that would benefit the sugar industry.[27]

Portuondo's project was only supported by Autonomist representatives, but it clarified the party's position and demonstrated that patronage and gradual abolition—far from being mechanisms to educate freed persons, which was acknowledged by Portuondo as impossible to achieve in a mill—were merely casuistic arguments to prolong slavery for the owner's benefit. The stance taken by the Autonomist party overrode private interest. For as long as slavery existed, there was a chance that a corruptible public employee could fix the papers of freed persons so that they would continue to be slaves; for as long as slavery existed, there were too many interests at stake to grant the island a greater share in its own government. If they wished to preserve the public order, moralize the administration, and achieve colonial autonomy, the abolition of slavery was essential. The true fear of extreme centralists lay not in bringing about autonomy, but rather in harming the interests of a colonial order that was highly beneficial to them.[28]

Once sessions resumed, the government presented a bill on abolition in early November. In contrast to the decision adopted by the Reform Board, it voted for immediate abolition with patronage, as proposed by Miguel Martínez Campos and Julio Apezteguía, but in a much more moderate form, owing to the concessions that had been made to Conservative Provost Romero Robledo, who had close links with overseas businesses. Once Havana was aware of the government bill, on December 4, 1879, another monographic session on abolition was held at the Central Board to lay down lines of action, particularly in view of a telegram sent to parliamentary representatives by Count Casa-Moré, president of the Constitutional Unión, pleading for an extension to patronage.[29] The party program was clearly in favor of immediate and simultaneous abolition, but how should they proceed when the government's proposal covered only part of the program, namely, immediate abolition, but accompanied by patronage? Once again, the board was divided, and again Cortina, on this occasion supported by José María Zayas, defended radical abolitionism. José Bruzón was sympathetic to the government position and favored a compromise, arguing that this was possible since nothing had been said about labor regulation in the program of August 2, 1879. He claimed that "the party had to take account of living conditions in the country when implementing its principles. . . . [A]s things stand, the landowner is not in a position to pay for non-slave labour . . . [and] immigration is not possible. Resources have to be found to replace that labour."[30] Days later, in a telegram that the Central Board sent to its parliamentarians, the deal was accepted: "Liberal Party enthusiastically supports first article on abolition. Simultaneous economic reforms: no coasting trade, abolition of export duties, customs reform. Modify Government bill with partial amendments, limiting potential duration and future working conditions and facilitating redemption of freedom from patronage, where existing. Central Board gives vote of confidence to representatives at Cortes."[31] Once again, the choice was gradualism; the Liberals renounced their maximum goal in order to obtain something else in its place, namely a modification of the colonial system. Ultimately, Martínez Campos still headed the government, and it was essential to support the guarantor of the Zanjón Peace, the man who had proposed sweeping changes in the colonial order by abolishing slavery, reducing budgets, lowering customs duties, and changing the nature of trading relations with the peninsula. Consequently, the contents of the telegram were about more than just abolition. For the most radical supporters of Autonomism, however, this represented yet another stain on the Central Board's record: "No; in the telegram of December 11, the leadership does not represent the Liberal Party of Cuba: the Liberal Party must respect the laws; but this party, in setting out its principles, through its representatives at the Cortes, was not able, without being unfaithful to its declarations, to support, even for a moment, any resolution of the social problem other than that presented in the circular of August 2, 1879."[32]

On December 9, all hopes were dashed. On that day, unable to present the economic reforms for Cuba to the Cortes, Martínez Campos left the government and was replaced by Antonio Cánovas. Cánovas was able to put the brakes on the economic reforms, but had no choice but to support the abolition bill already presented in the Senate, all the more so given the state of war in Eastern Cuba. The Autonomist rejoinder was given by senators José Silverio Jorrín and José Güell y Renté. The latter, in anticipation of events to come, while the bill was being studied by the senatorial committee, presented other initiatives intended not so much for acceptance by the government but to encourage debate. In reality, Güell y Renté's intervention was unfortunate in both content and form (he even asserted that there were 700,000 slaves living in Cuba, a figure that corresponded to the entire colored population), but it was nonetheless a declaration of Autonomist intent: immediate and simultaneous abolition, and six years' compulsory hire, during which the former master would incur the costs of clothing, health, and education, as well as an agreed economic remuneration. The senator also called for the regulation of courts for freed persons, the promotion of white immigration by means of land grants, and a law against vagrancy.[33]

In the debate, it was Jorrín who was mainly responsible for challenging the bill. His arguments revolved around demonstrating that the bill had profoundly altered the initial plan presented by Martínez Campos. This was an exaggeration, but demonstrated Autonomist support for the previous Government.[34] For Jorrín, the solution involved bringing the Puerto Rican abolition law to Cuba, agreeing to extend the labor regulation period, if necessary, and trading cash compensation for economic reforms, as Martínez Campos had intended. He rejected patronage as a form of covert slavery, in which the situation of the former slave could only deteriorate, because slaves' right to purchase their freedom would become more expensive. In Jorrín's view, "The senatorial committee's project is a step backwards in the historic Spanish movement to abolish slavery."[35] Within days, on receiving the telegram from Havana, Jorrín and Güell had toned down their opposition, although they continued to express their disagreement with the absence of compensation through economic reforms and the promotion of the white population, which was the only effective measure they could see to develop tenant farming and safeguard the future of the sugar industry.[36]

There remained a possibility that the project could be modified at the debate in the Chamber of Deputies, where Portuondo and Labra had already made their intentions clear. However, the withdrawal of opposition, owing to outrage over the prime minister's attitude, led to the law being passed without the support of any

Cuban representative: the Autonomists, annoyed that abolition was not accompanied by economic reform, joined forces with the opposition and the Conservatives and abstained from taking part in the debate. Labra, who seconded the protest, complained about this and took advantage of any public platform, including Madrid's Mercantile Association, to criticize what he was not able to oppose in the Chamber, stating that "owing to political circumstances I am not supposed to mention here, behind the doors of Congress—where I had hoped strongly to oppose, in line with pledges I have made for fifteen years, any project that involves gradual and deferred abolition of slavery" (Labra 1886, 2: 140, trans. by LMGM). Some sectors of Autonomism rejected the attitude of their representatives, considering their links with the political parties and dispositions of the metropolis more important than their duty as Cuban representatives (Betancourt 1887: 50–59).

On February 13, 1880, nominal abolition was passed as slavery continued to exist in the form of patronage—theoretically for eight years, though in practice reduced to six—for all those registered in the 1871 census. At the end of the fifth year after enactment of the law, a quarter of each slave contingent was freed by order of age, starting with the oldest. Sponsored persons had certain rights, including a small salary, healthcare, and maintenance and dress for themselves and their children, who also had the right to primary education. They were able to buy their freedom, and their patron was not allowed to free a sixty-year-old, sick, or disabled slave early without the latter's consent. Despite all of this, the day-to-day life of both slave and master—as Autonomists constantly denounced—remained very much the same. Autonomists continued to argue that patronage was a form of concealed slavery in which the work of the sponsored person was used to compensate the master for his future loss of property. It enabled masters to get around any of the advantages that patronage might have had for slaves, such as knowing when they would be set free, and it allowed the masters to obviate a whole series of rights and the possibility that slaves might use these to obtain their freedom. At the same time, patronage exacerbated the disadvantages, with a situation similar to or worse than the previous regime to which former slaves had been subjected, and breaches of the law were constantly reported.

Throughout the following years, Autonomists remained staunchly opposed to patronage. Not long after the Abolition Law was passed, in February and March 1880, Portuondo and Labra encouraged a debate about reforms, and as one historian would have it, "the basic solutions of the Cuban reforms emerged with less clarity than the disputes between the personalities involved" (Beck 1976: 283, trans. by LMGM). Although there was some truth in this, the debate nonetheless marked a change in attitude in the Autonomist strategy, because, as Labra stated to the party chairman, it was "necessary, then, to create the mood, broach the problems, discuss them and make people concerned about them."[37] The aim was for all parliamentary groups to clarify their overseas policy. Thus it was that the Liberals spoke out publicly against patronage, as Autonomists reminded them time and again when they came to power in February 1881.[38]

In May, 1880, the government published the regulation that would implement the Abolition Law. This, as Labra saw it, was the revenge wrought by Canovism and the Conservatives, who would have preferred a law more favorable to proslavery interests, and to achieve it overrode the opinions of the State Council and Administrative Council of the island of Cuba. Consequently, masters were granted powers that had not been contemplated in the previous regulation in 1842, and were given authority to apply coercive physical punishment—stocks and shackles—that had been abolished under the Moret Law, which the February 1880 law took over. Authorization was also given to extend the working day of the sponsored person during harvest time for as long as necessary. As a result, it was swiftly and constantly condemned by the Autonomists. This was flagrant proof that contradicted the government or anyone else who claimed that abolition had taken place (Labra 1881).

The plan was well organized. Its intention was to put a rapid and definitive end to patronage by constant condemnation and keeping the debate alive, while taking advantage of Liberal governments, which were better disposed to reform, to ensure that the benefits of the law reached all sponsored persons, and at the same time, obtaining other legal measures to alleviate their situation. Thus it was that in May 1881, a Royal Order was brought into effect governing public employees' presence on patronage boards, and in December the same year another one on the wages paid to sponsored persons, on periodic meetings of patronage boards, and on mill inspections. The circular of February 9, 1883, was more effective. This document fulfilled an earlier Autonomist demand by ordering the release of 40,000 slaves not registered in the 1867 census and, above all, by the abolition of the stocks and shackles, the most horrific aspect of the legislation of May 1880 (Labra 1885: v; Suárez Inclán 1884: 33–43).[39]

Objectives were gradually attained, but definitive abolition still failed to arrive. On two occasions, in June 1882 and in 1885, draft laws were submitted to abolish patronage, which, although never considered, provide a fitting summary of Autonomist reasoning: the absence of Cuban representatives when abolition was voted on; the legal equivalence that the Zanjón Pact had given to Cuba and Puerto Rico; the excesses of the May regulation which distorted the law of February 1880; the harm to sponsored persons that had resulted from the implementation of the law; documentation revealing deaths caused by physical punishment, despite its prohibition, and the infinite number of violations that had occurred, some of which had been substantiated in the courts and most in the press; the perpetuation of the enslaved status and the resulting social tensions generated; the increase in manumissions without any undermining of the economy, and the fact that most of these had been the result of mutual agreement. These were the arguments with which the Autonomists confronted the government to get patronage abolished, calling for slaves to be hired to work for a maximum of three years and to be granted political rights in five. The freed person's education, work, and the activity of support associations were promoted, and finally, the customs regime was modified to benefit the sugar crop.[40]

The legal arguments were completed with practical abolitionism, and legal coverage was provided for the claims lodged by sponsored persons. A tenuous chain of events was set in motion in Cuba when a sponsored person lodged a complaint and an abolitionist, often Autonomist, offered protection and filed the complaint with the island's courts. Cortina's firm had a clerk exclusively dedicated to this kind of lawsuit (Arce 1953: 49). When a lawsuit crossed the Atlantic, another party comrade would pick up the case in an appeal to the Supreme Court, and a favorable verdict was often achieved as a result. Thus it was that the case of the sponsored Faustino O'Farrill was taken to court in Havana by a member of the Central Board, Eliseo Giberga, and taken up in Madrid by Labra; the descendants of Esteban Santa Cruz de Oviedo were also defended by Labra at the Supreme Court and in Cuba by another member of the Central Board, José R. Izquierdo, when they claimed and were awarded the inheritance that was rightfully theirs as the children of their mothers' master. The significance of these lawsuits was often more political than legal, but they served to show the system's limitations (Labra 1886, 2: 269–89; 1894: 18–21, 34–36; Izquierdo, n.d.: xx).

The Autonomist press also publicized the violations, excesses, and absurdities of slavery legislation. On numerous occasions, they condemned the deaths of slaves in the stocks, the sale of slaves, disproportionate punishments, and the manner in which the status of a sponsored man who married a freed person was upheld but he remained in his master's servitude. In these reports, we also find a tenuous link that was started by an Autonomist daily in the provinces, only to emerge in the columns of *El Triunfo* or *Revista Económica* in Havana, and subsequently to make the leap to *La Tribuna* or *Revista de las Antillas* in Madrid, funded by Autonomist money. On occasion, the news found in its way into major metropolitan dailies, such as *La Justicia* or *El Liberal*, where the Autonomists also had contacts. Once the campaign had run in the press, the issue often ended up in the Spanish Cortes (García Mora 2005: 299–314).

It should not be forgotten that the conditions for the campaign were not ideal. Cortina never obtained an official permit to open a branch of the Abolitionist Society in Havana. The press did not enjoy full freedom, and the reproduction of an Autonomist petition for the abolition of slavery would lead to the closure of the publication bold enough to publish it. In Madrid, until the Liberals came to power in 1881, abolitionist meetings were impossible. As Scott rightly asserts, "these politicians and publicists remained a small minority, deprived of full freedom of expression, but they helped to maintain the slavery question alive, putting pressure on boards and, intentionally or otherwise, communicating information to sponsored persons" (Scott 1989: 176). Moreno Fraginals asserts that the campaign took place at precisely the moment of possibility, once slavery was collapsing and beginning to lose its point, during a period when the law became an "[essential] weapon for its ultimate abolition" (Moreno Fraginals 2003: 480).

The system itself was priming the machinery of its own dissolution. Scott considers that patronage was no more than a paradoxical combination of change and absence of change. On the one hand, the extension of servitude was a deterrent and a victory for masters because it avoided slavery, while on the other hand, patronage entailed sufficient legal mechanisms to differentiate it from slavery and bring about its end. Unlike slaves, sponsored persons knew when they would be freed and could go to a local board to demand their freedom if patrons failed to meet the obligations imposed on them by law. They also enjoyed the right of self-purchase, which stipulated the procedures to be followed and the amounts to be paid. In short, it gave the sponsored person, although in a limited way, the responsibility for his or her own freedom (Scott 1989: 167–79).

Thus it was that the slow, almost static situation that sponsored persons had been expected to endure until 1885, at which time the first quarter of slave contingents would have to be freed, did not actually unfold as planned. They enforced their rights to freedom in urban areas, where the boards of patronage were based, more than in rural areas. Between May 1881 and May 1885, some 88,472 sponsored persons had obtained their freedom, of which only 15,119 (17 percent) had obtained it as a result of the manumission of one-quarter of the slave contingent, as stipulated in Article 8 of the law. Among them, 31 percent had done so by mutual consent between patron and sponsored individual, and 17 percent through the patron's relinquishment (patrons reached many of the agreements and relinquishments so they would not be reported to the patronage boards); 13 percent of sponsored persons had achieved freedom by compensating the owner, and freedom was granted to a further 7 percent for patrons' failure to comply with the law. In the final year of patronage, which ran from May 1885 to May 1886, only 40 percent achieved freedom as a result of the "natural" implementation of the law; the remaining emancipations were due to the causes listed above (Villanova 1945: 129–32; Scott 1989: 209).

The expectations of landowners and colonial authorities for patronage were hard to achieve. A number of factors conspired against them. First, participation in the Ten Years' War had made the enslaved population aware of its rights. Second, the pressure of the abolitionists grew more intense, influencing, against the wishes of the colonial authorities, not only the metropolis but Cuba itself (Corwin 1967: 309–10). Finally, the economic situation also helped put an end to patronage. Restructuring of the sugar industry meant the end of a large number of facilities that were unable to modernize. Former slaves provided the basis for the agricultural proletariat that subsequently emerged. Few emancipated slaves had access to land of their own. Many abandoned the countryside and migrated to the city.

But at the same time that socioeconomic circumstances promoted the elimination of patronage, politics also played its part. In November 1885, the Liberals, who were always more receptive to overseas reform, returned to power and, in the April 1886 elections, the Autonomists achieved good parliamentary representation. At his debut in the Cortes, Montoro, defending the Autonomist program, once again called for an end to patronage, an initiative that was, for the first time, welcomed by the Cuban Conservatives, who accepted it, through their deputy Miguel Villanueva, claiming that they already had a plan in this regard, of which they had notified the government.[41]

We are unaware of the extent to which Villanueva's claims were true, but one month later, when discussions on the Cuban budget once again raised the subject of abolition, the Cuban Conservatives did indeed present an initiative. It would appear that, after a long campaign, the Autonomists had handed the initiative over to those who had always sought to defer a solution.[42] The situation became critical when three days later, the Constitutional Union deputies presented a project in which abolition was accompanied by an exacting system of labor regulation. The Autonomist minority was caught between a rock and a hard place. On the one hand, it could not refuse to sign a bill that called for the abolition of slavery. But on the other, the document in question was a casuistic application of their program. The situation was all the more delicate if they were to prevent public opinion from misinterpreting their position. Labra, the radical abolitionist, was in favor of signing the Conservative bill, aware that patronage could not last more than six months and that, generally speaking, in postabolitionary scenarios, any attempt to regulate the labor of freed persons was not worth the paper it was written on. Montoro, however, who on other occasions had been more inclined to compromise, now opposed the idea. It was Portuondo who came up with the solution: to present an additional article to the budgets, empowering the government to repeal patronage. The following day, Labra presented it. The Conservatives had no option but to accept this when the overseas minister gave his approval to the procedure. Thus it was that slavery was finally abolished. Some months later, on October 7, 1886, a Royal Decree brought it into effect.[43]

Once slavery was abolished, other issues remained, such as racial integration and the alignment of the civil rights enjoyed by freed persons. Labra, although now without the enthusiastic support of the leadership in Havana, would continue to use litigation to remove class and racial differences from the penal code, abolish segregationist legislation, and encourage the education of former slaves (1894). In Cuba, the Autonomists strove to create a national model to meet their requirements, while former slaves swelled the ranks of the proletariat, and their paths separated.

Notes

1. The price of slaves remained relatively stable throughout the first half of the nineteenth century; it then began to grow from an average of about 380 pesos in the five-year period between 1850 and 1854, to more than 600 in 1860–1865, later leveling off at about 530–570 pesos; see Bergad, Iglesias, and Barcia (1995: appendix).

2. On the creation of the Spanish Abolitionist Society and its relations with Cuba's liberal reformists, see C. Schmidt-Nowara (1999: 100–25).

3. The connection between abolition and free trade in Spain was established by A. Gil Novales (1968: 154–81).

4. In this respect, we share the argument put forward by J. A. Piqueras, who also believes that the abolitionism of the leaders of the 1868 Revolution could be due to their desire to consolidate a liberal and capitalist order (1992: 317–18).

5. On the abolitionist policy of the Mambises, see R. Cepero Bonilla (1948: 112–40).

6. On Maceo's stance and the Baraguá Protest, see J. Ibarra (1967: 121–26); on its impact on abolitionism in Britain and America, see P. S. Foner (1973, 2: 297).

7. The party program appears in L. Estevez y Romero (1974: 57). On Autonomism in general, see L. M. García Mora (2001: 715–48), M. Bizcarrondo and A. Elorza (2001), and M. de la Torre (1997).

8. On the creation of the Constitutional Union, we are reproducing the text published in L. M. García Mora (2009: 303–38).

9. On the creation of the Constitutional Union, see I. Roldán de Montaud (2000: 125–55).

10. A good summary of the strategies of the Autonomist leadership, from the party's foundation to the 1880 Abolition Law, can be found in "Veleidades," *Revista Económica* (Havana), December 14, 1879.

11. See "La cuestión social" and "Procedimiento en la cuestión social," *El Triunfo* (Havana), August 23 and September 1, 1878, respectively.

12. "La fórmula del Sr. Zayas," *Revista Económica* (Havana) 2 (81), May 7, 1879. For more on previous abolitionist projects, see Archivo Nacional de Cuba, Academia de la Historia, caja 107, no. 295: "Luis Armenteros: Proyecto de abolición indemnizada con arreglo a la Ley Moret. Pinar del Río, 15 de octubre de 1878."

13. See "Luchemos pues," *Revista Económica* (Havana), November 21, 1880.

14. Archivo Nacional de Cuba, Academia de la Historia, caja 107, no. 296: "Enmiendas que presenta el Sr. José Manuel Pascual a las bases del proyecto de abolición de la esclavitud. December 26, 1878."

15. See Archivo Nacional de Cuba, Donativos y Remisiones, caja 16, no. 42: "Actas de la Junta Central del Partido Liberal Autonomista. 1879. Sesión de 30 de marzo de 1879" and caja 14, no. 13: "Documentos varios relativos al Partido Liberal Autonomista. Julio 1879. Proposición sobre la cuestión social firmada por Ricardo del Monte, Leopoldo Cancio, José Manuel Pascual, Carlos Saladrigas y Enrique José Varona," Havana, July 15, 1879. See also "El proyecto del Sr. Montoso," *Revista Económica* (Havana), April 14, 1879.

16. See "El manifiesto del Sr. Zayas" and "Al Sr. Zayas," *Revista Económica* (Havana), April 14 and 20, 1879, respectively; the reply in Zayas's article "Claras explicaciones," *El Triunfo* (Havana), April 29, 1879; and the rejoinder "La fórmula del Sr. Zayas," *Revista Económica* (Havana), May 7, 1879.

17. See *El Triunfo* articles: "El proteccionismo en Campaña," "Alocuciones," and "No hay motivos" of February 6 and 8, 1879, respectively; "Gratas esperanzas," "¿Nos equivo-caremos?" and "¡Confianza!" March 7, 15, and 29, 1879, respectively.

18. See "Política activa y consecuente" and "El discurso de la Corona," *El Triunfo* (Havana), May 11 and June 5, 1879, respectively, and "Una circular," *Revista Económica* (Havana), June 15, 1879, trans. by LMGM.

19. See the circular of August 2 in I.. Estévez y Romero [14] (1974, 1: 81, trans. by LMGM).

20. In this part of the work on Labra, we are reproducing the text published in García Mora (2006: 125–37).

21. A new vision of Spanish abolitionism can be found in work by C. Schmidt-Nowara (1999; 2002: 291–307; 2000: 188–207).

22. On this, see Labra's observations in Sociedad Abolicionista Española (1881: 2–3).

23. See *Diario de Sesiones del Congreso de los Diputados*, 1879–1880 legislature, sessions of July 3, 12, and 14, 1879.

24. Archivo del Congreso de los Diputados, dossier 207, no. 52, legislature 1879–1880, and request for number of African slaves and controversy with Fabié in *Diario de Sesiones del Congreso de los Diputados*, legislature 1879–1880, sessions of July 19 and 24, 1879, respectively.

25. *Documentos de la Comisión creada por el real decreto de 15 de agosto de 1879 para informar al gobierno acerca de los proyectos de ley que habrán de someterse a las Cortes sobre reformas de la isla de Cuba, publicados en la Gaceta de Madrid de 13 de noviembre de 1879.* Madrid: Imprenta Nacional, 1879.

26. *Documentos de la Comisión creada . . .* (1879: 53).

27. Portuondo's plea in favor of radical abolitionism (1879).

28. On this, see R. M. de Labra (1882: 10–13) and Archivo Labra, "Carta de Antonio Govín a Rafael María de Labra, La Habana, 25 de agosto de 1881," where he asserts: "You, sir, are deeply hated by reactionaries, not so much for being an Autonomist, but as a distinguished abolitionist of universal renown."

29. On the pressure exerted by Romero Robledo and the telegram from Moré, see I. Roldán (1989), 173 and 179, respectively.

30. Biblioteca Nacional Jose Martí, Colección de Manuscritos de Montoro, XXXVII Actas 1879–1887: "Sesión de la Junta Central del Partido Autonomista. La Habana, 4 de diciembre de 1879"; trans. by LMGM.

31. Biblioteca Nacional Jose Martí, Colección de Manuscritos de Montoro, XXXVII Actas 1879–1887: "Sesión de la Junta Central del Partido Autonomista. La Habana, 4 de diciembre de 1879." The record from 4th includes the telegram sent to Madrid on December 11, trans. by LMGM.

32. "Segundo aniversario del partido liberal," *Revista Económica* (Havana), September 5, 1880, trans. by LMGM.

33. Diario de Sesiones del Senado, November 22, 1879.

34. With regard to this support, see the declaration made by Bernardo Portuondo at the Chamber of Deputies on February 4, 1880.

35. See Diario de Sesiones del Senado, December 12, 1879, p. 559, trans. by LMGM.

36. See Diario de Sesiones del Senado, December 16, 17, and 23, 1879, and January 30, 1880. On Jorrín's participation in the debates, see "Los debates y la carta," *La Política* (Madrid), December 16, 1879; "Información del Senado," *El Acta* (Madrid), November 24, 1879, and "Senado," *El Imparcial* (Madrid), January 23 and May 18, 1880.

37. Archivo Nacional de Cuba, Asuntos Políticos, legajo 253, expediente no. 10: "Carta de Rafael María de Labra a José María Gálvez, Madrid, 8 de marzo de 1880."

38. On the Liberal commitment, see speech by Víctor Balaguer in *Diario de Sesiones del Congreso de los Diputados*, February 13, 1880.

39. On the freedom of slaves not registered in the census, "Los 40.000 esclavos de Cuba," *La Tribuna* (Madrid), February 10, 17, and 20, 1883.

40. See *Diario de Sesiones del Congreso*, June 10, 1882, and June 7, 1885.

41. See speeches by Montoro and Villanueva in the *Diario de Sesiones del Congreso de los Diputados*, June 19, 1886. On the attitude of the Constitutional Union in regard to the elimination of patronage, see I. Roldán (1989: 212–17).

42. See *Diario de Sesiones del Congreso de los Diputados*, July 23, 1886, speeches by Miguel Figueroa and José Verguez.

43. See Biblioteca Nacional, José Martí, Colección de Manuscritos de Montoro, XLI Congreso Diputados: "Reunión de la minoría autonomista en el Congreso de los Diputados, Madrid, 24 de julio de 1886" and *Diario de Sesiones del Congreso de los Diputados*, July 27, 1886.

Works Cited

Amblard, Arturo. 1903. *Notas coloniales*. Madrid, Spain: Ambrosio Pérez.

Arce, Luis A. de. 1953. *José Antonio Cortina: Epoca y carácter, 1853–1884*. Havana, Cuba: Habana Selecta.

Beck, Earl R. 1976. "The Martínez Campos Government of 1879: Spain's Last Chance in Cuba." *Hispanic American Historical Review* (Durham) 56: 268–89.

Bergad, Laird W. 2007. *The Comparative Histories of Slavery in Brazil, Cuba, and the United States*. New York: Cambridge University Press.

Bergad, Laird W., Fe Iglesias, and María C. Barcia. 1995. *The Cuban Slave Market, 1790–1880*. New York: Cambridge University Press.

Betancourt, José Ramón de. 1887. "Manifiesto de París." *Discursos y manifiestos políticos de José Ramón Betancourt*. Madrid: tip. de F. Pinto, 50–59.

Bizcarrondo, Marta, and Antonio Elorza. 2001. *Cuba/España: El dilema autonomista*. Madrid, Spain: Colibrí.

Cepero Bonilla, Raúl. 1948. *Azúcar y abolición: Apuntes para una historia crítica del abolicionismo*. Havana, Cuba: Cenit.

Corwin, Arthur F. 1967. *Spain and the Abolition of Slavery in Cuba: 1817–1886*. Austin: Texas University Press.

Entralgo, Elías José. 1953. *La liberación étnica cubana*. Havana, Cuba: Universidad de La Habana.

Estévez y Romero, Luis. 1974. *Desde el Zanjón hasta Baire*. 2 vols. Havana: Editorial de Ciencias Sociales.

Foner, Philip Sheldon. 1973. *Historia de Cuba y sus relaciones con Estados Unidos*, 2nd ed., vol. 2. (orig. 1963, *A History of Cuba and its Relations with the United States*). Havana: Ed. Pueblo y Educación.

García Mora, Luis M. 1992. "Labra, el partido Autonomista Cubano y la reforma colonial, 1879–1886." *Tebeto: Anuario del Archivo Histórico Insular de Fuerteventura* (Puerto del Rosario) 5 (1): 397–415. http://dialnet.unirioja.es/servlet/articulo?codigo=2233858, accessed December 2010.

———. 1994. "Tras la revolución las reformas: el Partido Liberal cubano y los proyectos reformistas tras la Paz del Zanjón." In *Cuba, la perla de las Antillas*, edited by C. Naranjo Orovio and T. Mallo Gutiérrez. Madrid, Aranjuez, Spain: Consejo Superior de Investigaciones Científicas (CSIC); Doce Calles, 197–212.

———. 2001. "La fuerza de la palabra: El autonomismo en Cuba en el último tercio del siglo XIX." *Revista de Indias* (Madrid) 61 (223): 715–48.

———. 2005. "Intereses solapados: La Tribuna de Madrid y la autonomía colonial." In *Nación y cultura nacional en el Caribe hispano*, edited by Josef Opatrný. *Ibero-Americana Pragensia* (Prague) 15 (Suppl.): 299–314.

————. 2006. "Rafael María de Labra (1840–1918): La Abolición de la esclavitud y la autonomía colonial." In *Figuras de la Gloriosa: Aproximación bibliográfica al Sexenio Democrático*, coord. by Rafael Serrano García. Valladolid, Spain: Universidad de Valladolid, 125–37.

————. 2009. "Un nuevo orden colonial: del Zanjón al Baire, 1878–1898." In *Historia de Cuba*, coord. by C. Naranjo Orovio. Madrid: CSIC, Ediciones Doce Calles, 303–38.

García Mora, Luis M., and Antonio Santamaría García. 2002. "Esclavos por centrales: Mano de obra y tecnología en la industria azucarera: Un ensayo cuantitativo, 1860–1877." In *Azúcar y esclavitud en el final del trabajo forzado: Homenaje a M. Moreno Fraginals*, coord. by J. A. Piqueras. Madrid: Fondo de Cultura Económica, 165–85.

Gómez, Juan Gualberto. 1974. "La cuestión de Cuba en 1884." *Por Cuba libre*, 2nd ed. Havana, Cuba: Editorial de Ciencias Sociales, 173–242.

Govín y Torres, Antonio. 1955. "Discurso pronunciado por el Dr. Antonio Govín y Torres secretario de la junta central del Partido Liberal, en la reunión pública celebrada el día 9 de agosto de 1879, en el salón de La Caridad del Cerro." In *Discursos de Antonio Govín y Torres*, edited by J. Tarafa y Govín. Havana: Burgay, 29–39.

Ibarra, Jorge. 1967. *Ideología mambisa*. Havana, Cuba: Instituto del Libro.

Izquierdo, José R. n.d. *Pleito sobre filiación incidente al intestado de D. Esteban Sta: Cruz de Oviedo: Escrito de alegato presentado a nombre de Enriqueta Santa Cruz de Oviedo y demás hermanos*. [Havana]: s.n.

Klein, Herbert S. 1973. "Consideraciones sobre la viabilidad de la esclavitud y las causas de la abolición en Cuba en el siglo XIX." *La Torre: Revista de la Universidad de Puerto Rico* (San Juan) 21: 307–18.

Klein, Herbert S., and Stanley Engerman. 1983. "Del trabajo esclavo al trabajo libre: notas en torno a un modelo económico compartido." *HISLA: Revista Latinoamericana de Historia Económica y Social* (Lima, Peru) 1: 41–55.

Labra, R. María de. 1880. *Los diputados americanos en las Cortes españolas: Los diputados de Puerto Rico, 1872–1873*. Madrid, Spain: Imprenta de Aurelio J. Alaria.

————. 1881. *Un reto del esclavismo: El reglamento esclavista de 8 de mayo de 1880*. Madrid: s.n.

————. 1882. *La política en las Antillas: El Partido Liberal de Cuba*. Madrid: Aurelio J. Alaria.

————. 1885. *Mi campaña en las Cortes de 1881–1883*. Madrid: Aurelio J. Alaria.

————. 1886. "La abolición de la esclavitud en las colonias inglesas." *Discursos políticos, académicos y forenses*, vol. 2. Madrid: Marcelino Burgase, 139–64.

———. 1894. *La raza de color en Cuba*. Madrid: Fortanet.

———. 1897. *La república y las libertades de ultramar*. Madrid: Alfredo Alonso.

———. 1901. *La reforma política de ultramar*. Madrid: Alfredo Alonso.

Moreno Fraginals, Manuel. 2003. "La abolición de la esclavitud." In *Historia general de América Latina*, 6: *La construcción de las naciones latinoamericanas, 1820–1870*, edited by J. Z. Vázquez and M. M. Grijalva. Madrid: Ediciones Trotta; Paris: UNESCO, 465–81.

Novales, A. Gil. 1968. "Abolicionismo y librecambio (Labra y la política colonial española en la segunda mitad del siglo XIX)." *Revista de Occidente* (Madrid) 59: 154–81.

Piqueras, José A. 1992. *La revolución democrática (1868–1874): Cuestión social, colonialismo y grupos de presión*. Madrid: Ministerio de Trabajo y Seguridad Social.

———. 2007. *Félix Varela y la prosperidad de la patria criolla*. Madrid, Spain: Fundación Mapfre; Aranjuez: Doce Calles.

Portuondo y Barceló, Bernardo. 1879. *Voto particular sobre la reforma social en Cuba*. Madrid: Imprenta de las Heras.

Roldán de Montaud, Inés. 1989. "La Unión Constitucional y la abolición de la esclavitud: Las Actitudes de los conservadores cubanos ante el problema social." *Santiago* (Santiago de Cuba) 73: 131–217.

———. 2000. *La Restauración en Cuba: El fracaso de un proceso reformista*. Madrid, Spain: Consejo Superior de Investigaciones Científicas.

Santamaría García, Antonio, and L. M. García Mora. 1998. "Colonos: Agricultores cañeros, ¿clase media rural en Cuba? 1880–1898." *Revista de Indias* (Madrid) 18 (212): 131–61.

Schmidt-Nowara, Christopher. 1999. *Empire and Antislavery: Spain, Cuba, and Puerto Rico, 1833–1874*. Pittsburgh, PA: University of Pittsburgh Press.

———. 2000. "The End of Slavery and the End of Empire: Slave Emancipation in Cuba and Puerto Rico." In *After Slavery: Emancipation and its Discontents*, edited by H. Temperley. London: Frank Cass, 188–207.

———. 2002. " 'Nuestro objeto no es el interés, sino la civilización': La ideología liberal española y la emancipación de los esclavos en las Antillas." In *Azúcar y esclavitud en el final del trabajo forzado: Homenaje a M. Moreno Fraginals*, coord. by J. A. Piqueras. Madrid: Fondo de Cultura Económica, 291–307.

Suárez Inclán, Estanislao. 1884. *El Gobierno del Ministerio presidido por el Sr. Posada Herrera con respecto a la administración de las provincias de Ultramar*. Madrid: Fortanet.

Torre, Mildred de la. 1997. *El autonomismo en Cuba, 1878–1898*. Havana: Ed. de Ciencias Sociales.

Varela, Felix. 2007. "Consideraciones sobre el estado actual de la isla de Cuba" (orig. 1824, publ. in *El Habanero* [Filadelfia] 1 [1]: 14–19). In *Félix Varela y la prosperidad de la patria criolla*, by J. A. Piqueras. Madrid, Spain: Fundación Mapfre; Aranjuez: Doce Calles, 180–83.

Villanova, Manuel. 1945. "Estadística de la abolición de la esclavitud" (orig. 1885, publ. in *Revista Cubana*). In *Economía y civismo*. Havana, Ministerio de Educación, 129–32.

Archival Materials

Archivo Labra.

Archivo Nacional de Cuba, Academia de la Historia, caja 107, no. 295, 296.

Archivo Nacional de Cuba, Asuntos Políticos, legajo 253, expediente no. 10.

Archivo Nacional de Cuba, Donativos y Remisiones, caja 14, no. 13; caja 16, no. 42.

Biblioteca Nacional José Martí (Havana, Cuba). Colección de Manuscritos de Montoro, XXXVII Actas 1879–1887.

Biblioteca Nacional José Martí (Havana, Cuba). Colección de Manuscritos de Montoro, XLI Congreso Diputados 1886.

España, Comisión de Reformas de Cuba. Ministerio de Ultramar. *Documentos de la Comisión creada por el real decreto de 15 de agosto de 1879 para informar al gobierno acerca de los proyectos de ley que habrán de someterse a las Cortes sobre reformas de la isla de Cuba, publicados en la Gaceta de Madrid de 13 de noviembre de 1879*. Madrid: Imprenta Nacional, 1879.

España, Cortes Generales, Congreso. *Diario de Sesiones del Congreso de los Diputados*, 1879–1880, 1886.

Diario de Sesiones del Congreso, 1882, 1885.

Diario de Sesiones del Senado, 1879.

Sociedad Abolicionista Española. 1881. *Sesión de 25 de enero de 1881: discursos de los señores Chao, Aguilera, Portuondo, Aruan, Zapatero y Moya: discurso del Sr. Nabuco: "La esclavitud en el Brasil": Discurso del Sr. Labra: "La Sociedad Abolicionista Española en 1880."* Madrid: Presidencia de la Sociedad Abolicionista.

Passive Revolution and the Politics of Second Slavery in the Brazilian Empire

Ricardo Salles

The end of the eighteenth and the beginning of the nineteenth centuries in the Western world were marked by the processes of industrialization, notably in England; by market expansion, on national and international scales; by urban development; by the growing social and political importance of the middle classes; and by the formation of a bourgeois life style in general. At the same time and in close connection with these processes, the Atlantic world was shaken by revolutionary events: the American, French, and Haitian Revolutions, the Napoleonic turmoil, and the independence of Latin American countries. The Restoration of 1814–1815 in Europe didn't bury these events and their consequences, not only because a complete turn back to the Old Regime was virtually impossible, but because new revolutionary waves followed in 1830 and 1848. New national states were formed, and the old dynastic states and nations had to adapt to new social, political, and international realities. Even the Austrian Empire, and, to a lesser extent, the Russian Empire, which defeated and reverted the revolutions, could not be and were not the same again. In the Americas, the United States was a reality, reaffirmed after the "Second War of Independence." The independence of Latin American countries was consolidated, and even Haiti managed to survive international isolation and internal turbulence. The African slave trade, and shortly after, slavery itself, were abolished in most countries, with the important exception of the United States, Brazil, and the remaining Spanish colonies of Cuba and Puerto Rico.

All this authorizes the understanding of the "long" nineteenth century, up to 1850, as the "Age of Revolutions," and from that moment on, the "Age of Capital," to use the consecrated expressions of Eric J. Hobsbawm. On the other hand, as pointed out by Arno Mayer in his classic book, *The Persistence of the Old Regime: Europe to the Great War* (1981), the rise of capitalism and the bourgeoisie in Europe was an unequal, not linear, slow, and variegated process that lasted up to the outbreak of World War I and was marked by advances, setbacks, and compromises with the old aristocracies and monarchies. In the Americas, even though the rupture with the colonial order was more radical, several features associated with the colonial times persisted: the agrarian structure based on the *latifundium*, compulsory work, production for export, economic dependence on capital, and manufactured products originating in core economies. Even in the United States, with its extraordinary new capitalist development, slavery increased in parts of its territory, with a velocity and on a scale not experienced previously, until 1865, sustaining an agrarian and export economy in the South. In Cuba, slavery continued until 1886, and the colonial situation, although with a completely new basis and under new circumstances, was only overthrown in 1898.

In Brazil, African slavery, secularly disseminated throughout the territory, expanded mainly on coffee plantations until 1850, when the international slave trade was abolished. Nonetheless slavery, increasingly based on natural reproduction, remained the main form of labor and the main source of income until its abolition in 1888. At the political level, a dynasty of European origin—the Braganzas from Portugal—led the only successful monarchical experience in the Americas between 1822 and 1889, when it was overthrown by a military republican coup. This is probably the reason that recent Brazilian historical literature has stressed the persistence of political, social, and economic practices pertaining to the Old Regime throughout the nineteenth century, despite the different modernizing impulses attempted in the country, mainly in the political and administrative spheres (Fragoso and Florentino 1993; Martins 2006, 2007).

However, the direct association between compulsory work, agrarian production for export, and the persistence of archaic societies has been contested by researchers such as James Oakes (1990) in regard to the Old American South (1990), and Marta Petrusewicz (1996) in regard to the Kingdom of the Two Sicilies. Both have shown the contemporaneity and modernity of these economies, with the adoption of up-to-date market and entrepreneurial practices and technologies. In the particular case of slavery, Dale Tomich (2004) highlighted that if the first half of nineteenth century was marked by the development of industrial capitalism, liberalism, and abolitionism, it was also the moment in which a second slavery spread out, on a scale never experienced before, in the American South, Brazil, and Cuba. In fact, this second slavery grew to be intimately interwoven with the development of capitalism in Great Britain and in the North of the United States. A similar proposition is subjacent to Robin Blackburn's interpretation of modern slavery. He identified three periods in slavery history in Americas: the first one, called *baroque*, corresponded to its implantation in the New World by the Iberian monarchies in the sixteenth and seventeenth centuries. The second period, in the eighteenth century, was marked by the expansion of the French and British plantation system. The third moment was that of "the new American slavery" of the nineteenth century, which corresponds to Tomich's *second slavery* (Blackburn 2011). At this point, it is important to notice that this second slavery was a contested slavery, as it grew during the historical epoch of the Haitian Revolution and the abolitionist movement, which was active on both sides of the Atlantic.

The growth of the second slavery and other forms of coerced labor in agrarian economies, inextricably connected to the expansion of the world capitalist market, resulted in some regions in the formation of modern agrarian elites, imbricated in different ways with the construction or restructuring of national states. In this regard, Enrico Dal Lago (2005) pointed to the comparative dimension of the historical experiences of southern Italy and the Southern United States in the first half of nineteenth century, despite the singularities of each region. The economic, social, and political experience of Southern planters has also been compared, according to their specificities and interpretations, with Russia and Prussia in the nineteenth century, in the works of Kolchin (1990) and Bowman (1993), respectively.

Considered in this historiographical context, the purpose of this essay is to bring to light the historical experience of the Brazilian Empire, committed to the development of second slavery and to the power of the planters as a particular national dominant class formation, the imperial master class (*classe senhorial,* in a Gramscian sense).[1] More specifically, I will highlight the political and institutional features that made the Brazilian experience closer to those of Western Europe than to those of the new American national states of the nineteenth century.

To do so, I first explicate my understanding of the imperial master class. Then I consider the use of Gramscian categories of analysis for the European nineteenth century and its possible similarity to Brazil during the same period. The Gramscian conceptions of passive revolution and historical bloc are central in this regard.[2] I consider the building of the national state in the Brazilian Empire as occurring through the same process that historically produced the imperial master class's hegemony; this argument, too, is in accord with the Gramscian conception of class dominance, as fulfilled by and through the state, understood as involving a combination of coercion and consensus, and of civil and political society.[3] As I intend to show, Gramsci's historical categories of analysis, elaborated to understand the history of Europe, and particularly the history of France and Italy from the Revolution of 1789 until the decade of 1880, apply, with the necessary adaptations, to Brazilian history of the nineteenth century.[4]

This essay is not, however, an exercise in comparative history. I rather see it as a tentative essay in theoretical history. According to Dale Tomich, theoretical history distinguishes itself from historical theory, "which is concerned with formulating theoretical categories that are appropriate for the comprehension of a historically distinct object of inquiry." Theoretical history, on the other hand, "is concerned with using such categories to reconstruct processes of historical development" (Tomich 2004: 18–19). As I understand it, this distinction cannot be rigid, and the historian is or should be constantly changing from one to another in combinations that depend on the focus of the analyses. What I do is discuss a theoretic historical framework, as formulated by Antonio Gramsci to cope fundamentally with European's historical capitalism and modernity, particularly its political and cultural aspects, and I consider its validity for interpreting the history of the Brazilian Empire and its place in the general historical context of the nineteenth century, which was marked by the development of historical capitalism and of second slavery.

◆ ◆ ◆

Slavery in Brazil dated from the early colonial period. Until the mid-nineteenth century, it was heavily dependent on the international African slave trade and influenced by the practice of manumissions. The large-scale international slave trade kept slave prices relatively low, allowing people from different socioeconomic strata to buy and own slaves in different proportions. It also facilitated the possibility that some slaves, accumulating some money, could buy their own or their relatives' freedom, and that their masters could easily replace them. Both these factors led to the formation of a low social group, directly or indirectly of slave ancestry. Until the 1860s, this social group remained fundamentally within the orbit of the great slave owners and the imperial government. This was due either to the power of the great slave owners or the fact that they, too, even if only mildly dependent on slavery, played subaltern roles in maintaining the slave social order (Cunha 1985; Marquese 2007). This order—in conjunction with specific political conditions—led in turn to the formation of the imperial master class as a particular historical form of national dominant class. In this respect, I follow the definition of Ilmar Rohloff de Mattos (1987), who coined this term to differentiate it from a strictly economic, static, and structural conception of planters in general. For Mattos, even though the master class was a class of planters, its formation and identity went far beyond the mere corporative realm, being concomitant with and inextricably connected to the building of the imperial national state.

Despite the fact that these historical developments took place on the American continent during the revolutionary period, I argue that the Brazilian experience was also part of the general institutional and political framework that Antonio Gramsci, considering the European experience at that same historical moment, designated as "passive revolution." For Gramsci, this formula, or canon, of historical interpretation derived from the global impact of the French Revolution and Napoleon's impact on European history. He borrowed the expression from Vincenzo Cuoco's work, *Saggio storico sulla rivoluzione napoletana del 1799*, published in 1801. Cuoco considered the short and failed Neapolitan revolution, in which he took part, to be a passive revolution, comparing it to the successful and active French Revolution. According to Cuoco, the Neapolitan revolutionaries were supported by the presence of the foreign French troops on the Italian peninsula, but not by the people, in contrast to what happened in France during its revolution. That was the reason the Neapolitan revolutionaries were easily defeated by the reactionary forces. Gramsci merged Cuoco's formula with another one, "revolution-restoration," coined by the French historian Edgar Quinet in his 1865 book *La Révolution*. In Quinet's view, the French Revolution went through a period of revolution, from 1788 to 1792, when the National Convention was summoned, and another of restoration, from 1792 to 1794, when "the people," except at spasmodic moments, were absent from the main scene (Meneses 2004).

Gramsci combined and extended the reach of the two formulas to cope with Italian and even European history for most of the nineteenth century. In that sense, "passive revolution" expresses a national reaction to the French Revolution (which tended to establish a permanent hegemony with Napoleon) that attempted to go beyond it. In Italy, "passive revolution" expressed the rise of popular initiative as a historical fact, although without overcoming the limits of its subordination. The consequence was that the rise of industry and the bourgeoisie took place as a "reaction of the dominant classes to the sporadic and inorganic subversion of the masses, as restoration," conceding to some of the popular demands (Voza 2009: 725). Seemingly, in Europe, the process of passive revolution, during the Restoration period, expressed the rise of the bourgeoisie and capitalism in accommodation with sectors of the aristocracy, which therefore assumed the inevitability of this ascension, to the detriment of a rising popular and democratic protagonism (Gramsci 1977: 41, 133, 134 passim).

These events corresponded to the birth of a specific new liberal political culture that I call "restrictive class liberalism."[5] This liberalism did not impose formal or corporative barriers to political participation, except on slaves in slave countries and regions, and in some cases on their offspring. However, class condition—in terms of property, *éthos*, education, and most of the time, some social status—was valued, and with time turned to social prejudice. Constitutionally or formally, this class condition resulted in income restrictions on the franchise, and membership in institutions such as chambers, senates, councils, and other prerogatives that were lifelong or acquired via nomination, usually by the monarch. This liberalism drew from different intellectual sources and affiliations, including Edmund Burke, with his strong criticisms of the radicalization of the French Revolution; the utilitarian and "liberal"[6] Jeremy Bentham, in Britain, in the late eighteenth century; and Benjamin Constant, in France, with his doctrine that sought to combine monarchy and representation in the last decade of eighteenth century and the first decades of nineteenth. But most importantly, it drew from historical experience. In France, from 1820 to 1850, François Guizot, in addition to contributing original intellectual insights, was its man of action and statesman. Restrictive class liberalism had the French Revolution as its point of departure; the revolution was seen as an inescapable and foundational historical event, and at the same time, in regard to Jacobinism and the outcome of Napoleon, something to be corrected and avoided in the future. To cope with this historical task, class-restrictive liberalism aimed to combine both the traditional role of the old monarchies, considered key for political stability, and the inevitable and sometimes desirable impulses toward forms of national representation based on citizen equality in the civil society, which arose from the growing importance of middle classes in European civilization. As the French Revolution was its starting point, the Restoration (1814–1830) and the July Monarchy (1830–1848) in France constituted its main political references (Rosanvallon 1985; Démier 2000, 2012; Waresquiel and Yvert 2002; Furet 2008; Wallerstein 2011).

At the same historical moment, what was happening in France fed the political imagination of the political elite in Brazil (Carvalho 2002; Barbosa 2001; Mattos 1987). In particular, this group of intellectuals and political leaders was organically related to the imperial state, and in this way to the imperial master class as a dominant class. The actions of this group, mainly through its conservative wing, led the building of the imperial order. The core of this order, the imperial master class, was a particular historical class formation centered on a group of coffee planters of the Paraíba River basin in southeast Brazil, comprising the provinces of Rio de Janeiro, Minas Gerais, and São Paulo, and the city of Rio de Janeiro, the imperial court and its main port and commercial center. Regardless of its regional identity, the imperial master class was a nationally dominant class, in the Gramscian sense. This doesn't mean it was homogeneously spread all across the national territory; rather, it means that its political rule was national, that is, organized from the national state, submitting to and incorporating the interests of other social groups in the Brazilian Empire. In that sense, the historical experience of the imperial master class surpassed the corporative scope of its immediate practices, grounded in its economic position and fixed to a specific territory. It also went beyond the limits of its family and social networks and its particular habits, social behaviors, and forms of material and immaterial consumption.

Other social groups—large-, medium-, and small-scale slave owners, and also a vast range of the free population who did not possess slaves—were subordinately incorporated into the imperial national order. Slavery was its common denominator, but not everyone participated on equal terms. Slaves, submitted by force, were in practical terms excluded. Freedmen were also partially excluded, because they did not enjoy full citizenship. Poor white or mulatto men and women were also partially excluded politically by restrictions based on income, or they suffered informal but equally effective forms of domination. Both slaves and poor people, however, made an impression and influenced society and politics. By means of daily actions and resistances and more or less articulated collective struggles, they opened spaces and gained formal and informal rights. Some of these struggles originated among themselves, others developed from conflicts between the ruling elites. Over all, Brazilian imperial social order was based on a complex combination of conquests from below and concessions from above. Among them was the diffused, though selective, practice of manumissions.

From one point of view, very dear to the predominant contemporary Brazilian historiography on slavery, slave agency was able to force masters' concessions, including manumissions, in a process that ended up undermining slavery. From another point of view, which I espouse, elasticity was the mark of Brazilian slave order. Everyone wanted to own slaves, but very few could, and even fewer would. Even former slaves manumitted by their own efforts or by their master's benevolence could buy slaves of their own. The possibility of slave ownership, or at least the possibility of inserting oneself into the slavocrat order, was the soundest warranty of freedom (Marquese 2007; Salles 2007). The African slave trade that lasted until its effective prohibition in 1850 produced an almost unlimited supply of captives at relatively low prices. This condition favored manumission. It also favored poor people, who could afford to buy slaves, and planters, who could bear the cost of freeing and replacing slaves. The general result of all these factors, until the mid-1860s, was the formation of a kind of solidarity, or at least indifference, among free people of different social strata regarding slavery. Among slaves, manumissions, up to that period, functioned as a kind of escape valve in relations with their masters.

This slave social fabric was one of the main factors that favored the transformation of a regional group of coffee planters, integrated in the international market of commodities, into a national dominant class, because it counted on the solidarity of slave owners of different social groups and regions in the country. British pressure to end the transatlantic slave trade, formally approved by law in the Brazilian Parliament in 1831 but reestablished on a larger scale from approximately 1835 on, also helped to cement these solidarities. But this solidarity was not a spontaneous process derived only from favorable economic and social conditions. The concrete action of a group of intellectuals, in the Gramscian sense of a political elite organic to the state as a formation of class dominance, led this process. This elite, in its conservative branch, was the main ruling group of the Brazilian Empire between 1838, the date when the conservative movement of the Regress took office during the last years of the Regency (1831–1840), and 1888, when the conservative cabinet of the Baron of Cotegipe, which stood against the abolition of slavery in the last years of the Second Empire, was overthrown.

This elite gathered around the service of the imperial state, and its members had different social backgrounds, usually coming from the dominant sectors of society. It formed from several distinct regions of the country, not just the basin of the Paraíba

River Valley and the court of Rio de Janeiro. Regardless of its diverse origins and autonomy, granted by the specific forms of sociability of a political career, this elite always gravitated around that social space. "*O Império é o café, o café é Vale*" ("The Empire is coffee, and coffee is the Valley") was a common saying at that time. Its political action always took into consideration the interests and expectations of this region and the class as a whole, even when it contradicted its immediate and corporate interests. Such was the case when the majority of the conservative party forced the approval of the law of September 28, 1871, which declared the wombs of slave women free. The law set a political horizon, though distant, when slavery would end. Facing international isolation after the defeat of the Confederate states in the American Civil War and having encountered enormous difficulties promoting large-scale recruitment of soldiers to the war with Paraguay (1864–1870), mostly due to the country's institution of slavery, this sector of the elite saw the gradual and slow end of slavery as the best way to avoid a crisis that was certain and could be fatal to the imperial order. Despite the fact that most of the representatives of the provinces of Rio de Janeiro, Minas Gerais, and São Paulo opposed the law, the bonds that united the political elite, particularly the Conservative Party, and planters were soon reestablished. By mid-1870s, the "Free-Womb" Law (*Lei do Ventre Livre*) became the last bunker in defense of slavery confronting the mounting abolitionist movement. Until the end of that decade, the issue of slavery practically vanished from the political agenda (Salles 2008). When it reappeared via an incipient abolitionist movement, the Conservative Party, first as the opposition to Liberal cabinets, until 1885, and then as government, from that date to 1888, managed to resist the pressure for immediate abolition, which would finally come on May 13th, 1888.

The similarity between the questions posed by Gramsci in relation to European history and those raised in this essay does not lie only in the theoretical realm. It also occurs in the field of historiography itself, since both of the problems treated here, as well as those that received his attention, occurred in the same historical period. This is true not only with regard to the chronological time of the first half of the nineteenth century, but also because both investigations deal with the same historical problems. As we saw, Gramsci was concerned in particular with the unfolding of the French Revolution and the Restoration period, with the formation of national states, with the rise of the bourgeoisie, and with the establishment of industrial capitalism as a dominant mode of production. More than anywhere else in the Americas, Brazil felt the impact of Napoleon's war. In 1808, Napoleon's troops invaded Portugal and the royal family fled to Rio de Janeiro, which became the court and the head of the Portuguese Empire. This event had great significance in Brazilian history, as it marked a singular route to independence, in which the monarchical form of government, under a European dynasty, was preserved.

Reflecting on Italian history at the same moment in time, Gramsci highlighted the "tardive" and relatively peripheral development of industrial capitalism and the construction of a territorial national state on the peninsula.[7] Although the Brazilian state-building process was not tardive compared with its German and Italian counterparts, and it did not deploy the conditions for the development of capitalism, the same Gramscian criteria of historical interpretation can be used to compare their histories. In the first place, both Brazil and Italy, even if other conditions differed, shared peripheral positions in the international system of historical capitalism. In Italy, a set of historical conditions and events—the repercussions of the French Revolution, French invasions, and the Napoleonic wars; the advent of the national question, from both the perspective of the role of territorial states in the international arena, as traditional ruling elites considered it, and as a demand of the middle classes and the masses for more and new political space—resulted in processes of social and political compromise among dominant social groups. In Brazil, the same set of historical circumstances added to new specific conditions—such as the establishment of the Portuguese court in Rio de Janeiro, shortly followed by independence from Portugal, and the development of a new upsurge of slavery, both as a result of and as a formative force of international market expansion—led to the formation of the imperial master class as a national dominant class, which was, significantly, articulated to the national state-building process, and also to forms of social and political compromise.

The development of a second slavery, in close connection with the expansion of the international capitalist market, constituted a solid and dynamic material and economic force that stimulated the formation of new historical blocs, in a way similar to the development of industrial or protoindustrial capitalism in some regions of Europe.[8] Briefly, Gramsci's concept of historical bloc refers to the complex and historical combinations of social forces, alliances, and class antagonisms, modes of production, state formations, and cultural patterns that occur embedded within a specific time, territory, and international interstate context. This is not to say that the development of second-slavery economies and politics was a mere byproduct of the development of historical capitalism. On the contrary, it means that historical capitalism, the world-system, and the interstate system in the nineteenth century should be seen also through the prism of second slavery (Tomich 2004). In Brazil, in articulation with the process of national state building, under the auspices of imperial master class, the expansion of second slavery resulted in the development of national slavery (Salles 2008a: 41–75, esp. 43–46).

Gramscian criteria of historical interpretation apply to the history of nineteenth-century Brazil in terms similar to the history of Italy during the same period, in regard to the role played by old social groups attached to governmental functions in the process of national and state formation. In both Italy and Brazil, ruling elites that originated from the Old Regime were the main leaders of the process of national state building. In Italy, the elite aggregated around the Piedmont-Sardinian monarchy, and in Brazil, the Luso-Brazilian elite gathered around the Braganza dynasty. Confronting external pressures in the post–French Revolution and post–Napoleonic world, and having to deal with internal social forces galvanized and potentiated to a large extent by these events, these elites, in different peripheral situations, had to, in Gramscian terms, go through a process of *aggiornamento* (updating) to survive. They had to accept or undertake the establishment of class-restrictive liberal monarchical regimes. From a social point of view, these groups integrated themselves or allied, in different ways and to varying degrees, with economically ascending classes. In Italy, the Piedmont aristocracy allied with the bourgeoisie and the middle classes in the north, and also with modernizing sectors of the agrarian bourgeoisie and aristocracy in the central and southern peninsula. In Brazil, the Luso-Brazilian elite, which played a key role in the process of national independence and affirmation of the imperial state, allied with the slave owners and planters, notably those from the southeast. In some cases, they even became planters themselves. On the other hand, in both the Kingdom of Italy and in the Empire of Brazil, old upper classes, such as traditional landlords in southern Italy and slaveholders in other provinces in Brazil, kept their local and corporate power, even if their position was subordinate to the new national ruling class.

In 1822, with the support of the merchants of Rio de Janeiro, high-ranking state bureaucracy, and planters, notably those established in the provinces of Rio de Janeiro, São Paulo, and Minas Gerais, Prince Dom Pedro, heir of the Portuguese throne, proclaimed Brazilian independence. This was a way to face the pressure exerted by the Portuguese Cortes, fruit of a liberal revolution in 1820, to limit monarchical powers and at the same time resist the efforts of the Cortes to curtail Brazilian autonomy, which had been exercised since 1808, when the Court came to Rio de Janeiro fleeing Napoleon. In this way, independence satisfied very different expectations: provincial wishes for more autonomy in relation to Lisbon as well as Rio de Janeiro; the attempt of the prince and his entourage to preserve privileges and powers; the intention of Rio de Janeiro's merchants to preserve their interests; the desire of many planters for autonomy and greater influence in politics and administration; and last but not least, popular and radical demands for more political rights.

Let us take a closer look at the Brazilian historical process, after the independence from Portugal in 1822. In 1824, then-emperor D. Pedro closed down the National Constituent Assembly and promulgated a centralist and restrictive liberal constitution. The practical interpretation of the constitution and its enforcement by D. Pedro and his court entourage had distinct traits of constitutional absolutism. Rebellion exploded and was severely repressed in the northeast of the country, riots took place in the Court, and discontent grew among different social strata, including planters in the Southeast. Liberal opposition amounted. At the end of 1831, the emperor was forced to abdicate in favor of his minor son, Pedro II. The significance of the fact that his government had negotiated a treaty with Great Britain that forbade the international slave trade and cut one the most important ties that linked his reign to the planters cannot be underestimated in this episode. In 1834, the proposal of a liberal amendment to the constitution provoked serious disputes between those who wanted a federalist monarchy and those who, even though they were willing to accept some minor concessions to provincial autonomy, stood for centralization. In 1838, in the midst of a series of provincial rebellions and even a large slave revolt, the faction in favor of centralization seized the regency by election. The supporters of centralization were known as *regressistas* (partisans of regression) in opposition to the *progressistas* (partisans of progress). The *regressistas* won the decisive support of the majority of the coffee planters of the Paraíba River basin by committing to reopening the international slave trade, which was central to the expansion of coffee plantations in the region (Parron 2011). They formed what was soon to be known as the Conservative Party. In 1840, the opposition to the *regressistas* managed to declare Pedro II an adult, even though he had just turned fifteen, as a maneuver to overthrow the conservative regency. Even though they protested against breaking constitutional rules, the conservatives refrained from taking extreme measures against the coup, opting to oppose the new government only in parliament and in the press. Their tactic worked very well, and by the end of 1841, the young emperor had summoned the conservatives to form a new government. The liberals revolted in Minas Gerais and São Paulo, but were defeated by the conservative government with the strong and active support of the majority of the Paraíba River valley planters.

This process meant the consolidation of an imperial historical bloc, a new social, political, and cultural hegemony, as it unfolded in three simultaneous and inextricably interwoven levels. First, this new historical bloc was established on the material and cultural level in general. It resulted in the formation of the imperial master class, centered around the development of a second slavery bound to the international capitalist market. At this point, it is important to point out that Brazil was not experiencing, either potentially or partially, anything like a bourgeois revolution, a process of industrialization or modernization in contrast with an archaic or conservative vocation. The point is to understand the main features of the national development of a second slavery as it connected to the international commodity market, in terms of the development of historical capitalism that I have been trying to emphasize so far. Nineteenth-century second slavery was modern and up to date. That modernity provided sufficient dynamism to sustain the "revolution" side of the Gramscian formula of passive revolution.

In short, that meant the establishment of a set of social and cultural practices with slavery at the very center. Slavery was considered a form of discipline and of civilizing labor. It was viewed as a necessary and unavoidable step to guarantee a young and agrarian civilization in America and its insertion into the general framework of material and moral progress characteristic of the Western century. One day in a distant future, as happened in Europe's historical march toward more refined levels of civilization, there would be conditions to overcome slavery, but not at that present moment. Brazilian slavery even had one positive side effect. According to the dominant self-image in society, due to long-established practice of manumissions and to the Christian mentality prevailing among slave owners, slavery in Brazil had a positive impact on Africans. Living in barbarity and practicing enslavement among themselves, African slaves ended up being civilized when brought to Brazil. The elasticity of Brazilian slavery, propitiated by the international slave trade, as seen above, was key to these practices and conceptions.

The new historical bloc meant the institutionalization of a liberal, representative, and socially restrictive monarchy. This process was on pace with the political culture of the era of Restoration in Europe, including, and above all, the July Monarchy in France. Pierre Rosanvallon (1985), analyzing the role of Guizot in French political history between 1820 and 1848, characterized this era as having a political culture of its own. This political culture was a tentative combination of civil equality on the one hand, and political and income restriction in the balloting process, accompanied by restricted political institutions on the other. As a political culture, this liberalism aimed to distance itself from any democratic, radical doctrine of how to organize society and government based on abstract rationality. Experience, history, and realism were the key considerations to a good and balanced government. The aim was to avoid a new revolution and to refrain from Jacobinism. In the second place, restrictive liberals recognized that there was no point in trying to revive the prerevolutionary world of privileges. This was gone for good. The task was to close the curtain on the revolution, not to reverse it. Political distinction had to be based on recognition of natural and acquired capacities. Power and government had to be embedded in society. The bourgeois and middle classes of society constituted the basis for this political culture.

In this regard, it is worth mentioning that the Brazilian voting and parliamentary system in the same period allowed lower-income people to vote and permitted more political participation from below than occurred in Europe (Carvalho 2002). This was based on access to slaves by different social strata in Brazil, though that occurred without compromising the social hierarchy; rather, it was fundamental to it. This allowed a less restricted, but not democratic, balloting and political system that nevertheless produced power that was more politically stable for the political elites.

One last remark with respect to class-restrictive liberalism: what Rosanvallon has seen as an autonomous political culture at a particular moment in French history, *Le moment Guizot* (1985), Gramsci saw as a decisive moment in a broader historical epoch of passive revolution (Gramsci 1977: 281). Gramsci's approach seems to have some advantages. First, it enlarges the geographical scope of the issue at hand, inserting it into the general context of European revolutions and counterrevolutions (as proposed here, this must be done to incorporate the Americas into the general framework of analysis). Second, it widens its time scope, inserting it in the *longue durée* of the formation of historical capitalism, with the set of historical revolutions and political transformations that took place throughout the nineteenth century, which again, as stated here, did not take place only in Europe. Third, besides enlarging it, Gramsci's approach deepens the reach of analysis, relating the political cultures, languages, doctrines, and the role of political elites to material, social, and cultural processes of transformation that not only occurred at that same time, but constitute the social condition within which they appeared, as Guizot himself and his *doctrinaire* fellows were well aware.

Finally, the new imperial historical bloc was not the spontaneous result of objective cultural and material processes, but rather resulted from the political and social actions and struggles of the moment. In this respect, the *regressistas* group, soon to become the core of the Conservative Party organized around the Paraíba River basin, played a decisive role. Between 1838, when they first came to regency government aiming to guarantee the constitution and the centralized monarchy, and 1889, when the monarchy was overthrown, they were the dominant political party of the empire. They were in the government thirty-one out of fifty-one years, or 61 percent of that period. During that time, they faced internal disputes and even a dissidence that allowed the formation of a new moderate liberal wing, which would come to govern between 1862 and 1868. But, most importantly, during the whole period, besides balloting reforms that fundamentally kept voting restrictions, the main political institutions of the centralized monarchy were maintained: for instance, royal power, lifelong membership in the Senate and State Council, and the nomination of the presidents of the provinces by the central government. Even regarding slavery, all the reforms put into practice were, directly or indirectly, the fruits of foreign or popular pressure. These reforms, however, were conducted by conservative governments, following the practice of reform-mongering as a way to prevent serious crises. At different conjunctures, they understood that the expansion, maintenance, and when the time came, gradual end of slavery was the quintessence and the social source of their political power.

This political dimension constitutes the "passive" side of the process of national state building in nineteenth-century Brazil. This concerns the hegemony and intellectual and moral direction imposed by the conservatives over the liberals on the process as a whole. Let us take a closer look at the historical period considered above, from 1838 to 1889, dividing it in particular moments.

The period from 1838, when the *Regresso* movement seized the Regency office, to 1862, when conservative dissidents allied with the liberals and managed to form a new cabinet, was the peak of conservative preeminence over Brazilian politics. The basis for this preeminence was support from the Paraíba River basin planters, particularly from coffee planters, and the positions they held in the office and in the Assembly of the key province of Rio de Janeiro. During that time, they faced and defeated provincial attempts to separate from the Empire: in Rio Grande do

Sul (1835–1845), in the liberal revolt of 1842 in the very core of the Empire, in São Paulo and Minas Gerais, and finally in an isolated liberal uprising in Pernambuco in 1848.[9]

In 1843, in the Senate, Bernardo Pereira de Vasconcelos, one of the leading figures of the *Regresso*, mocked a colleague who advocated for incentives to bring white immigrants to the country and who at the same time claimed that barriers should be raised to prevent the entrance of Africans. The example of the United States, where white immigrants chose to come to the free states, was mentioned. Vasconcelos replied that doing so would stimulate "barbarizing tendencies that will result from the abolition of the African slave trade." Ironically, another senator said, "So, Africa civilizes!" Vasconcelos promptly replied: "That is true; Africa does civilize America." (*Anais do Senado*, vol. IV, 346, in Escosteguy Filho 2010: 121). Even after the abolition of the international slave trade, the conservatives, the ones who pushed the decision through National Assembly, made it clear that the end of international trade did not affect their commitment to the institution of slavery in Brazil. On May 26, 1855, in a speech at the Chamber of Deputies, the marquis of Paraná, himself a planter in the Paraíba Valley and chief of the cabinet, stated, "what is convenient to the present interests of the Brazilian society is to maintain the laws that sustain slavery in the Empire for a long period of time." (Anais da Câmara dos Deputados, 145–47).

During this period, although conservative governments were constantly opposed, sometimes even by force of arms, liberals tacitly accepted the backbone of state institutions and imperial politics. They were unable to build a political and institutional alternative. In 1868, when they were expelled from the government as a result the emperor's action against the majority they held in the National Assembly, they radicalized their discourse.[10] The question of slavery finally became an issue in their program, although they proved to be incapable of implementing concrete measures when they returned to the government again in 1879. That same year, with the support of urban popular groups and the lower middle class of society, an abolitionist movement arose. In response, republicans formed a political party; the imperial political order, both socially and politically, was at stake.

Unlike the liberals, the conservatives built their political cohesion and strength on their realistic view of slavery. Although they were rarely open supporters of the institution, they, or their families, were more often slave owners themselves, and as such, they dealt with it as a fact of life, as something inevitable in Brazilian historical and geographical conditions, something that could not be irresponsibly attacked without compromising the whole social and political order.

All in all, the conservatives stood at the head of imperial cabinets in nineteen of the twenty-four years from 1838 until 1862. These were the years in which the ties that connected the political elite, especially its conservative wing, to the master class were tighter.

Over the next twenty years, until 1885, the liberals headed the government for twelve years.[11] Although they had the emancipation banner in their political program from 1868, until 1884 they did nothing to end slavery, not even gradually. They opposed the Free-Womb Law, which was proposed and passed by the conservative viscount of Rio Branco in 1871, and in 1884 they failed to pass the law that would free slaves older than sixty years. This law would be passed the following year by the conservative cabinet of the baron of Cotegipe, João Maurício Wanderley. A sugar planter from Bahia with close connections to the conservatives of the province of Rio de Janeiro, he was called to take office to lead the emancipationist reform. Cotegipe's proposal guaranteed the slave-owners' interests, because the law also approved a stipulation that the slaves who benefited from the law would have to work for their former masters until they turned sixty-five. This measure had the support of some liberal representatives. So it is no surprise that one of them, Martinho de Campos, who occupied several political positions including president of the province of Rio de Janeiro, minister of finance, and even the presidency of the Council of Ministers, declared in 1882 that he was a *escravocrata da gema*, a hard-core slavocrat (Costa 1998: 308). During this period, the ties between many sectors of the intellectual and political elites and slavery were loosening.

Finally, between 1885 and 1888, the abolitionist movement, and from 1887 on, slave revolts took the forefront of the political scene. At this point, the intellectual and political field was irremediably divided by the abolitionist movement and by the active presence of slaves themselves in the political arena, supported by that same movement. The conservative Cotegipe was one of the last men standing in defense of slavery, or at least in defense of its prolonged, negotiated, and indemnified end. He did not succeed. In short, abolition was conceded on May 13, 1888, by João Alfredo, also conservative, who replaced Cotegipe. All in vain: the proclamation of the Republic by a military coup the following year, on November 15, was just an epilogue to the Empire that was born with slavery and perished with slavery.

◆ ◆ ◆

This approach shows both the autonomy and the dependency of the intellectual and political field in regard to its relation to the master class, understood at this point at its corporate level, as an objective and relative position in the relations of production. The autonomy and political preeminence of the intellectuals, as a group or social stratum in the Brazilian Empire, notably in its superior political ranks, must always be understood and evaluated in the context of its organic relations toward the master class. Such organic relations are historical, not mechanical, spontaneous, or invariable. They are an index of historically formed and built relations, sometimes more firm, at other times more loose, with peak moments and periods of stability, crisis, and rupture, and other periods that do not conform to any fixed definition. Therefore, individuals are not fit, as from the perspective of a static sociological conception, into this or that category; rather, their actions have to be evaluated at every conjuncture in their organic relation to social classes, and particularly to the state.[12]

The use of Gramscian categories of analysis also shows the active role some of the most prominent intellectuals played in the conformation of the imperial master class and the imperial historical bloc. Their relation with the class was not only, or even primarily, a matter of family origins or personal social position as land and slave owners, nor was it a question of what social networks they fit in, although this was important in many cases. As intellectuals, they played a directive and leading role producing a worldview based on their political and cultural actions, class interests, and identity. They did so as they related, as intellectuals, to the state; to broader cultural and intellectual practices and institutions nationally and internationally; and to other classes and social groups outside the immediate realm of corporate class practices. In that sense, class interest and identity as such only came to be as they were produced by the actions of intellectuals. The actions of intellectuals, in turn, can only be totally understood and explained in their historical reach and significance if related to the formation, expansion, and maintenance of the social power of the imperial master class in relation to the slaves and other social groups of Brazilian society subordinated in this process.[13]

At this point, it is of fundamental importance to understand the long-term role played by slaves in this historical development. Their role justifies the conceptualization of the process as a passive revolution. Their social agency, at least until the 1880s, was dispersed and fragmented. In that regard, characterization of agency—whether conscious or unconscious of its implications—as resistance does make sense. With the exception of a series of slave rebellions in Bahia at the beginning of the century, which had their peak in the Malê revolt in Salvador in 1835, slave agency never had a general or political purpose and never seriously threatened the political order of the empire. The revolts and the perils they represented never went beyond provincial borders. Despite that, the politics of the Brazilian Empire cannot be fully understood without constant referral to the presence of slaves in its social and political life. In social life, this is true as concerns the daily, private, and local administration forming the master habitus (Muaze 2011: 320 and passim; Muaze 2008). Crimes, runaways, revolts, and disobedience were always present to remind masters and authorities that the slave was their "irreconcilable enemy," as put by a planter's committee set up in Vassouras in 1854 to monitor slave actions (Mattos 1987; Salles 2008a: 177 et seq., esp. 188).

On the general political, cultural, and social plane, slavery and slaves had different effects, according to time and space, depending on what issues made the national and the international agenda. One thing is certain: slavery and slaves represented a powerful force inhibiting a democratic radicalization of Brazilian liberalism. They represented the *non plus ultra* that narrowed the potential social base of the liberals, so that they hesitated to stand for the abolitionist or even the emancipationist banner and appeal to the masses. This facilitated the production of a politically conservative and socially restrictive political hegemony, which cannot be fully comprehended without considering the social hegemony exerted by the master class in society. This deep trait of Brazilian political and social life in the nineteenth century characterized the process of national state building as a passive revolution.

In the United States, at this same period, different political, demographic, and economic circumstances led to a strange paradox. Southern and slave states, except for Virginia and North Carolina, were the first to experience a democratic institutionalization in their political evolution. A certain egalitarianism fomented by the war for independence, the more fluid economy and society in the new western states, and more pronounced political competition due to the Second Party system, led to the result that "by 1850 all slave states save Virginia and North Carolina had adopted white manhood suffrage for elections to both houses of their state legislatures" (Bowman 1993: 151, 145 et seq.). In Europe, limits to suffrage were initially generated by the apprehensions caused by the experiences of Jacobinism and of Napoleon that shaped European politics until 1848. From that moment on, the main political consideration in European life was the menacing presence of the dangerous classes. During the decades between 1880 and the 1890s, however, this presence was greatly institutionalized. Dominant liberalism turned democratic, or was in the process of so doing.

During the 1820s and the beginning of the 1830s, politics in the Empire of Brazil coincided with what happened in Europe, particularly with what happened in France. On both sides of the Atlantic, one could follow the same main political trends: democratic radicalism, restrictive liberalism, and restoration. From 1848 on, politics in the two countries diverged. As monarchical restrictive liberalism faced nascent opposition from below in Europe, especially in France, it gained more and more consistency and stability in the Brazilian Empire. When in 1848 France faced a republican and democratic revolution that overthrew the monarchy, and a few months later faced an attempted social revolution, in Brazil the Second Empire with its limited and restricted liberalism was at its apex. Slavery was abolished in French colonies in that year. In Brazil, even with the reluctant abolition of the international slave trade two years later, its golden age was about to begin.

Slavery provided the social ground that permitted restricted liberalism to be consolidated in Brazil, whereas it was contested and finally collapsed in France. The fact that radical and democratic ideals, not to say socialist ideals, started to make some progress in Brazil only by late 1870s is not due to an atavistic backwardness of its intellectual life. Rather, it represents the ways in which Brazilian second-slavery society and European society in its transition to capitalism, France in particular, played different roles and had different experiences on the common field of historical capitalist modernity. It also shows, on the other hand, that the politics of second slavery, as it took place in Brazil, the United States, and Cuba, does not constitute a separate reality from that of historical capitalism in the nineteenth century. This is not to say that an understanding of Brazilian politics would not profit from comparison with North American and Cuban experiences. It only means, as I have tried to show, that there are no mechanical relations between those realities and that the terms of comparison can be and should be more ample.

Notes

1. There is no direct English translation of what Ilmar Rohloff de Mattos means by "*classe senhorial*" in *O Tempo Saquarema* (1987). Literally, it would mean "seigniorial," or "manorial," though without a feudal connotation. The expression "master class" would be closer to the literal meaning of "*classe senhorial*" as planters or masters in general ("*plantadores*" or "*senhores*" in Portuguese). By "*classe senhorial*," however, Mattos means a particular historical slave-owner class formation, in a given time and place, distinguishing them from the planters and masters in general. To cope with this translational difficulty I will use, when appropriate, the expression "imperial master class" to mean "*classe senhorial*" in Mattos's sense.

2. Luiz Werneck Vianna was possibly the first scholar to systematically use the concept of passive revolution to explain the Brazilian path to capitalist modernity (1996); see also Vianna (1995). For the use of the historical analytical category of historical bloc, see my *Nostalgia imperial* (1996).

3. I depart from the work of Ilmar Rohloff de Mattos (1987), who used Antonio Gramsci's conception of politics and E. P. Thompson's formulation of class formation to consider the construction of the imperial national state and the formation of the mas-

ter class ("*classe senhorial*") as two sides, inextricably connected, of the same historical process.

4. What follows is a modified synthesis of my paper "O Império do Brasil no contexto do século XIX: Escravidão nacional, classe senhorial e intelectuais na formação do Estado nacional" (2012).

5. Immanuel Wallerstein (2011) labeled a similar definition of this political culture as the "ideology of centrist liberalism," understanding ideology as a political metastrategy.

6. "Liberal" appears here in quotes, as the word wasn't coined until the first decades of the nineteenth century. Wallerstein, in a footnote and using different sources, traces the origins and the uses of terms "liberal" and "conservative" from the late eighteenth to early nineteenth century (2011: 2). In this essay, I will use the term "liberal" to refer to both a general political culture and a particular political tendency. The term "conservative" will also be used in this latter sense, as a particular political tendency within the more ample liberal culture.

7. "Tardive" appears in quotes because it implies a linear vision of the historical process. I use the expression as a convenience, since it is not the focus of my attention, and as it is consecrated in Marxist historiographical tradition. This kind of approach to the German and Italian experiences of the development of capitalism, which are also labeled as "from above" to stress the central role played by state governments, supposes that they are conceived in comparison to model experiences of bourgeois revolution: the French Revolution in political terms and the Industrial Revolution in regard to the development of capitalism in Britain. This perspective has been contested by recent historiography, which questions the very notion of bourgeois revolution as a simplification to understand the general process of industrialization added to or driven by the formation of national states. Departing from a Marxist perspective, Arno Mayer, in *The Persistence of the Old Regime* (1987 [1981]), had already criticized the simplistic view of nineteenth-century history as a paved road leading straight to bourgeois domination and industrial capitalism. Gramscian historical reflections, as they generalize the passive revolution characteristic of Italian history to other parts of Europe and emphasize the political accommodation between previous ruling groups and the ascending bourgeoisie as key to the development of capitalism, are also implicitly critical of this simplification.

8. I use the expression "protoindustrial capitalism" to designate those social and economic environments for which, even though it is not immediately present on a large scale, industrialization is an issue in the agenda of social groups and governments. For instance, in

early nineteenth-century France, one cannot detect the existence of an industrial bourgeoisie on any considerable scale, but industrialization was nevertheless an issue.

9. Although the end of the Farroupilha War in 1845 in Rio Grande do Sul occurred under a liberal government, the decisive figure in the defeat and pacification of the ragtag *farroupilhas* was the baron of Caxias, Luís Alves de Lima e Silva, a conservative general and a right-hand man of the conservative leadership, who had familial bonds to planters in the province of Rio de Janeiro and was also responsible for the defeat of the liberal uprisings of 1842.

10. The nomination or dismissal of the president of the Council of Ministers was a prerogative of the royal power held by the emperor, which he could exercise at will, regardless of the majority in the National Assembly; but Dom Pedro II seldom used it.

11. As emancipationist reforms I understand, as the abolitionists of the period did, the procrastinating nature of measures taken to anticipate and therefore avoid possible future crises. The first was in 1871, when the Free-Womb Law was passed under a conservative government. The concessions of minor reforms, such as the 1885 law, attempted to diminish abolitionist pressure.

12. In that sense, I am deliberately trying to avoid the most common trap of "applying" Gramsci, and I am characterizing particular individuals as organic (directly connected to fundamental social classes) or traditional intellectuals (more autonomous, relating to previously formed intellectual strata). The organic relation to a social class in a given moment can produce the traditional intellectual, depending on the circumstances and even on the individual's trajectory in another historical situation. Conversely, traditional intellectuals, formed in traditional or past situations, can attach themselves, either consciously or unconsciously, to processes of formation of new historical classes and social groups, depending, again, on historical circumstances.

13. Class interests and identity here do not necessarily result in explicit class self-identification as such.

Works Cited

Barbosa, Silvana M. 2001. *A Sphinge Monárquica: O poder moderador e a política imperial.* Unpublished PhD diss., Universidad Estadual de Campinas, Departamento de História/Instituto de Filosofia e Ciências Humana, Brazil.

Blackburn, Robin. 2011. *The American Crucible: Slavery, Emancipation and Human Rights.* London: Verso.

Bowman, Shearer D. 1993. *Masters and Lords: Mid-19th-Century U.S. Planters and Prussian Junkers.* New York: Oxford University Press.

Câmara dos Deputados. *Anais da Câmara dos Deputados.* http://www2.camara.gov.br/.

Carvalho, José Murilo de. 2002. "Introdução." In *Visconde do Uruguai,* org. by J. M. de Carvalho. Coleção Formadores do Brasil. São Paulo, Brazil: Editora 34.

Costa, Emilia Viotti da. 1998. *Da senzala à colônia,* 4th ed. São Paulo, Brazil: Ed. Unesp.

Cunha, Manuela Carneiro da. 1985. *Negros, estrangeiros: Os escravos libertos e sua volta à África.* São Paulo: Brasiliense.

Dal Lago, Enrico. 2005. *Agrarian Elites: American Slaveholders and Southern Italian Landowners 1815–1861.* Baton Rouge: Louisiana State University Press.

Démier, Francis. 2000. *La France du XIXᵉ siècle: 1814–1914.* Paris: Éditions du Seuil.

———. 2012. *La France de la Restauration, 1814–1830: L'impossible retour du passé.* Paris: Gallimard.

Escosteguy Filho, João Carlos. 2010. *Tráfico de escravos e direção Saquarema no Senado do Império do Brasil.* Unpublished MS diss., Universidade Federal Fluminense, Instituto de Ciências Humanas e Filosofia, Departamento de História, Niterói, Brazil. http://www.historia.uff.br/stricto/td/1391.pdf.

Fragoso, João, and Manolo Florentino. 1993. *O arcaísmo como projeto: Mercado atlântico, sociedade agrária e elite mercantil no Rio de Janeiro, c. 1790–c. 1840.* Rio de Janeiro, Brazil: Diadorim.

Furet, François. 2008. *Revolutionary France, 1770–1880.* Oxford, UK: Blackwell Publishers.

Gramsci, Antonio. 1977. *Quaderni del carcere.* 4 vols. Torino, Italy: Einaudi.

Kolchin, P. 1990. *Unfree Labor: American Slavery and Russian Serfdom.* Cambridge, MA: Belknap Press.

Marquese, Rafael de Bivar. 2007. O poder da escravidão: Um comentário aos "Senhores sem escravos." *Almanack Braziliense* no. 6: 14–18. http://www.almanack.usp.br/almanack/PDFS/6/06_forum-02.pdf.

Martins, Maria F. V. 2006. "A velha arte de governar: O Conselho de Estado no Brasil Imperial." *Topoi* 7 (12): 178–221. http://www.revistatopoi.org/.

———. 2007. *A velha arte de governar. Um estudo sobre política e elites a partir do Conselho de Estado (1842–1889).* Rio de Janeiro: Arquivo Nacional.

Mattos, Ilmar Rolhoff de. 1987. *O Tempo Saquarema.* São Paulo: Hucitec.

Mayer, Arno J. 1981. *The Persistence of the Old Regime: Europe to the Great War.* New York: Pantheon.

———. 1987. *A Força da tradição: A persistência do Antigo Regime (1848–1914)* (Portuguese trans. of *The Persistence of the Old Regime: Europe to the Great War*). São Paulo: Companhia das Letras.

Meneses, Jaldes de Reis. 2004. "Gramsci e Tocqueville." On the website Gramsci e o Brasil. http://www.acessa.com/gramsci/index.php, accessed May 22, 2013.

Muaze, Mariana. 2008. *As memórias da viscondessa: Família e poder no Brasil Império.* Rio de Janeiro: Jorge Zahar Ed.

———. 2011. "O Vale do Paraíba Fluminense e a dinâmica imperial." On the website INEPC, Inventário das Fazendas, Textos autorais. http://www.institutocidadeviva.org.br/inventarios/?page_id=8.

Oakes, James. 1990. *Slavery and Freedom: An Interpretation of the Old South.* New York: Knopf.

Parron, Tâmis. 2011. *A política da escravidão no Império do Brasil, 1826–1865.* Rio de Janeiro: Civilização Brasileira.

Petrusewicz, Marta. 1996. *Latifundium: Moral Economy and Material Life in a European Periphery.* Ann Arbor: University of Michigan Press.

Rosanvallon, Pierre. 1985. *Le Moment Guizot.* Paris: Gallimard.

Salles, Ricardo. 1996. *Nostalgia imperial: A formação da identidade nacional no Brasil do Segundo Reinado.* Rio de Janeiro: Topbooks.

———. 2007. "Da liberdade de se ter escravos à liberdade como direito." In *Nação e cidadania no Império: Novos horizontes*, edited by José Murilo de Carvalho. Rio de Janeiro: Civilização Brasileira.

———. 2008a. *E o Vale era o escravo: Vassouras, século XIX: Senhores e escravos no coração do Império.* Rio de Janeiro: Civilização Brasileira.

———. 2008b. Escravidão e política no Império. *História, Ciências, Saúde-Manguinhos* 15 (1): 231–35.

———. 2012. "O Império do Brasil no contexto do século XIX: Escravidão nacional, classe senhorial e intelectuais na formação do Estado." *Almanack* (revista eletrônica semestral) no. 4: 5–45.

Tomich, D. 2004. *Through the Prism of Slavery: Labor, Capital, and World Economy.* Lanham, MD: Rowman & Littlefield.

Vianna, Luiz Werneck. 1995. "O Ator e os fatos: A Revolução passiva e o Americanismo em Gramsci." *Dados* 38, no. 2.

———. 1996. "Caminhos e Descaminhos da Revolução Passiva à Brasileira." *Dados* 39, no. 3. http://dx.doi.org/10.1590/S0011-52581996000300004.

Wallerstein, Immanuel. 2011. *The Modern World System*, 4: *Centrist Liberalism Triumphant, 1789–1914*. Berkeley: University of California Press.

Waresquiel, Emmanuel de, and Benoît Yvert. 2002. *Histoire de la Restauration, 1814–1830: Naissance de la France moderne*. Paris: Perrin.

The Contraband Slave Trade
of the Second Slavery

Leonardo Marques

Historian Luiz Felipe de Alencastro argues that one of the greatest crimes of the nineteenth century—and one often forgotten—was the illegal enslavement of the more than 700,000 Africans brought to Brazil after 1831, when a federal law formally banned the slave trade to the country (2010). The crime was even greater if we look at the issue from a hemispheric perspective and include the more than half a million enslaved Africans who were disembarked in Cuba after 1820, when the slave trade to the Spanish colony was also formally abolished. The number of individuals illegally enslaved in the Americas then goes up to almost 1,300,000, a number that becomes even bigger if we include their descendants. Most slaveholders and merchants responsible for these disembarkations would never be brought to justice for their crimes, but most of the people illegally disembarked in both countries would remain enslaved until either their deaths or the final abolition of slavery in the Americas during the 1880s.[1]

The main factor behind these massive flows of enslaved human beings was the expansion of coffee and sugar production in Brazil and Cuba, most of which was exported to the growing urban centers of the North Atlantic. The transformation of historical capitalism in the long nineteenth century was marked by the expansion of slavery not only in Brazil and Cuba, but also in the United States, a process described by Dale Tomich as the "second slavery" (Tomich 2003). The integration of these three slave societies into the more-or-less self-regulating market of the nineteenth century led to the adoption of new technologies, novel forms of labor organization, and growing specialization in the production of sugar, coffee, and cotton (in, respectively, Cuba, Brazil, and the United States) as planters strove to remain competitive in this new context. Historians working with the concept of second slavery have explored not only the interconnections among these slave societies, but also the transformations of slavery as a system and its relationship to the capitalist world-economy as a whole (Schmidt-Nowara 1999; Tomich 2003; Marquese 2004; Kaye 2009; Berbel, Marquese, and Parron 2010; Baptist 2014).

This new context also shaped the emergence and development of the contraband slave trade of the second slavery in fundamental ways. First, the transatlantic slave trade became illegal across the Atlantic as a result of the consolidation of British hegemony in the aftermath of the Napoleonic Wars (Huzzey 2012; Tomich 2016). However, while the United States effectively closed its doors to the importation of enslaved Africans (leading to the emergence of a massive domestic slave trade), Brazil and Cuba continued to heavily depend on it. Second, the context of growing anti–slave trade pressure in the international arena on the one hand, and expansion of the world economy on the other, contributed to a more intense internationalization of the traffic. By the 1850s, the old national divisions that had characterized the business in the eighteenth century had basically disappeared. Slave traders of all nationalities could take advantage of British financial innovations while U.S.-built vessels became a mainstay of the traffic. European manufactured products, from Swedish iron bars to British textiles, became a significant part of the cargoes used in slave-trading operations on the coast of Africa (Eltis 1987: 50). Finally, despite the successful domestication of the slave trade in the United States, the country would play a key role in the geopolitical configuration that allowed the contraband slave trade of the second slavery to flourish (Rothman 2004; Fehrenbacher 2001; Marquese and Parron 2011).

Historians have explored multiple aspects of this contraband slave trade—from international diplomatic tensions to the national political configurations that allowed the emergence of the illegal traffic to Cuba and Brazil (Bethell 1970; Murray 1980; Berbel, Marquese, and Parron 2010). Few works have explored the organization of this illegal slave trade, and those that have usually offer synchronic depictions of it (Howard 1963; Franco 1980; Tavares 1988; Ferreira 1996; Rodrigues 2005). Even fewer have dealt with the subject in an integrated fashion, that is, incorporating the histories of the three greatest slave societies of the nineteenth century—Brazil, Cuba, and the United States—and showing how their interconnections shaped the history of the traffic (Eltis 1987). The present chapter provides an overview of the history of the contraband slave trade of the second slavery, paying special attention to its transformations over time. Thus, by distinguishing three main moments of the contraband slave trade (1820–1834, 1835–1850, and 1851–1867), I show not only how new strategies and forms of organization emerged, but how the histories of Cuba, Brazil, and the United States intersected over time. This traffic, as I hope to show, became entrenched in some of the main institutions of nineteenth-century capitalism, such as the balance-of-power system and the ideal of a self-adjusting market (Polanyi 2001: 3).

The Birth of the Contraband Slave Trade, 1820–1835

The end of the Napoleonic Wars marked an important turning point in the history of the transatlantic slave trade. By that time, a few countries had already formally abolished the slave trade, most notably Haiti (which also ended slavery altogether), Britain, and the United States. British efforts to establish a plan for the concerted action of European powers against the slave trade at the Congress of Vienna, however, met with the opposition of plenipotentiaries from Portugal, Spain, and France, who insisted that the traffic could only be ended gradually. With the failure to establish a multinational plan for the suppression of the traffic, and without the context of war that justified the apprehension of suspected slavers in previous years, the British government entered an era of diplomatic efforts that accompanied its global economic and political expansion. These efforts were reflected in the establishment of a treaty system encompassing a large number of states, from slave-trading empires such as Portugal and Spain to African chiefdoms and Arab "rulers" in the Persian Gulf. The forms of these treaties varied. The Netherlands, Portugal, and Spain all signed treaties with Britain in 1817 that included mechanisms for international enforcement in the form of the mutual right of search and mixed commissions to judge vessels suspected of engaging in the slave trade. The Netherlands had already agreed to stop the trade in 1814, with the treaty of 1817 only adding these enforcement instruments. Portugal and Spain agreed to prohibit the business north of the equator, but Spain also committed to abolishing the business entirely in three years after the signing of the treaty, May 20, 1820 (Kontorovich 2009).

From the beginning, however, other states looked suspiciously at British intentions, as reflected more clearly in the refusals by France and the United States to sign treaties containing the mutual right of search or the establishment of mixed commission courts. Acceding to that would be similar to assenting to British global domination. During the War of 1812, John Quincy Adams famously compared the right of search to the transatlantic slave trade and concluded that, in some contexts, the former was actually worse (Fink 2011: 10–23). The country only came to accept the establishment of the mutual right of search and mixed commissions with the British in 1862, after the beginning of the U.S. Civil War. The French in turn only established conventions with the British allowing the mutual right of search and the seizure of vessels equipped for the slave trade in, respectively, 1831 and 1833 (Kielstra 2000: 76, 157–60). In the meantime, French participation in the slave trade resumed, with vessels under French colors disembarking an estimated 166,805 enslaved Africans in the Americas between 1814 and 1831. Almost 40 percent of these were taken to Cuba, especially Santiago de Cuba, a privileged destination for French refugees after the beginning of the Haitian Revolution.

The significant presence of French slave traders in the traffic to Cuba after the Napoleonic Wars was an indication of the persistence of a structural problem of the Spanish Empire: its weak connection to Africa. After a first slave-trading peak in the seventeenth century—to a large extent a product of the Iberian Union

(1580–1640) that united the crowns of Spain and Portugal—the traffic to Spanish colonies decreased and henceforth carried mainly by non-Spanish slave traders under exclusive contracts called *asientos* until 1789, when a royal *cédula* opened the slave trade to all nations. The traffic then became the duopoly of British and U.S. merchants until both countries passed anti–slave trade laws in 1807. Together these traders accounted for more than four out of five slaves disembarked in the Spanish colony between 1789 and 1807. This situation started to change with the British and U.S. slave trade acts of 1807. Cuban-based merchants sought to acquire the slave-trading skills and knowledge of British and U.S. dealers to build an effective branch of the Spanish slave trade, a process that took place mainly between 1808 and 1820 (Ortega 2006). By the late 1810s the Spanish came to dominate important aspects of the slave trade to Cuba. Manuel Moreno Fraginals tracks the names of seventy-six Spanish individuals and companies prominent in the traffic to Cuba by that time (Moreno Fraginals 1988: 345–47).

However, Spanish slave traders still had to deal with two main problems: the persistent weak connection to African suppliers and the illegality of the business after 1820 (as prescribed by the Anglo-Spanish treaty of 1817). The first problem persisted until the total suppression of the transatlantic slave trade in 1867, leading to a permanent Portuguese presence in the traffic to Cuba. A few Spanish slave traders were able to build important ties to traders in parts of West Africa, which partially solved this problem during the first decades of the contraband slave trade. Many of these initial connections were with British and U.S. traders who had become part of a creolized merchant community in Upper Guinea during the 1810s and increasingly operated as middlemen for the growing Spanish slave-trading community. The growth of a Spanish branch of the slave trade was even reflected in the growing importance of the Spanish language in the region. Already in 1811, the Upper Guinea merchant John Pearce, a descendant of a Yani woman and a U.S. slave trader, was sending his sons to schools in Matanzas to learn Spanish. The growing importance of the language gave some advantages to factories whose dealers were capable of communicating with the visiting Spanish captains and supercargoes (Mouser 2013: 11; Barry 1998: 136). Spanish merchants such as the Zangronis family managed to establish themselves on the African side of operations, although never to a degree comparable to the massive Portuguese presence in central supplying regions. In the 1830s, Juan José Zangronis would actually move to Ouidah to act as the directly supplier of slaves to his father and brother in Cuba. According to a British missionary, Zangronis became the second-largest slave trader in the region, second only to the great slave trader Francisco Felix de Souza, the *Chachá de Ajudá*, of whom he became an associate (Moreno Fraginals 1988: 344–54; Law 2004: 173).

The second problem—the prohibition of the traffic according to the terms of the Anglo-Spanish treaty of 1817—was solved by a series of political arrangements. The fundamental step came with the establishment of the *régimen de las facultades omnímodas*. This measure gave absolute powers to the captains general of the island, a transformation that had its origins in the Liberal Triennium of the early 1820s. In 1823 Joaquín Gómez, one of the main slave traders in the island, presented a proposal for strengthening the powers of the captain general to assure that Cuba would remain within the Spanish Empire. Gómez and the *Deputación Provincial de la Havana* (a group representing planters from the rural districts) argued that this was a necessary measure to curb social disruptions caused by conspirators seeking independence as well as threats of slave rebellion. The regimen was approved in 1825 and, among other things, left all the control over the contraband slave trade in the hands of the captain general. This had the effect of limiting the opportunities of the British government to pressure the Spanish government, because only captains general could decide what measures coming from the metropolis should effectively be applied in the island. Captain General Francisco Dionisio Vives y Piñón, for example, refused to publish in Cuba a communication sent by the Spanish government that stated that Africans illegally introduced into the island had the right to freedom. José Antonio Saco, who had been publicly condemning the traffic since 1832 as a crucial step for "whitening" Cuba, was deported from the island, and a general silence over the contraband slave trade was imposed until its suppression in the 1860s (Piqueras 2005: 132–34; Berbel, Marquese, and Parron 2010: 144–49). Between 1824 and 1825 the number of enslaved Africans carried to the island more than doubled. Many of the same individuals who had been carrying the traffic before 1820, such as the Zangronis and Pedro Blanco (especially famous among historians for his role in the case of the *Amistad*), simply continued their slave-trading operations in the following decades (Gámez Duarte 2004: 320–21; Rediker 2012).

Unlike Spain, Portugal refused to abolish the traffic altogether in its treaties with Britain during the 1810s. Brazilian independence in 1822 further complicated matters. From the beginning, recognition of independence by the British would only come with a commitment to abolish the slave trade. The British made similar agreements with most other recently independent Latin American countries, but the Brazilian case was more complicated. The commerce in human beings carried to Brazil had no counterpart in terms of strength and longevity, leading William Wilberforce to refer to the country as the "slave trade personified." If the early treaties between Britain and Portugal abolishing the slave trade left the South Atlantic branch untouched—Portuguese slave traders were allowed to carry on their business below the equator and with Portuguese possessions in Africa—British abolitionists took Brazilian independence as an opportunity to intervene more effectively, a move that had been cut short by the Portuguese during the previous decade. A treaty was signed and ratified between late 1826 and early 1827, with Brazil agreeing to abolish the trade within three years after ratification (Bethell 1970: 27–61).

In 1830 Dom Pedro officially decreed the abolition of the slave trade to Brazil. The three-man regency that replaced him—Dom Pedro abdicated the throne in 1831—agreed on the necessity of a national law regulating the slave trade. National sovereignty would be reaffirmed in response to a treaty that many saw as a foreign imposition. The law passed in 1831 was actually more radical than the terms of the treaty of 1826. The year 1831 saw a dramatic decrease in the number of importations with the disembarkation of 6,178 enslaved Africans. Estimates are that 46,192 Africans were disembarked in Brazil between 1831 and 1834, less than the total number of slaves disembarked in the country in the year of 1830 alone. According to Leslie Bethell, the decrease was the product of a glut in the market, oversupplied in the wake of abolition (Bethell 1970: 72). The early years after the 1831 law, however, saw some serious efforts from Brazilian authorities to curb the contraband slave trade, with a large number of speeches in Parliament denouncing its persistence. In the aftermath of the 1835 *Malê* slave revolt the Brazilian foreign minister signed additional articles to the treaty of 1826, facilitating the seizure of vessels suspected of engaging in the slave trade based on their equipment (Mamigonian 2002; Parron 2009: 80–84).

U.S.-built ships became increasingly predominant in the slave trade during this first era (and perhaps even before that). My estimates, which I have discussed at length elsewhere, are that U.S.-built ships were used in 1,070 slave voyages in the 1830s (63 percent of the total), 671 in the 1840s (52 percent), and 269 in the 1850s (91 percent). Together they were responsible for the disembarkation of more then 900,000 enslaved Africans in the Americas (Marques, forthcoming). Already in the 1810s the growing British pressure stimulated the demand for U.S.-built vessels among slave traders across the Atlantic. According to historians Lance Davis, Robert Gallman, and Karin Gleiter, the tradition of fast sailing vessels in the United States was "formed during the disputes with England of the late eighteenth and early nineteenth centuries. Merchantmen were built to elude British men-of-war" (1997: 265). With multiple seizures and convictions in British courts during the 1810s, the appeal that these vessels had to slave traders could hardly be overemphasized. In Cuba, the transfer of slave-trading expertise and resources to Spanish merchants was frequently accompanied by the sales of U.S.-built ships (Marques 2013: 85–155). In Rio de Janeiro and Bahia, U.S. companies had been taking advantage of the sale of U.S. vessels (as well as slave-trading equipment) since the 1820s. Foreign merchant houses such as Maxwell, Wright & Co. and Birckhead & Co. frequently announced U.S.-built vessels and slave-trading equipment in the classifieds section of the *Jornal do Commercio*, one of the main newspapers in Rio. In a series of advertisements for the U.S. brigantine *Seaman* in 1828, Maxwell, Wright & Co. described the vessel as well fit for the slave trade. And these actions were in direct contravention to U.S. laws, which prohibited intentional sales of vessels for the slave trade. It would be very hard for them to prove that they did not have the intention to sell these ships to slave traders, had someone taken these announcements to U.S. courts. But the connections between regular commerce and the slave trade had not yet become the object of political tensions (Marques 2015).

From Cuba to Brazil, 1836–1850

The political arrangement that allowed the emergence of a massive contraband slave trade in Brazil was concluded in the second half of the 1830s. The first signs of change came in 1834, when the municipal chamber of Bananal, in the state of São Paulo, sent a representation to the Parliament asking for the revocation of the 1831 law. The following year Bernardo Pereira de Vasconcelos also suggested that the law be revoked. Vasconcelos was one of the main founders of the *Regresso*, a forerunner of the Brazilian Conservative Party. While speeches against the law continued to be given by conservative politicians in the Parliament and published in newspapers, petitions calling for its revocation also came from the municipal chambers of the cities of Valença, Mangaratiba, Bananal, Barra Mansa, Paraíba do Sul, and Vassouras. The common element uniting all of them was coffee. As demand for the product rose in the international market, coffee plantations spread throughout the Zona da Mata in Minas Gerais and the Vale do Paraíba, an area stretching from the province of Rio de Janeiro to northern São Paulo. As coffee production in the area developed, demand for labor rose. The ascension of the *Regresso* in 1837 would finally lead to the entrenchment of slaveholding and slave-trading interests in the Brazilian administration, paving the way for the growth of the contraband traffic (Eltis 1987: 195–56; Parron 2009: 128–29).

The slave-trading community that operated in Rio de Janeiro—and supplied most of the slaves for these coffee plantations—went through significant transformations in the aftermath of the 1831 law (unlike Cuba, where, as we have seen, many of the same individuals were involved in the slave trade before and after 1820). The main slave traders of the first quarter of the nineteenth century had diversified their investments and abandoned the business by the late 1820s. Part of their investments actually went to the coffee plantations that radically transformed the Vale do Paraíba in the following decades (Marquese and Tomich 2009). When demand for African labor in those plantations increased in the 1830s, a renewed slave-trading community emerged. Not only did most of leading figures of this group appear after 1831, but also the ownership of slave-trading voyages became more concentrated than ever before (one of the consequences of British anti–slave trade pressure). Between 1838 and 1844 the four leading firms controlled 60 percent of all slave-trading operations, with the famous slave trader Bernardino de Sá (one of the few who had been involved in the business before 1831) at the top. In the following seven years, this percentage rose to 67 percent with Manoel Pinto da Fonseca, the greatest slave trader of the contraband era, who was responsible for 36 percent of all voyages, ascending to the top of the slave-trading community. (Bernardino de Sá organized 22 percent of the voyages of the previous period.) A similar process took place in Cuba. While seventy-six firms within five major groupings controlled the business before 1820, a dominant single business became the norm after that year, with its owners and partners changing over time. The organization of the trade also changed, with joint stock companies increasingly replacing the individual and family operations that characterized the pre-1820 slave-trading communities around the Atlantic (Eltis 1987: 150–51).

In Cuba, the silence over the contraband slave trade was reinforced by the exclusion of the colony from the new Spanish constitutional phase that began in 1837. This marginalization protected the island from electoral processes in Spain and from the circulation of ideas against slavery or the slave trade. Thus, the concession of absolute powers to the captain general and the exclusion of the island from the areas contemplated by the Spanish Constitution of 1837, historian José Antonio Piqueras argues, were the key instruments in silencing critical voices (2005: 132–34). Despite the common view that these measures were attacks on Cuban society, they had the support of slave-trading and slaveholding elites in the island, who considered them a lesser evil. While the Spanish colony continued to be governed from the metropolis, it operated in complicity with the slaveholding interests of the island (Schmidt-Nowara 1999: 20–21).

The new political strategy was all the more necessary in the face of growing British pressure, which led to the 1835 extra provisions to the Anglo-Spanish treaty of 1817. In one of them Spain committed itself to pass legislation abolishing the slave trade, a law that was only passed ten years later (which raised distribution costs by eliminating the open tolerance with which Cuban officials treated the illegal traffic) (Murray 1980: 199–200; Eltis 1987: 201). Another provision had a more immediate impact by allowing the capture of vessels equipped for the slave trade. As a result, leading slave traders had to develop new strategies that involved non-Spanish merchants to a much greater extent than before. Before 1835 the vessels that carried slave-trading equipment and goods used in the exchange for slaves in Africa were usually the same that transported human cargoes back to the Americas. The first consequence of the provisions of 1835 was the division of slave-trading operations in two parts, with vessels of other nationalities—especially from the United States, the only country that continued to refuse the establishment of a treaty with the British that included the mutual right of search—carrying slave-trading equipment and goods to Africa in the first leg of the voyages. These vessels were then sold on the African coast (or, in many cases, sold in Cuba but deliverable in Africa), from where they returned to Cuba with captives, usually under a different flag. Others maintained their original nationality and returned in ballast after delivering their cargo in Africa. A few of them may have maintained their original nationality and returned with slaves on board them, but evidence of this is scarce.

Merchants and shipbuilders from Baltimore, who had been at the forefront of the shipbuilding industry with their notoriously fast clippers, were probably the first to take advantage of this new context. The high demand for Baltimore schooners and brigantines led to the efflorescence of the local shipbuilding industry in the late 1830s, precisely when the rest of the United States faced an economic depression. Their connection to the transatlantic slave trade became increasingly evident, with rumors that some vessels had been specifically designed for the illicit commerce in human beings to Cuba. Already in October 1836 the British commissioners in

Cuba, Edward W. H. Schenley and R. R. Madden, reported to the Foreign Office the arrival of four U.S. vessels in the Spanish colony, the *Emanuel* and *Dolores* from New York and the *Anaconda* and *Viper* from Baltimore. All four had been built in Baltimore. The first two were sold to Spanish slave traders and sailed under Spanish colors to Africa. The other two, however, sailed fully equipped for the slave trade under U.S. colors, although their cargo was really owned by Pedro Forcade, a Frenchman involved in the Cuban traffic.[2]

Schenley and Madden also wrote to the U.S. consul in Cuba, Nicholas Trist, to denounce the cases. The reply from Trist was short and direct: the U.S. government had no intention of discussing those issues. The problem nonetheless continued to be raised by the British government in the following years, especially because many of the documents authenticating the voyages were frequently found aboard captured slavers with the signatures of Nicholas Trist. The U.S. consul, however, had always been very open about his views on the role of U.S. representatives overseas, which were shared by the foreign merchant community in Havana. In his view, the sales of U.S. vessels should meet no interference. If Britain intended to act against this commerce, they should first prohibit their own factories from producing the bolts and shackles used aboard slavers. Trist agreed that U.S.-built vessels were present in the slave trade to Cuba, but concluded that the small number of English ships was due to the fact that Britain did not have the tradition of building fast merchant vessels. "But for this circumstance," he argued, "Great Britain would just as well supply the slave traders here with ships, as she does with muskets, gunpowder, manufactures and other articles." Trist must have rejoiced at the appearance of British-built steamers in the last years of the contraband slave trade.[3]

The reappearance of the U.S. flag in the slave trade in the second half of the 1830s had nonetheless drawn attention to the issue of indirect participation in the transatlantic slave trade, generating debates that brought to the forefront the extension of U.S., French, and British involvement in the illegal business. Despite the conspiratorial tone of Trist's accusations, his observations that the British were as immersed in the slave trade as the Americans definitely had some truth to them. British legislators had been trying to curb the indirect participation of

British subjects since the early nineteenth century to no effect. British merchants continued to provide a large part of the goods used by slave traders in Cuba and Brazil, and in fact, merchants in Sierra Leone recycled ships condemned by the Courts of Mixed Commission and sold them back to slave traders. The controversies around the indirect participation of U.S. citizens in the illegal business soared in the late 1830s and generated a backlash against the indirect involvement of British merchants. A select committee was appointed by the British Parliament to investigate the issue. Some abolitionists certainly considered that this indirect participation should be suppressed despite the costs, with Lord Brougham trying to pass new legislation in 1843 precisely to that end. However, as had been the case earlier in the century, the strands of British abolitionism more attuned to the precepts of laissez faire had the last word. Brougham's efforts in Parliament were rejected, while that same year, Pedro de Zulueta, cofounder of a British company accused of supplying goods to slave traders, was acquitted by the British courts (Eltis 1987: 57, 84).

The U.S. flag would also soon appear in the traffic to Brazil, once British pressure on the Portuguese and Brazilians increased. The 1839 Palmerston Act unilaterally extended to the Portuguese flag the practice of seizing suspected slavers based on their equipment. Also starting in 1839, British commissioners in the Mixed Commission of Rio de Janeiro and Sierra Leone reinterpreted the existing treaties between Brazil and Britain in such a way that capture of vessels equipped for the slave trade became possible for the first time. In 1845, tensions between Britain and Brazil would reach a new level with the passing of the so-called Aberdeen Act, which empowered British courts to adjudicate Brazilian vessels captured by the British navy (Bethell 1970: 167–68). The strategies, put into practice in Cuba in the second half of the 1830s, were also quickly carried over to Brazil because, in fact, a number of slave traders involved in the traffic to Cuba redirected their operations to Rio de Janeiro in the early 1840s. Francisco Rovirosa, who also appears in the documents as Ruviroza y Urzellas, was the most successful one, becoming the fourth-largest slave trader in Rio by the mid-1840s (Eltis 1987: 151–57). Like Rovirosa, the greatest slave traders of the 1840s in Brazil, such as

Manoel Pinto da Fonseca and José Bernardino de Sá, frequently employed U.S. vessels as auxiliaries to the slave trade for years before turning them into slavers under new flags. A few of them may have managed to carry slaves under the U.S. flag, but to a much smaller degree than has been depicted in recent works on the subject (Horne 2007; Graden 2007).

As in Cuba, this new context opened up opportunities for foreign merchants and individuals willing to operate in the shady area connecting legitimate commerce and the transatlantic slave trade. How far these merchants could go without breaking the law remained open to interpretation. Many considered the chartering as well as the sale of vessels to slave traders as perfectly normal business under the laws of the United States as long as these ships did not return with enslaved Africans on board or had their nationality switched once their ownership changed hands. These merchants established close connections to well-known slave traders in Brazil. Thus a petition published on the *Jornal do Commercio* attesting to the integrity of Manoel Pinto da Fonseca—the greatest slave trader of the contraband era—was signed by a long list of merchants from Rio de Janeiro, among them some British and American houses such as Maxwell, Wright & Co., Forbes, Valentino & Co., and James Birckhead (signing as Diogo Birckhead) (Marques 2015). Maxwell, Wright & Co., in fact an Anglo-American house, was especially important, for they combined better than anyone else commercial activities that ended up being strictly connected in the two decades of the contraband slave trade to Brazil: the selling and chartering of vessels to slave traders and the exportation of coffee. By consigning and selling ships to Manuel Pinto da Fonseca and other slave traders, they facilitated the transportation of goods and slave-trading equipment in outbound trips under the U.S. flag, contributing to the success of illegal slave-trading voyages in a context of increasing British pressure. As we have seen, disembarked slaves were often taken to the Vale do Paraíba coffee plantations or related sectors. Most of the coffee produced by these slaves was afterward exported to the United States by the same Maxwell, Wright & Co., which by the mid-1840s had become the main coffee exporters in the country (Jarnagin 2008; Marquese 2013).

What became increasingly clear from the investigations of U.S. diplomatic representatives in Brazil was that African slaves were frequently taken on board with the connivance of American captains and under the protection of the U.S. flag. Some called for the prohibition of the sale of U.S. vessels on the African coast, but it was highly unlikely that measures such as these could be passed in the context of expanding commerce and the laissez-faire ideals that marked the nineteenth century. French merchant houses also sold merchandise and, occasionally, vessels to slave traders in Brazil during the 1840s, generating similar debates in France. The minister of foreign affairs, François Guizot, argued that, as in Britain, "no disposition of the law covers commerce with slave stations, as long as there is no actual purchase or sale of slaves taking place" (Jennings 1976: 519). When, in 1849, Palmerston pressured the Sardinian government to take measures against the indirect participation of its merchants in the slave trade, he received a reply along similar lines. The Sardinian minister for foreign affairs argued that if they were to stop their vessels from carrying provisions and articles used in the trade for slaves by Brazilian merchants, the exclusion should apply to ships of all nations. And while Sardinian vessels could be used by slave traders in Brazil, "as these vessels are generally of excellent construction," if their sales were executed using the established forms and according to prescribed consular acts, passing into third hands in a legal manner, "the sellers cannot reasonably be called to account for the use which the purchasers might make of them under a foreign flag."[4]

In a sense, it was Britain itself that continued to set the terms for what constituted legitimate and illegitimate commerce. While British resources continued to find their way into the slave trade, it was unlikely that any other nation would take more radical measures against this symbiosis of legitimate commerce and the slave trade. Only the suppression of the contraband slave trade as a whole could bring that to an end. In the case of Brazil, this process was triggered by a series of incidents involving the British navy and Brazilian authorities in Brazilian territorial waters, the most famous of which was an exchange of fire in Paranaguá in 1850. The attacks had an immediate impact and combined with new political developments in Brazil to stimulate the definitive suppression of the traffic to the country in the early 1850s (Bethell 1970; Mamigonian 2009; Berbel, Marquese, & Parron 2010).

Slave Trading in the Slaveholding Republic, 1851–1867

If Britain was able to push Brazil to abolish the traffic without major international obstacles other than diplomatic tensions with Brazil itself, Cuba was a completely different story. The long dream of incorporating the island into the United States had been shared throughout the century by figures as diverse as Thomas Jefferson and John Quincy Adams. By the 1850s the desire to incorporate the island became strongly attached to slavery expansionism (which, in some cases, led to Southern visions of a slaveholding empire involving the U.S. South and multiple Caribbean and Central American regions). At the same time, some slaveholders in Cuba considered annexation to be the best way to protect slavery against British abolitionism and slave rebellion (issues that came to be seen as completely interconnected after the *Escalera* conspiracy). Many Cuban exiles also supported annexation and, at times, the filibustering epidemic of the 1850s. As a consequence, British pressure to abolish the Cuban slave trade never took the aggressive and open form that it had taken in Brazil. British authorities were fully aware that a more violent action would provide the necessary pretext for the annexation of the island by the United States. Geopolitical tensions involving Britain, Spain, and the United States, therefore, protected the island from stronger antislave trade measures (Ramiro Guerra 1964: 496–500; Johnson 2013).

Most captains general in Cuba during the 1850s would not enforce the law to the point where planters could be economically damaged. It is important to note, however, that in the absence of the penal law of 1845, which helped inflate the prices of slaves (the lieutenant-governor of Trinidad, for example, allegedly received $51,000 in bribes for allowing one disembarkation in 1860), this volume could have been two or three times larger. It was precisely because some authorities refused to cooperate that bribes became so essential to the Cuban slave trade, with officials occasionally trying to enforce the law within the limits imposed by the geopolitical tensions between the United States, Britain, and Spain. Officials had to find a balance between showing the will to extinguish the illegal trade (to maintain the strategic support of Britain against external threats) and keeping the support of Cuban slaveholders (who occasionally called for annexation as a way to protect slavery in the island)(Corwin 1967: 118–19; Eltis 1987: 202–3).

It was in this turbulent context that, with the abolition of the Brazilian slave trade, some of the deported slave traders attempted to transfer their operations to Cuba, an effort that was quickly cut short by Cuban authorities. This failure was a direct consequence of the new requirements of the business in its final phase. With the penal law and the increased bribes, only well-connected individuals such as Julián Zulueta, Francisco Feliciano Ibañez, José Luis Baró, Mariano Borrell, Francisco Martí, and Nicolás Martínez de Valdiviso, most of whom owned estates and had strong connections to local authorities, had the ability to safely organize the disembarkation of slaves on the island. Captain General Francisco Serrano— who had, according to British authorities, facilitated the illegal disembarkation of enslaved Africans on the island—was a relative of the aforementioned Borrell (Eltis 1987: 149–50; Ferreira 1996; Quiroz 2003: 489–90).

Thus, with Brazil and Cuba practically closed to Portuguese slave traders, most of those willing to continue in the illegal business established their bases of operations in Lisbon and, especially, New York during the early 1850s. U.S. ports became increasingly important for the outfitting of slave voyages over the decade, surpassing their Cuban counterparts after the mid-1850s. The key figures in this transformation were these Portuguese slave traders, at times referred as the "Portuguese Company" in the sources. Although usually described by historians as a single large group, it apparently had been composed of many different companies and partnerships formed throughout the 1850s. Some of its main figures were Antonio Augusto de Oliveira Botelho, Manuel Fortunato de Oliveira Botelho (Antonio Augusto's brother), Joaquim Teixeira Miranda, John Albert Machado, Gaspar José da Motta, J. Lima Vianna, the members of Abranches, Almeida & Co., José Luccas Henriques da Costa, and, perhaps the best-known of them all, Manoel Basílio da Cunha Reis (Howard 1963: 49–50; Eltis 1987: 157–58; Ferreira 1996).

Portuguese slave traders in Brazil during the 1840s were tightly connected to the African end of their networks. Cuban importers of the 1850s, by contrast, generally did not have any control over slave establishments in Africa. As we have seen, that had been a persistent problem for the Spanish slave trade since the eighteenth century. Slave factories were either independently owned or held by the Portuguese slave traders of New York. The prominent role of the latter was especially true for West Central Africa (which became by far the main exporting region during the final years of the trade). Many members of this group had previously been in charge of slave factories owned by Brazilian companies during the 1840s, but had gone on to become owners of slave expeditions themselves. José da Silva Maia Ferreira, for example, known as the father of Angolan literature, was among the group of migrants who moved from Africa to New York in the aftermath of the Brazilian suppression of the transatlantic slave trade. The years of Maia Ferreira in the city are generally associated with his nomination as Portuguese vice-consul to New York in 1856. Before that date, however, Maia Ferreira was part of the slave-trading network of Portuguese residents of New York, being listed with a few others by Benguela authorities in 1855 for his involvement in the transatlantic slave trade (Marques 2013: 279–80).

With the relocation of Portuguese slave-trading networks to the U.S., contrabandists had direct access to U.S. vessels and depended less on U.S. intermediaries. Some of these migrants became naturalized U.S. citizens, owning and employing U.S. vessels in slave expeditions. They played multiple roles, organizing their own voyages and acting as brokers or in other intermediate functions to Spanish slave traders interested in using the U.S. flag to cover their operations. Besides the direct access to U.S.-built ships, the existence of a legitimate trade (especially in palm oil) between the United States and Africa offered the perfect cover for their illicit operations (Brooks 1970).

This symbiosis of legitimate commerce and the slave trade proved particularly helpful once Anglo-American tensions rose again in the late 1850s. As the obstacles to suppression of the traffic in a world of sovereign nation-states became clear, the British themselves, who had been the greatest advocates of this new world order, eventually decided to violate those limits. After Palmerston became the British prime minister for a second term in 1855 and the Crimean War came to an end the following year, the British navy resumed its more aggressive attitude towards the transatlantic slave trade. With the U.S. flag covering most of the slave trade to Cuba, British actions inevitably led to the boarding and seizures of U.S. vessels.

The international frictions that emerged in this context were explored and maximized by slave traders themselves, who pressured both governments with claims for losses in what they claimed was legitimate commerce with Africa. In the case of the *North Hand*, Guilherme de la Figanière, an associate of the great Portuguese slave traders of New York, wrote to the U.S. secretary of state, Lewis Cass, in 1858 complaining that "so long as improper direct British interference with our vessels continues, and unwarrantable suspicion is created against them, our legitimate trade with Africa will not only be injured—as I know to my cost—but destroyed." John Albert Machado, a Portuguese slave trader who became a U.S. citizen, also made his contributions to heighten tensions. When his vessel *Thomas Watson* was seized and taken to Sierra Leone by the British navy earlier that same year, he immediately contacted the U.S. secretary of state to complain about the destruction of his lawful business. He also took the opportunity to make a claim for the *Mary Varney*, another vessel captured by the British that had been employed, according to him, in a lawful voyage to Africa. Both vessels had actually been restored, but Machado asked for $80,000 compensation for the interference in the voyage of the *Thomas Watson* and $50,000 for the *Mary Varney*. The values were considered too high by the British government, especially because Machado did not furnish any vouchers or accounts of his losses, and waited four years before making a claim for one of the vessels (Marques 2013: 317–18).

These 1858 Anglo-American tensions—stimulated in part by the deliberate actions of slave traders—generated angry responses from all sides in the U.S. Congress. A few congressmen actually called for the seizure of British warships as a payback. Unlike in Brazil ten years earlier, the loud reactions in the United

States led the British government to back off. Malmesbury emphasized the difficulties faced by British officers in a letter to the U.S. representative at Britain, but assured him that new instructions had been issued to the commanders of British cruisers and that his government recognized the principles of international law as spelled out in a previous letter sent by U.S. Secretary of State Lewis Cass. The U.S. government celebrated the declaration as a capitulation of the British. While in fact British officers continued to occasionally board U.S. vessels, they did it on a much smaller scale after mid-1858 (Fehrenbacher 2001: 185–87). Only the advent of the Civil War would shift the geopolitical configuration that kept those tensions, and therefore the contraband slave trade, alive.

Conclusion

Like slavery itself, the slave trade that supplied the labor force for plantations in the Americas went through significant changes between the eighteenth and nineteenth centuries. While part of the traffic in human beings took place across imperial borders in previous centuries—whether legally with the Spanish *asiento* or illegally through smuggling—and the crews aboard slave ships had always been from various nations, the internationalization of the business reached a new level in the nineteenth century. In Cuba, this process started even before the slave trade became illegal, since its construction depended on the transference of slave-trading expertise and resources from Britain and the United States. But it would eventually also affect Brazil. The new phase of historical capitalism under British hegemony that characterized the long nineteenth century, based as it was on a renewed interstate system (supposedly regulated by the law of nations) and a more or less self-regulating market, led to a symbiotic connection of the contraband slave trade as a whole to the manufactured products, credit, and resources coming from the North Atlantic.

The imperial and national political configurations that allowed the contraband slave trade to emerge in Cuba and Brazil during the first era of the traffic would soon be affected by developments in the international arena, as the British state sought to establish a new moral, economic, and political order across the globe. The new pressures that came with the 1835 provision to the Anglo-Spanish treaty, which allowed the seizure of vessels equipped for the traffic, led slave traders to seek not only fast clippers from Baltimore, but also the U.S. flag to cover their illegal operations. After that year the role of U.S. captains, mates, brokers, and other middlemen steadily increased. After all, the country continued to be the only one that persistently refused to establish the mutual right of search or Mixed Commission Courts with Britain. The subsequent unilateral actions of the British Foreign Office against Portugal and Brazil starting in the late 1830s immediately stimulated the transference of these strategies to the Brazilian traffic (since many individuals were involved in the slave trade to both Cuba and Brazil).

The U.S. contribution to the transatlantic slave trade continued to expand in the interstices of Anglo-American tensions. The country, however, continued to position itself against the transatlantic traffic. John C. Calhoun openly criticized the slave trade to Brazil and Cuba. As secretary of state, he had to investigate the cases of U.S. involvement in the slave trade to Brazil and order a few arrests. In the aftermath of the Webster-Ashburton Treaty of 1842, Calhoun argued that Brazil and Cuba already had enough slaves and that it was actually in the U.S. interest to have the slave trade to those countries closed. The fraudulent use of the U.S. flag would not be an issue anymore and U.S. cruisers on the African coast would have the sole purpose of protecting U.S. commerce in the region. Moreover, he argued, Cuba and Brazil were rivals on the production of many articles, including cotton. "Brazil possesses the greatest advantages for its production, and is already a large grower of the article," continues the report of his speech, "towards the production of which the continuance of the market for imported slaves from Africa would contribute much." For Southern slaveholders the demise of the transatlantic slave trade to Brazil meant just the weakening of another competitor (Marques 2013: 227–28). Thus, while the new conditions of the nineteenth-century capitalist world-economy led to the expansion of slavery in new parts of the Americas—the second slavery—it also generated competition and tensions between those same areas.

The U.S. contribution to the slave trade and the tensions generated by this participation would reach a new level in the aftermath of Brazilian suppression of the traffic in 1850. The strong opposition offered by the United States to British pressure in the 1840s—and its emergence as a "slaveholding republic" in international relations more generally—induced slave traders to reconfigure their networks to include the United States in more effective ways. These traders, many of them involved in the traffic to Brazil during the 1840s, realized the advantages of slave trading in the slaveholding republic. By relocating to the United States, slave traders, most of them Portuguese, would have easier access to U.S. vessels and a much stronger basis for conducting their operations in face of growing British pressure. In New York especially, they created a vast network involving diplomats, shipping companies, and innumerable agents spread across the Atlantic, managing to exploit and prolong international frictions involving the United States and Great Britain to supply captives to Cuban plantations.

The highly internationalized nature of the traffic in this final era was the culmination of a process of adaptation to the restructuring of the world-economy and to the emergence of a geoculture of the international system in the nineteenth century (Arrighi 1994: 163–246; Wallerstein 2011: 21–141). These broader transformations, however, also unleashed the forces that ultimately led to the suppression of slavery, and consequently the contraband slave trade, in the Americas.

Notes

1. All estimates come from the *Voyages* database (www.slavevoyages.org), unless otherwise noted. I would like to thank Dale Tomich, Rafael Marquese, David Eltis, and FAPESP for grant #2014/17522-2, São Paulo Research Foundation (FAPESP).

2. Schenley and Madden to Palmerston, October 25, 1836, BPP, Slave Trade, 1837 (001), vol. LIV, Class A, 191–92.

3. Her Majesty's Judge to Palmerston, August 22, 1838, BPP, Slave Trade, 1839 (180), vol. XLVIII, Class A, 126; A Calm observer, *A Letter to Wm. E. Channing, D.D.: In Reply to One Addressed to Him by R. R. Madden, on the Abuse of the Flag of the United States in*

the Island of Cuba, for Promoting the Slave Trade (Boston: Published by William D. Ticknor, corner of Washington and School Streets, 1840), 8–9.

4. Azeglio to Abercromby, January 15, 1850 [Inclosure 1 in No. 230, BPP, Slave Trade, 1850 (1291), vol. LV, Class B, 318.]

Works Cited

Alencastro, Luiz Felipe de. 2010. "O pecado original da sociedade e da ordem jurídica Brasileira." *Novos Estudos—CEBRAP* (Centro Brasileiro de Análise e Planejamento) 87 (July): 5–11.

Arrighi, Giovanni. 1994. *The Long Twentieth Century: Money, Power, and the Origins of Our Times.* London; New York: Verso.

Baptist, Edward E. 2014. *The Half Has Never Been Told: Slavery and the Making of American Capitalism.* New York: Basic Books.

Barry, Boubacar. 1998. *Senegambia and the Atlantic Slave Trade.* African Studies Series, 92. Cambridge, UK: Cambridge University Press.

Berbel, Márcia Regina, Rafael de Bivar Marquese, and Tâmis Parron. 2010. *Escravidão e política: Brasil e Cuba, c. 1790–1850.* São Paulo: Hucitec: FAPESP.

Bethell, Leslie. 1970. *The Abolition of the Brazilian Slave Trade; Britain, Brazil and the Slave Trade Question, 1807–1869.* Cambridge, UK: Cambridge University Press.

Brooks, George E. 1970. *Yankee Traders, Old Coasters & African Middlemen; a History of American Legitimate Trade with West Africa in the Nineteenth Century.* African Research Studies, no. 11. Brookline, MA: Boston University Press.

Corwin, Arthur F. 1967. *Spain and the Abolition of Slavery in Cuba, 1817–1886.* Austin: Institute of Latin American Studies: University of Texas Press.

Davis, Lance E., Robert E. Gallman, and Karin Gleiter. 1997. *In Pursuit of Leviathan: Technology, Institutions, Productivity, and Profits in American Whaling, 1816–1906.* Chicago: University of Chicago Press.

Eltis, David. 1987. *Economic Growth and the Ending of the Transatlantic Slave Trade.* New York: Oxford University Press.

Fehrenbacher, Don Edward. 2001. *The Slaveholding Republic: An Account of the United States Government's Relations to Slavery.* Oxford, UK: Oxford University Press.

Ferreira, Roquinaldo Amaral. 1996. "Dos Sertões ao Atlântico: Tráfico ilegal de escravos e comércio lícito em Angola, 1830–1860." Unpubl. MA diss., Universidade Federal do Rio de Janeiro, Brazil.

Fink, Leon. 2011. *Sweatshops at Sea: Merchant Seamen in the World's First Globalized Industry, from 1812 to the Present.* Chapel Hill: University of North Carolina.

Franco, Jose. 1980. *Commercio clandestino de esclavos.* Havana: Ed. de Ciencias Sociales.

Gámez Duarte, Feliciano. 2004. "El desafío insurgente: Análisis del corso hispanoamericano desde una perspectiva peninsular, 1812–1828." Unpubl. diss., Universidad de Cádiz, Spain.

Graden, Dale Torston. 2007. "O envolvimento dos Estados Unidos no comércio transatlântico de escravos para o Brasil, 1840–1858." *Afro-Ásia* 39: 9–35.

Guerra, Ramiro. 1964. *Manual de historia de Cuba: Económica, social y política [desde su descubrimiento hasta 1868],* 2nd ed. Colección Histórica. Havana: Ed. Nacional de Cuba; Ed. Consejo Nacional de Universidades.

Horne, Gerald. 2007. *The Deepest South: The United States, Brazil, and the African Slave Trade.* New York: New York University Press.

Howard, Warren S. 1963. *American Slavers and the Federal Law, 1837–1862.* Berkeley: University of California Press.

Huzzey, Richard. 2012. *Freedom Burning: Anti-Slavery and Empire in Victorian Britain.* Ithaca, NY: Cornell University Press.

Jarnagin, Laura. 2008. *A Confluence of Transatlantic Networks: Elites, Capitalism, and Confederate Migration to Brazil.* Atlantic Crossings Series. Tuscaloosa: University of Alabama Press.

Jennings, Lawrence C. 1976. "French Policy towards Trading with African and Brazilian Slave Merchants, 1840–1853." *The Journal of African History* 17 (4): 515–28.

Johnson, Walter. 2013. *River of Dark Dreams: Slavery and Empire in the Cotton Kingdom.* Cambridge, MA: Belknap Press.

Kaye, Anthony E. 2009. "The Second Slavery: Modernity in the Nineteenth-Century South and the Atlantic World." *Journal of Southern History* 75 (3): 627–50.

Kielstra, Paul Michael. 2000. *The Politics of Slave Trade Suppression in Britain and France, 1814–8.* Basingstoke, UK: Macmillan; New York: St. Martin's Press.

Kontorovich, Eugene. 2009. "The Constitutionality of International Courts: The Forgotten Precedent of Slave-Trade Tribunals." *University of Pennsylvania Law Review* 158 (1): 39–115.

Law, Robin. 2004. *Ouidah: The Social History of a West African Slaving "Port" 1727–1892.* Athens: Ohio University Press; Oxford, UK: James Currey.

Mamigonian, Beatriz Gallotti. 2002. "To Be Liberated African in Brazil: Labour and Citizenship in the Nineteenth Century." Unpublished PhD diss., University of Waterloo, Canada.

———. 2009. "In the Name of Freedom: Slave Trade Abolition, the Law and the Brazilian Branch of the African Emigration Scheme (Brazil–British West Indies, 1830s–1850s)." *Slavery & Abolition* 30 (1): 41–66.

Marques, Leonardo. 2013. "The United States and the Transatlantic Slave Trade to the Americas, 1776–1867." Unpublished PhD diss., Emory University, Atlanta, Georgia.

———. 2015. "The Contraband Slave Trade to Brazil and the Dynamics of US Participation, 1831–1856." *Journal of Latin American Studies* FirstView (August): 1–26.

———. forthcoming. "United States Shipbuilding, Atlantic Markets, and the Structures of the Contraband Slave Trade." In *The Rise and Demise of Slavery and the Slave Trade in the Atlantic World*, edited by Kristin Mann and Philip Misevich. New York: Rochester University Press.

Marquese, Rafael de Bivar. 2004. *Feitores do corpo, missionários da mente: Senhores, letrados e o controle dos escravos nas Américas, 1660–1860.* São Paulo, Brazil: Companhia das Letras.

———. 2013. "Estados Unidos, Segunda Escravidão e a Economia Cafeeira do Império do Brasil." *Almanack* (revista eletrônica) no. 5. http://www.almanack.unifesp.br/index.php/almanack/article/view/990.

Marquese, Rafael B., and Tâmis P. Parron. 2011. "Internacional Escravista: A Política Da Segunda Escravidão." *Topoi* 12: 97–117.

Marquese, Rafael, and Dale Tomich. 2009. "O Vale do Paraíba escravista e a formação do mercado mundial do café no século XIX." In *O Brasil Império*, edited by Keila Grinberg and Ricardo Salles. Rio de Janeiro: Civilização Brasileira.

Moreno Fraginals, Manuel. 1988. *O engenho: Complexo sócio-econômico açucareiro cubano.* São Paulo, Brazil: Hucitec.

Mouser, Bruce L. 2013. *American Colony on the Rio Pongo: The War of 1812, the Slave Trade, and the Proposed Settlement of African Americans, 1810–1830.* Trenton, NJ: Africa World Press.

Murray, David R. 1980. *Odious Commerce: Britain, Spain, and the Abolition of the Cuban Trade.* Cambridge, UK: Cambridge University Press.

Ortega, José Guadalupe. 2006. "Cuban Merchants, Slave Trade Knowledge, and the Atlantic World, 1790s–1820s." *CLAHR: Colonial Latin American Historical Review* 15 (3): 225–51.

Parron, Tâmis Peixoto. 2009. "A Política Da Escravidão No Império Do Brasil, 1826–1865." Unpubl. MA diss., Universidade de São Paulo, Brazil.

Piqueras Arenas, Josep Antoni. 2005. *Sociedad civil y poder en Cuba: Colonia y poscolonia.* Madrid: Siglo XXI de España Editores.

Polanyi, Karl. 2001. *The Great Transformation: The Political and Economic Origins of Our Time,* 2nd Beacon paperback ed. Boston, MA: Beacon Press.

Quiroz, Alfonso W. 2003. "Implicit Costs of Empire: Bureaucratic Corruption in Nineteenth-Century Cuba." *Journal of Latin American Studies* 35 (3): 473–511.

Rediker, Marcus. 2012. *The Amistad Rebellion: An Atlantic Odyssey of Slavery and Freedom.* New York: Viking.

Rodrigues, Jaime. 2005. *De Costa a costa: Escravos, marinheiros e intermediários do tráfico negreiro de Angola ao Rio de Janeiro, 1780–1860.* [São Paulo, Brazil]: Companhia das Letras.

Rothman, Adam. 2004. "The Domestication of the Slave Trade in the United States." In *The Chattel Principle: Internal Slave Trades in the Americas,* edited by Walter Johnson. New Haven, CT: Yale University Press.

Schmidt-Nowara, Christopher. 1999. *Empire and Antislavery: Spain, Cuba, and Puerto Rico, 1833–1874.* Pittsburgh, PA: University of Pittsburgh Press.

Tavares, Luís Henrique Dias. 1988. *Comércio Proibido de Escravos.* Ensaios 128. São Paulo, Brazil: Editora Atica; Conselho Nacional de Desenvolvimento Científico e Tecnológico.

Tomich, Dale W. 2003. *Through the Prism of Slavery: Labor, Capital, and World Economy.* Lanham, MD: Rowman & Littlefield.

———. 2016. "Civilizing America's Shore: British World-Economic Hegemony and the Abolition of the International Slave Trade (1814–1867)." In *The Politics of the Second Slavery,* edited by Dale Tomich. Albany, NY: State University of New York Press.

Wallerstein, Immanuel. 2011. *The Modern World-System, 4: Centrist Liberalism Triumphant, 1789–1914.* Berkeley: University of California Press.

Spaces of Rebellion

Plantations, Farms, and Churches in Demerara and Southampton, Virginia

Anthony E. Kaye

The comparative history of slave rebellions is often framed around conditions purportedly conducive to slave rebellion. Revolts tended to break out, revisionist scholars observed, when the metropolis was at war, the master class was divided, or famine was abroad in the land; or in slave societies with high ratios of black to white people or of African-born to Creole slaves. But the patterns of slave rebellion in history were not as neat as these categories imply. At the time of Bussa's Rebellion in 1816, Barbados had not witnessed a slave rebellion since the end of the seventeenth century, notwithstanding a population where slaves outnumbered white people by over three to one, and when England had been at war for 70-odd years of the previous 115. Although Jamaica is renowned for perennial slave rebellions, the Baptist War in 1831 was, depending on the criteria, the culmination of conspiracies, maroon wars, and revolts that had broken out about once every five years, or every decade; or it could be considered the first major uprising in seventy years (Patterson 1970: 289–325; Genovese 1992: 11–12; Watts 1987: 311, table 7.5; Reckord 1968: 108; Brown 2008: 3; Mullin 1995: 260).[1] Fine-grain analysis of *how* slaves carried out rebellions is rare in comparative histories.

Human geography—how people made, used, and contended over social spaces—clarifies a stark question about two slave rebellions at distant points on the Atlantic rim. Similarities between the Demerara Rebellion in 1823 and the Nat Turner Rebellion in 1831 existed in the soil. The coasts of South America and tidewater Virginia were both sea beds millennia ago. As the Atlantic Ocean receded, it left behind similar soils, heavy clays, along the coast of Guyana and in the north end of Southampton County, in Virginia (Reinhart 1987: 4–6, 14–26, 40–42). Rivers carved up the coasts and marked the boundaries of these revolts. In British Guyana, rebels mobilized up and down the East Coast from the Demerara to the Mahica rivers. In Virginia, Turner and his confederates cut a swath across the southern end of Southampton below the Nottoway River. From a bird's-eye view, the rebels adopted similar strategies: to mass in the countryside from plantations across the East Coast to Georgetown for a drive on the town, the colonial capital of Demerara, and from the hinterland for a drive on Jerusalem, the county seat of Southampton. At the crux of this comparison is a contrast between these two revolts as bracing as the distance between them. In Demerara, 10,000–12,000 slaves on three dozen plantations launched a massive insurrection remarkable for its lack of violence, at least on the rebels' part. In Virginia, some sixty slaves from two dozen farms and plantations waged one of the most violent rebellions in United States history, slaughtering men, women, and children with fence rails, firearms, and axes. In Virginia, rebels killed about sixty people, while rebels in Demerara put sixty in the stocks and killed only two, possibly three.[2] Why did rebels in Southampton feel compelled to kill so many white people, and rebels in Demerara so few?

The rebels' divergent strategies were bound up with struggles over social space waged at work and in church. One cadre of rebels in Demerara alluded to Christian doctrine to explain why they eschewed violence. " 'It is contrary to the religion we profess,' " they told an Anglican minister who crossed their path early on the third day of the revolt; " 'we cannot give life, and therefore we will not take it.' "[3] The everyday practice, not just the doctrine, of Christianity also shaped the terrains of struggle from whence these rebellions were launched. At

Bethel Chapel, slaves from up and down the East Coast congregated, circulated information, cultivated leaders, and enlisted a white missionary in their struggles with slaveholders. They made the chapel a site of negotiation, whereas owners in Southampton made Baptist churches sites of discipline. The spatial organization of religious worship compounded that of the spatial organization of production. In the everyday labor of carving out plantations on the Atlantic rim and producing staple crops in Demerara, slaves laid out a grid where they converged at certain focal points and ranged widely over the coast. The small scale of mixed agriculture in Southampton, by contrast, dispersed slaves on small farms, and they congregated in small churches scattered over the county. Slaves' familiarity with the terrain in Demerara enabled them to imagine sweeping white people off the plantations into Georgetown without violence. On the dispersed terrain of Southampton, rebels felt compelled to fight their way from one large slaveholding site to another all the way to Jerusalem.

Demerara and Virginia occupied interstices in plantation America. Southampton perched in a niche between the cotton kingdom and the Chesapeake, in the Virginia Tidewater but not of it. The county did not adopt the tobacco culture that defined the Tidewater gentry until the mid-eighteenth century, nor did it follow the shift to wheat. Southampton was also in the cotton kingdom, but not of it. It was on a tier of Virginia counties along the North Carolina border, the northernmost latitudes where cotton was extensively grown. Optimal conditions were further south, and Virginia cotton was only profitable when prices were high. Cotton sold at a premium after the War of 1812 and remained above fifteen cents per pound through 1825. Cotton from Virginia and North Carolina was enough of a fixture in the Atlantic market to acquire its own grade in England (Hilliard 1984: 67–68, maps 94–95; Gray and Thompson 1941, 2: 888–90, fig. 11). Production in Southampton was characterized by small-scale, mixed agriculture.

Planters in Demerara worked another niche in the Atlantic economy, where the scale of production was larger and the stakes higher than in Southampton. Empires and staple economies converged in Demerara. French Guyana and Brazil lay to the southeast, Dutch Suriname to the west. Demerara was Dutch until the

Netherlands ceded it to the British in 1803. Planters in Demerara were mixed agriculturalists too, approaching midcourse by 1823 in a shift from a diversified plantation colony to sugar monoculture. About half the plantations on the East Coast produced sugar, some exclusively, most with cotton or coffee or both (Higman 1995: 63–64, 68–70, table 3.8; Costa 1994: 47–48). The plantations were undergirded by a grid laid under Dutch rule in Demarara's environmental niche between tropical rain forest, mountain highlands, infertile savannahs, mangrove swamps, and ocean coastline.

The metropolitan merchants among absentee proprietors in Demerara had advantages over resident planters in reaping profits from this niche in Atlantic sugar markets. The abolition of the British slave trade choked the supply of laborers in Britain's plantation colonies and made long-term prospects for sugar production uncertain throughout the empire. Meanwhile, as the value of plantations declined, merchants in England picked them up at bargain prices in Demerara from indebted planters, or from heirs eager to convert a newly acquired stake in the uncertain sugar industry into a reliable income. Merchants advanced supplies to planters in return for consignments of tropical commodities; they converted clients' debts into mortgages and, in many cases, an ownership interest in plantations. John Gladstone, a Liverpool merchant, member of Parliament, and father of the future prime minister William E. Gladstone, obtained a half-dozen estates in Demerara from clients and their heirs during the 1810s. He reallocated slaves between plantations, capitalized on his estates' relative advantages and economies of scale. In 1816 Gladstone gained sole proprietorship over estate Success, a center of the revolt, converted it from coffee to sugar, and doubled its force of slaves to 330 people (Viotti da Costa 1994: 46–48, 58–314; Hall 1973: 106–35; Checkland 1954: 216–29, esp. 216, 222–29; 1971: 123, 194–95).[4]

Only the herculean labors of a vast force of slaves reclaimed arable land set precariously against the Atlantic, six feet below sea level at high tide.[5] Water converged on the coastal strip from every direction: the ocean in front, rainwater from the inland forest at the rear, rivers cross-cutting the lowlands. Demerara took its name from one of the rivers that bisected the coast. The British adopted the

Dutch West India Company's rules of settlement, arraying slaveholdings on long, narrow strips perpendicular to the Atlantic, the Demerara, or the Mahaica River. Narrow fronts minimized plantations' exposure to the ocean and rivers. The typical plantation was an elongated rectangle just 1,200 feet across (Mohamed 2008: 87, 94; Rodney 1981: 1, 6).[6]

To hold back the waters, slaves dug a network of canals and dams on each plantation: the "front dam" to beat back the Atlantic surf, the "back dam" to staunch runoff from the interior, and in between, the "middle walk." Canals bordering each plantation connected the dams, bore off the converging water to the sea or diverted it onto the plantation for irrigation. A latticework of trenches channeled the water and divvied up and connected the cane fields. Slaves shoveled some 100 million tons of sodden clay to construct this massive hydraulic system. It required constant maintenance, too. Breaches in the dams had to be filled and eroded parapets rebuilt. Silt piled up in canals and trenches, along with sand from the ocean and dirt from rains, runoff, and rivers. Shovel gangs dug out the sediment with skill as well as brawn to keep a canal, say, at an even pitch that prevented pooling and kept water flowing into or out of the fields or down to the ocean (Dalton 1855, 1: 227–28; Rodney 1981: 2–5; Mohamed 2008: 94–11, esp. 109–11; Viotti da Costa 1994: 47–48).

The plantation grid facilitated slaves' mobility and social intercourse. The nomenclature of middle *walks*, *navigation* trenches, and the company's *path* spoke to how the system of drainage and irrigation did double duty as means of transportation and communication. Canals were a link as well as a boundary between plantations. Slaves traveled between field and factory and between plantations by canal. They navigated the length and breadth of the estate by water or on foot via the middle walk. This walk ran between the front and back dams, parallel to the sideline dams, through the center of each plantation, a raised embankment flanked by two navigation trenches. These, in turn, branched off at right angles toward the sideline dams. Between every other estate along the coast, slaves maintained the Company's Path, a broad dam originally mandated by the Dutch West India Company. The estates backed onto canals that intersected with the road to

Georgetown, which ran close to the corridors of power. "A person cannot come from the east coast without passing near" the governor's residence, a physician pointed out to a court martial after the rebellion. In town, streets were routinely called dams.[7] The plantation landscape, laced with paths across plantation lines up and down the East Coast from Georgetown up to the Mahaica River, configured a terrain of struggle where slaves could mobilize swiftly and extensively.

The rebels' strategy rested on the fulcrum of a plantation landscape that afforded them considerable leverage. Leaders used canals, dams, and roads to collect and circulate intelligence from as far as England between Georgetown and estates along the East Coast. On the eve of the revolt, representatives from different estates convened at Success middle walk, a social and geographic nexus where rebels could draw people into their discourse. Although planters and managers commanded the spaces from the seacoast to the dwelling houses, boiling houses, mills, and cane fields, their presence and their power to the rear of the estates became attenuated over the provision grounds, the uncleared lands, and the bush. During tense moments in the revolt, rebels contemplating their next move, as well as slaves awaiting the outcome, went "aback" where the authorities could not easily get at them.[8]

Jack Gladstone, a carpenter on Success, worked this terrain in advance of the revolt. When a runaway entreated him to negotiate a return to Success, Gladstone sent the fugitive "aback," beyond the manager's reach. When rumors of emancipation began to circulate among slaves in the summer of 1823, he worked his sources to collect information from halfway up the East Coast to the West Coast and Georgetown in between. When the rumor first reached him, Gladstone went to town to talk up the governor's manservant, who read his owners' papers from time to time. A member of Bethel Chapel who lived on Success brought word from an estate up the coast: the overseer had said "the great men" in England had agreed to free the slaves, but the planters were holding out. To rally forces on estates near the Mahaica, Gladstone sent a messenger with a letter urging a contact up on Dochfour to be prepared for rebels down the coast in Gladstone's vicinity to strike next evening.[9]

The terrain of struggle was less auspicious in Southampton. Compare the diversified plantation production of Demerara to the mixed commercial agriculture in Southampton, where slaves were dispersed on modest-sized farms.[10] The terms of work in composite farming enabled slaves to get around to an extent, shifting between crops and tasks, conveying grains and other goods to mills and markets. Yet the greatest source of mobility was not a tight plantation grid, as in Demerara, but a domestic slave trade among slaveholding families in Southampton. The terms of work thus configured different terrains of struggle where rebels conceived different courses for their revolts. Turner, navigating a terrain where slaves were widely dispersed on small farms and plantations that routinely shifted in ownership and residence, understandably concluded that the extent of his mobility and social ties would not permit him to recruit widely in advance. The rebels would have to cut a swath to Jerusalem in the event, threading their path among the small farms to relatively large slaveholdings, where recruits might be found in numbers along the way.

Southampton's dispersed slaveholdings were the product of a vigorous local slave trade among kinfolk. For planters and small slaveholding farmers in a niche of mixed agriculture at the edge of an emergent cotton South, it paid to circulate slaves in both the interregional trade and locally. Recent scholarship, properly underscoring the domestic slave trade between the border states and the Deep South as a Second Middle Passage, have paid little attention to what might be called a Second Domestic Slave Trade. This was a *domestic* slave trade in a dual sense, within the South and among the households of slaveholding kin. Parents and siblings who stayed behind in the Upper South exchanged slaves between households and between generations within families and particular localities, such as Southampton. Slaveholding men and women bequeathed bonded people to adult sons and daughters starting their own households. Among small slaveholding families, as well as planters, the Second Domestic Slave Trade was the key to entering the master class and accumulating human property.

Nat Turner himself passed through this domestic trade. His parents belonged to Benjamin Turner, and Nat lived on his farm until the age of nine. Many farmers, like Benjamin Turner, began to divide their estates before they died. Benjamin Turner bestowed 360 acres on a son, Samuel, along with eight slaves, including Nat

Turner, his mother, and his paternal grandmother. In 1822 Samuel Turner died, and his widow sold Nat Turner out of the Turner family to Thomas Moore. Thus Nat Turner had three owners between 1809 and 1822, all in the southwest corner of Southampton corner. He moved just two miles south when he was bequeathed from Benjamin to Samuel Turner, and another two miles when he was sold onto Moore's 720-acre farm.[11] Slaveholdings remained small, in part because this domestic slave trade dispersed slaves among households in generational cycles within Southampton.

In the annual routine of mixed agriculture, slaves moved among different tasks, and different sites to an extent, producing cotton, corn, sweet potatoes, fruit, and swine. Shifts came in tight succession: planting corn, sweet potatoes, and cotton from late winter into May; plowing and chopping out weeds through early August, when slaves shook trees to drop their fruit; and then manufacturing alcohol began. Mixed agriculture encouraged temporary exchanges of labor between households with gluts and shortages. Slaves went to work on other farms, selling their own labor by the task or the day, or were hired out by owners. Agriculture and manufacturing were generally separated in Southampton's small-scale production, and slaves moved farm produce to sites where it was processed, such as the mills along the James and the Nottoway rivers. Alcohol production, ubiquitous in the Tidewater since the second half of the eighteenth century, was a mainstay on Southampton farms and plantations during the early republic. Every farmer kept apple orchards, and most had peach trees as well.[12]

Brandy making in Southampton, rather than cotton growing, most closely resembled sugar production in Demerara. Both enterprises integrated agriculture and manufacturing. The technology of turning fruit into alcohol bore certain similarities to grinding sugar cane and condensing the juice into granulated sugar. Fruit presses operated on the same principle as grinding mills on sugar plantations. Laborers fed fruit into rollers, grinding it into pulp and juice. Englishmen who manufactured and employed the early fruit presses during the seventeenth century had implicitly acknowledged the analogy to sugar production by naming their new contraption the *ingenio*, Spanish for sugar mill. A semblance of sugar production prevailed in distilling too. Apple and pear juice left in covered vats fermented into hard ciders, which turned to vinegar unless quickly consumed or distilled. Distilling cider was analogous to boiling cane juice and transferring the condensed liquid between containers. In the early nineteenth century, Tidewater farmers began to use condensers to speed distilling and increase the yield of alcohol from fruit juice, as sugar planters did in processing cane (Meacham 2009: esp. 24–39, 51–63, 102–9).[13]

Alcohol was also inscribed in the terms of struggle between slaves and owners by the time of the Turner Revolt. Slaveholders employed liquor—ubiquitous on farms across the county, valued among the products of labor—as a tool of discipline. Slaves did much of the work to make brandy and duly received it as a reward for arduous labor and as a gift during slack seasons in summer and Christmas. Yet owners had also grown wary of alcohol as a cause of insubordination by slaves. Masters' talk of "saucy," "quarrelsome," and "impudent" slaves implicitly acknowledged how alcohol diminished bondpeople's inhibitions (Meacham 2009: 120–32, esp. 130–31).

The terrain of mixed agriculture in Southampton shaped the contours of the rebellion in elemental ways. Liquor by no means caused the Turner Revolt, but certainly lubricated it. Turner launched the revolt on the fortieth anniversary of the Haitian Revolution. Had he embarked on July Fourth, as he originally intended, the fruit would have remained on the tree (Greenberg 1996: 48; Howe 2007: 324). But by late August there was brandy in the barrels at farms along the rebels' path. The rebels' course was laid out, in part, by the exchange of slaves among kindred households. By daylight the insurgents had backtracked through the two households Turner had passed between in 1822, launching the uprising at the home of his present owners and killing the widow who had sold him from the Turners to the Moore family. Although the small scale of mixed agriculture meant slaves were literally few and far between, Turner and his comrades had sufficient mobility to know the lay of the land around their own neighborhood and to plot their course through farms with relatively large slaveholdings. Conversely, the limits of slave mobility may explain why the rebels did not find their way to the largest slaveholdings outside their neighborhood.

The terrain of struggle was contoured in churches as well as production. In this arena too, slaves in Demerara achieved a relatively favorable balance of power. Religion, like production, concentrated slaves in Demerara and dispersed them in Southampton. Slaves from the estates converged on the lone church on the East Coast, Bethel Chapel, and made it the arena for cultivating valued allies in the persons of their minister and a cadre of enslaved church officers, who led the rebellion. In Southampton, Christian slaves convened with slaveholders in several small churches dotting the countryside. Although slaves formed a majority in most congregations, slaves in Demerara constituted the entire membership at Bethel.[14] These revolts also reflected different compromises with slavery struck by American and British evangelicals. Antislavery ministers were long gone from Southampton by Turner's day but remained abroad in missions across the British Empire, including Demerara. Whereas Bethel Chapel was a site of negotiation, churches in Southampton had become sites of discipline.

During the Age of Revolution, evangelicals came to terms with the contradictions of preaching salvation in slave societies. Methodists and Baptists persisted through the 1780s with a message that slavery was incompatible with the Gospel, but in the early 1790s rendered policies on slavery unto Caesar. John Wesley's *Discipline* had prohibited Methodists from buying and selling slaves. He had sided with the empire against the colonies and, joining those whose opposition to slavery was sharpened during the contest with America, chided self-styled patriots for contending for their liberties while holding slaves (Lyerly 1998: 122; Hempton 1996: 78–82; Vickers 2009: 26–27).[15] Wesley's Toryism encouraged American Methodists to seek their own way on slavery after the Revolutionary War. In 1784 they added rules to the *Discipline* giving members one year to manumit their slaves and a second year in Virginia, home to more slaveholders and Methodists than any other state in the republic. Despite the compromise with Virginia, antislavery seemed ascendant. In 1785 the Baptist General Committee of Virginia deemed "hereditary slavery to be contrary to the word of God" and, after a protracted debate over the "equity" of slavery in 1790, urged Baptists "to extirpate the horrid evil from the land" and the state legislature "to proclaim the general Jubilee." David Barrow brought the antislavery politics among Virginia Baptists most dramatically to the Southampton vicinity, where he was the minister of the Black Creek church and the outstanding opponent of slavery. In 1786, Black Creek followed the general committee's lead and deemed slaveholding "unrighteous." Four years later Barrow was a member of the general committee that exhorted Baptists and the state legislature against slavery (Najar 2005: 162–64; Daniel 1972: 65–66).

As long as evangelicals contested the legitimacy of slavery, Baptist churches groped for even-handed discipline of slaves and slaveholders. In Southampton, proceedings between Nero and his owner John Lawrence speak to the persistence of this struggle within congregations such as South Quay Baptist, as well as between the two men. Nero, even after the church censured his "disobedience & harsh language" to his owner in 1780, persisted in the belief that he could get a hearing for his grievances against Lawrence. Nero made accusations of "misconduct" against Lawrence, who was duly censured in turn. Two years later, Lawrence brought charges of disobedience against Nero, who was censured a second time. But the congregation was unmoved by Lawrence's next round of charges in 1786, which produced "no proof" that Nero was "guilty of a crime." Two months later the church directed Lawrence to "produce all the witnesses he has" against Nero but dismissed the charges yet again. Over six years, then, the church censured Nero twice yet sided with him three times, defending him against charges by Lawrence twice and censuring the owner once. South Quay finally excommunicated Nero in 1791 when he threatened to run away and take some of his fellow slaves with him. For a time though, power flowed in two directions in Baptist churches such as South Quay. Owners brought brethren slaveholders to bear to discipline slaves, who could prevail on the church to intercede on their behalf with owners (Scully 2001: 342–43).

When evangelicals resolved their own contest over slavery, Baptist churches increasingly became arenas for one-sided discipline of slaves. By the end of the 1790s, evangelicals in Virginia had recast antislavery as a matter of individual conscience and ceded policy on slavery to the state legislature. Methodist petitions in 1785 urging the legislature to abolish slavery provoked a backlash of proslavery petitions equating Methodist antislavery with Toryism. Methodist leaders suspended the requirement for members to free their slaves. In 1798, a revised *Discipline* condemned slavery as an "enormous evil," yet advised preachers evangelizing the enslaved to uphold slaves' duties to masters. Methodists hoped to carve out a space to advocate manumission as a sign of conversion and urged state legislatures to abolish slavery for the last time two years later. Baptists had already remanded the slavery question to the legislature in 1793. The Baptist General Committee, in response to regional associations' objections to its call for legal means to abolish slavery, resolved that the entire matter "belongs to the legislative body." Baptists' compromise with slavery put antislavery ministers such as David Barrow at odds with their congregations. In 1798 Barrow resolved to leave for Kentucky, explaining in a letter to his congregation that he could no longer provide for his family without resorting to slaveholding (Lyerly 1998: 55, 125–35; Najar 2005: 164–66; Allen, Jr. 1963: 440–51).

Even as Baptists ostensibly ceded the politics of slavery to secular authority, they redeployed church discipline to police slaves on the ground with new zeal. The shift was manifest in the proceedings initiated at South Quay one day in March 1810 against five slaves. In addition to cases of theft, fighting, and attending horse races, three men were charged with offenses related to alcohol: one man for selling spirits, two other men for "excessive drinking." Churches in Southampton and adjoining counties were especially zealous against intemperance. Between 1772 and 1840, drunkenness was second only to theft among charges laid to black men, 13 percent in those counties, compared to 6 percent in Virginia as well as the other states.[16] Small-scale distilling made alcohol pervasive around Southampton, every slaveholding household being a site of struggle over drinking, and Baptist owners made their churches an arena for this contest with slaves.

The churches played no role in the Turner Revolt, nor could they. He was born two years after Barrow left for the western country, the antislavery men were gone from the pulpits now, and the churches belonged to the slaveholders. Turner and his parents were part of an evangelical fellowship during his boyhood. Thereafter his accounts of his religious strivings are strikingly solitary in *The Confessions of*

Nat Turner, his interview after the rebellion. In his attempts to cultivate a following among evangelicals for the rebellion, he steered clear of the churches. Their small enslaved congregations, scattered over the countryside, firmly in slaveholders' control, held little promise as a social base for organizing the revolt (Kaye 2007: 705–12; Scully 2007: 661–84). In Demerara, by contrast, slaves from estates across the East Coast converged on a single chapel. Moreover, Bethel Chapel also hints at what was lost in Southampton with the departure of antislavery ministers. For slaves could enlist even a mildly antislavery missionary, such as John Smith, in their struggles with owners and thereby make their chapel less a site of discipline than a site of negotiation.

British missionaries evangelized slaves based on their own division of labor with political authorities. In contrast to Southampton, where antislavery ministers had decamped by the turn of the century, ecumenical tendencies in the evangelical movement enabled men with an antislavery temper to join the mission to slaves. The London Missionary Society (LMS), which conducted the station at Bethel Chapel in Demerara, had to accommodate a constituency of several evangelical sects, including those that avoided any position on slavery, and British Methodists, who remained vocal in their antislavery long after their American brethren had stayed their tongues. Wesley, in the last letter of his life in 1791, urged William Wilberforce to persist in the abolition campaign "till even American slavery (the vilest that ever saw the sun) shall vanish away." Wesley's successors embarked on a campaign to make British Methodism respectable. They erected an ecclesiastical hierarchy to discipline revivalists whose enthusiasm was unbecoming to an emergent high church or smacked of political radicalism. They built new churches to settle ministers and congregations. They galvanized provincial societies to raise money to send missionaries abroad. The architects of British Methodism as a high church were antislavery men. Richard Watson was their leading advocate of both foreign missions and antislavery. In 1817 in his *Defence of the Wesleyan Missions in the West Indies*, he eloquently testified to "the state of oppression under which [the slave] groaned." John Smith, who began his mission in Demerara that year, was neither a Methodist nor an abolitionist, yet voiced similar sentiments to Watson's. "Ever since I have been in the colony," Smith wrote to his LMS superiors shortly after the revolt broke out, "the slaves have been most grievously oppressed."[17]

Smith's mission reflected the ecumenical strand in British evangelicalism. He was a member of an Independent church, converted by Methodist preaching, and conducted a Congregationalist ministry under the nondenominational auspices of the LMS. As an apprentice cabinetmaker in London during the 1810s, he taught Sunday school at his Independent chapel and had a powerful experience of conversion contemplating a guest sermon by a Methodist minister. In 1813 Smith first applied to the London Missionary Society, founded by Independents, Methodists, and Presbyterians, although Congregationalists were increasing their sway. He preached as an itinerant for two years before the LMS accepted Smith and sent him to study under a Congregationalist minister. The society's instructions to Smith were short on specifics and emphatic that he should have nothing to do with the slaves' "temporal condition."[18]

Contrary to the instructions of the LMS, as well as Smith's better judgment, slaves quickly drew him onto a terrain of struggle where contentions over the length of the work week and slaves' attendance at chapel were joined. In the transition to sugar production, managers struggled to expand, in addition to their workforce, the workday and the work week. Manufacturing sugar required evening labor during the harvest, which made Bethel members late for evening services and their attendance light. On Sundays, managers kept slaves from going to chapel with a variety of work, tasks of reproduction either squeezed out of the weekly routine of staple production or left over from it. Slaves were kept at their labor digging trenches, weeding fields, boiling the juice from Saturday's crushed cane, drying cotton and coffee, and packing sugar for market. They had much work to do as well in preparation for the beginning of the coming week, making hogsheads, collecting *begasse* for fuel in the boiling house, and washing the coppers. On Sundays when the work weeks did not collide, slaves were often collecting their allowance of food and clothing from the planters, working their provision grounds or gardens, or marketing their surpluses in town.[19] As slaves drew Smith into contests over work time and chapel attendance, they drew his antislavery sentiments out of him.

Smith quickly came alive to the spatial dimension of his congregation's attempt to make Bethel Chapel a site of negotiation. Shortly after he arrived in Demerara, he sought a physical separation between the sites of his ministry and of slaves' contentions with owners. He requested permission to move the chapel on estate Le Resouvenir across the road, so "that I might be farther from the Negroes, and know less of what was transacted on the estate." But the chapel stayed put. Two years on, Smith was seeking an emotional distance in lieu of a physical one. "I wish the negroes would say nothing to me of their troubles, which arise from the severe usage of their managers," he wrote in March 1819. He tried to respond "with apparent indifference, and behave with coolness to those who relate it."[20] Meanwhile slaves brought him their complaints about floggings for trifling offenses and the mounting burden of labor with the transition to sugar production. Their most persistent grievance was against managers who prevented them from going to chapel and punished them for it.[21]

Smith made important concessions to planters in the related struggles over labor time, and attendance at chapel. He discontinued an evening service on Sundays after his first year in Demerara and another during the week the year before the rebellion. Sunday labor was, strictly speaking, against the law in Demerara, subject to a fine, although rarely enforced. In October 1818, the LMS published his letter lamenting that attendance had recently fallen off due to plantation managers keeping slaves at their labors on Sundays. When the *fiscaal*, a colonial officer charged with investigating complaints about mistreatment of slaves, demanded proof of the charge against specific planters, Smith demurred.[22] Smith urged slaves to uphold the Sabbath, at least when owners permitted it. They should not do business, their owners' or their own, on Sunday, they should work and trade for themselves on Saturday when they were allowed to, but work masters' crops when owners and managers insisted on it, even on the Sabbath.[23]

For all these concessions, Smith believed planters and managers strayed into his spiritual domain by preventing slaves from attending Sunday services. In October 1819 Quamina and Seaton, deacons at Bethel and leaders of the rebellion, told Smith their manager had forbidden all the slaves on Success from going to chapel.

On Christmas Eve, Smith returned home with his wife to find several troubled slaves waiting: "their managers had given them orders not to come to chapel any more." He promised try to get to the bottom of the order not to attend chapel "and get it altered." Slaves' prerogative to attend Sunday services was heatedly contested yet again at the time of the revolt. From the pulpit and in private conversations with slaves, Smith endorsed the governor's circular requiring slaves to obtain passes to go to Sunday services, but objected to it privately for "putting it into the power of the managers to prevent" slaves from "coming at all." At the court martial, he marveled at planters' audacity transgressing on the Lord's Day. "Are their masters greater than God?" he asked indignantly.[24] Smith's objection to planters and managers claiming the last word on slaves' attending chapel indicates how far his understanding of his own sphere had encroached on powers slaveholders arrogated to themselves.

Discipline at Bethel, in contrast to Baptist churches in Southampton, focused primarily on intimate relations. As the controversy over Sunday labor suggests, neither the congregation nor the parson could avoid questions of plantation discipline. Smith also annexed such questions to church discipline when he denied members sacraments, such as a seat at the Lord's Supper, for working their provision grounds or going to market on Sunday, or queried managers about prospective candidates for baptism or membership. On occasion, he also obliged managers who asked the minister to have a word with a recalcitrant laborer in the congregation. Drinking, which so preoccupied Virginia churches such as South Quay, received scant attention at Bethel. For Smith, what was at stake in slaves' intimate relations was an orderly Christian life. In February 1823 he assured the LMS that his congregation was "fast abandoning their wicked practices for more regular habits of life, as is evident from the number of marriages."[25]

Slaves themselves, especially men, had brought their relations with spouses to Bethel before Smith made them the crux of chapel discipline. When he convened the congregation to settle outstanding quarrels at the end of his first month at Bethel, most of the cases members raised were between husbands and wives, jealousies, and couples who had separated. The next Sunday another man complained his wife had left him, as it turned out, because he had beaten her.[26] A few weeks later, another man brought the case of his unfaithful wife to the congregation, although he wanted the parson's opinion most. Cipio had found her in bed with another man over a year ago and left her, "put her away" in slaves' parlance, but waited to resolve the matter "until a missionary arrived to advise him," according to Smith. After nearly a year of members bringing conflicts between spouses to Bethel, it finally dawned on Smith that he might formalize intimate relations in chapel discipline. He spent a November morning reflecting on "the evils arising from the want of marriage among the Slaves" and resolved to give the subject due attention in preparing candidates for baptism. In March 1820, the congregation agreed to rules making marriage a condition of membership. Cohabiting without marriage became grounds to deny candidates admission to Bethel and to exclude members, who could not put away their spouse "without first having the consent of the church."[27]

Whereas Baptist slaveholders in Southampton used proceedings in church to tighten their hold over enslaved members, slaves in Demerara employed church discipline to reinforce the bond between husband and wife. The number of marriages performed at Bethel markedly increased under the new rules. Smith married just eight couples in 1817–1819, then twenty-seven in 1820 and seventy in 1821. Members used Smith's recognition of their marriages to make claims on owners to uphold the tie between spouses. One proprietor alluded to such claims, and implicitly acknowledged their power, when he wrote Smith to object to the minister performing marriages on the grounds that it taught slaves "the pernicious principle, that their owners have no right to separate them."[28] At Bethel, enslaved members gained leverage to impose limitations on that fundamental right for owners of human property, the owners' power to sell them.

Bethel Chapel was also the site where slaves laid a network of leadership over the network of communication embedded in the plantation landscape. Teachers connected Bethel, like the canals and dams on the plantation grid, to estates up and down the East Coast. Witnesses before the court martial identified teachers on at least ten plantations over some fifteen miles, from several estates around Le

Resouvenir, to Nonpareil half-way up the coast, to Dochfour near the Mahaica River. According to one deacon, "almost every estate" had one. Seaton, the teacher on Success, counted fifty-one slaves under his instruction.[29] Although Smith told the court martial that "deacons were in no respect superior to any other member," slaves regarded chapel members and their officers as a hierarchy. To one member, the deacons were "head of all." Their stronghold was Bethel and vicinity. They lived on estates within a mile of Le Resouvenir, where the chapel was located. They performed their official duties—handing out the sacraments, taking collections, leading prayers and psalms after Sunday services—inside the chapel itself.[30]

Bethel's lay leadership extended their sphere of duties along with their ambition. Teaching scripture was no part of the deacons' charge, Smith claimed. "They were not teachers by virtue of their office, nor did they, as such, ever teach any one to my knowledge." Yet all three deacons who testified to the court martial cited teaching among their primary responsibilities. Romeo's commitment to teaching may explain why one member thought he was a teacher rather than a deacon. Jason, the one freedman among the deacons, saw his duty as nothing less than "to make" candidates for baptism "sensible." Bristol, another deacon, specified his responsibilities to candidates as teaching them the catechism and to read too. Outside chapel, he took the liberty of explaining Smith's sermons and texts to slaves "on my own estate," Chateau Margo. Although Smith told the court martial "the people chose" their teachers, Bristol appropriated that power as well: "on my own estate I appoint them," he noted.[31]

The rebels' political achievement was to distill the everyday struggles over labor time and attending chapel in the stakes of the rebellion. Slaves on Chateau Margot were often heard to say they would not have to break the Sabbath if they had both Saturday and Sunday off. Bristol, the deacon who lived there, told the court that the slaves revolted "Because they had no other time to wash their clothes, or do anything else, except on the Sabbath." Asked why they could not do so on Sundays, he replied, "Because they had to go to chapel." Up the coast by the Mahaica, one grievance predominated among those enumerated to the Anglican minister by the insurgents who said they had no right to take life: "A hardship of being restricted from attendance on [Smith's] chapel, was, however, very generally the burthen of complaint."[32]

The outbreak of the revolt revealed Bethel as the locus of this conjuncture between the aims of the rebellion and the struggles over work time and chapel attendance. After services on Sunday August 17, 1823, the overflow crowd went quickly away.[33] A large contingent from a number of estates made their way to the middle walk on adjoining Success for a meeting convened by the chapel's lay leaders, including Quamina, the head deacon and father of Jack Gladstone, who had learned of "the paper" from the governor's servant. The talk at the meeting parsed the rumor that planters had suppressed an emancipation edict from the metropolis and suggested participants were leaning toward a revolt. So Quamina left to tap into the network of communication emanating from Bethel and find out what was in the wind from the powers that be in England, to see the parson and determine once and for all whether "the paper" contained "any free." Smith alluded to the colonial office's prohibition against whipping enslaved women and drivers carrying whips in the field, but made clear there were no provisions for emancipation. Smith also hoped to tap the network of communication and urged Quamina to spread the news along the coast and forestall a revolt. But Quamina left Smith thinking the revolt could force the hand of the powers that be in Demerara. "I will drive the managers to the court," Quamina told a companion as they left Smith's house, "and see what is the best they can do for these slaves."[34]

The revolt, including the rebels' restraint, followed a course hewed in the making of the converging networks of communication and leadership in the plantation grid and Bethel Chapel. The rebellion broke out toward evening the next day, Monday, August 18, when a cadre of fifty slaves surrounded the manager's house on Success. As they called him out, confiscated his weapons, and put him into the stocks, Quamina and his son, Jack Gladstone, were most active holding back the crowd, "keeping the rest back, and preventing them doing any injury to me," the manager recalled. Similar scenes played-out on other estates. Rebels seized managers, overseers, and their firearms, locked the white people in their houses, or clapped them in the stocks.[35] A cadre of leaders traveled between estates maintaining order.[36]

Meanwhile other insurgents took down bridges, a precaution that greatly slowed the progress of militia and regular troops from Georgetown up the coast.[37] As troops made their way from one plantation to the next up to Mahaica on Tuesday, the second day of the revolt, the slaves retreated aback en masse.[38]

The Turner Revolt was also marked from the outset by the conjuncture between the terrains of production and worship. Southampton had neither a single locus of worship nor a plantation grid that integrated a network of transportation and communication with central strongholds such as the middle walk at Success. Navigating a dispersed geography contoured by mixed commercial agriculture and small churches, Turner convened a half-dozen men from adjoining farms in his immediate neighborhood. At Cabin Pond, a liminal space at the edge of a large plantation, they talked through the night undisturbed. From this point of departure, the dispersed geography and terms of work hewed the rebels' path in subtle but important ways.

The ubiquitous production of alcohol in Southampton enabled the rebels to partake at several points on route to Jerusalem. It was early enough in the season that hard cider was still around, undistilled and unspoiled. The drinking began at the feast on Cabin Pond, washing down the pork with brandy, and continued at the Travis farm, the rebel's first stop. Upon arrival "they all went to the cider press and drank, except myself," recalled Turner, a teetotaler. If this was dubious, rebels could still have taken strength from the conviction. Around sunrise they arrived at the farm of his previous owner, Eliza Turner, where three of the men "went to the still." When Turner, having divided his forces, rejoined them at the Harris plantation, he found forty men, "who shouted and hurraed as I rode up, some were in the yard, loading their guns, others drinking." Liquor did not play a solely detrimental role in the rebels' work. They might have drunk in the belief, widespread in the early modern period, that alcohol increased physical strength (Greenberg 1996: 48–50; Meacham 2009: 10).

As the rebels made their way along Barrow Road (see map) toward Jerusalem, the disadvantages as well as the uses of alcohol surfaced. Turner may have counted on the effects of liquor when he changed tactics from a stealth advance, catching slaveholders unawares, to assert control over the route of march, unleashing "terror and devastation wherever we went." As they pulled out from Harris's at the head of the road, Turner directed fifteen or twenty mounted men to lead the column and approach each house "as fast as their horses could run," not only to prevent victims from escaping but "to strike terror to the inhabitants" (Greenberg 1996: 50–51). As much as the spirituous effects of liquor contributed to Turner's cordon of sound and fury, they also distrained the ranks. The forty rebels now included many from his neighborhood and others outside it.[39] Drinking may have increased solidarity *within* these cadres as much as between them. Turner, declining to partake, held himself aloof from the comradery among the drinkers. When the force reached the Parker farm at the end of Barrow Road, factions pulled in different directions. Turner was struggling to control the course of the revolt, and alcohol probably contributed to this predicament.

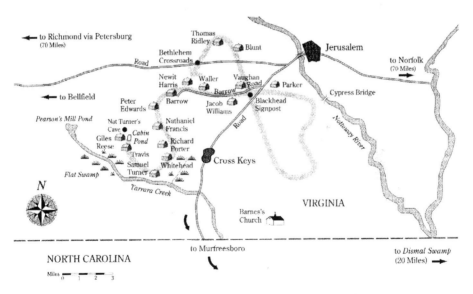

Path of Nat Turner's Rebellion. Source: Oates (1975).

Barrow Road also marked a shift in the type of farms attacked by the rebels. To this point, Turner threaded a course through Southampton's larger slaveholdings. To gather new recruits quickly, he sent his forces where the slaves were. Had the rebels attacked households randomly, they would have come across a slaveholding with ten slaves or more about every tenth farm, yet they beat a path to slaveholdings that size every second farm. Only 9.8 percent of the households south of the Nottoway had at least ten over the age of twelve, yet nearly half the invaded households had that many: fifteen at the Whitehead farm, ten at Nathaniel Francis's, seventeen at Peter Edwards's, and thirty-one at Newit Harris's at the head of Barrow Road.[40] As the rebels made their way between relatively large slaveholdings, they bypassed small ones. When Turner divided his forces at Whitehead's, for example, he sent one detachment to Richard Porter's farm with thirteen slaves, and bypassed another Porter household with only two.[41]

Along Barrow Road, the rebels hit relatively small farms and bypassed larger slaveholdings. Three farms had fewer slaves than adjoining properties or ones equidistant from Jerusalem. At the Parker farm, for instance, Turner wanted to continue on to Jerusalem, but the rebels paused to recruit in the quarters here, although the adjoining plantation had over twice as many slaves.[42] Some of the rebels had family among the thirteen at Parker's, and recruiting along kinship lines was a promising strategy, to be sure, but to that point it had not been the strategy employed. As for Turner, either they had ventured far enough outside his neighborhood that he no longer knew where the largest slaveholdings were, or those nearest the road to Jerusalem were relatively small. Meanwhile, white militia caught up with the rebels at the Parker farm and dealt them the first of several reversals. The terrain of dispersed slaveholdings, where potential recruits were few and far between, had caught up with the rebels too.

The divergent courses of these revolts reflect stark contrasts in the terrains of struggle in British Guyana and Virginia. In Demerara, slaves gained a purchase on their terrain working a plantation grid that connected estates in a network of communication and transportation. At Bethel Church, the enslaved congregation drew their minister into the struggle over Sunday labor and cultivated a network of teachers and deacons that, like the plantation grid itself, radiated across the East

Coast. On a terrain where slaves circulated among the estates, assembled in church, and exchanged information from Georgetown to the Mahaica River, rebels could envision mobilizing in overwhelming force, driving slaveholders to town without bloodshed, and negotiating their freedom. The terrain of struggle was comparatively unfavorable in Southampton, where slaves navigated a dispersed geography of small farms and small churches that were also sites of discipline. Turner saw few prospects for assembling a sizeable force in advance and recruited by making a show of force, slaughtering owners on large slaveholdings. The small scale of production made liquor ubiquitous in Southampton, a fixture on the terrain of struggle, and an important feature of the revolt. The rebels used alcohol to unleash violence along their path and a furious cacophony along Barrow Road.

The spatial dimensions of slave revolts offer one approach to move beyond the familiar factors cited as conducive to slave rebellion. These dimensions remind us that all rebellions arose from an everyday terrain of struggle. These revolts underscore, moreover, how that terrain was configured by terrains of production and religion that opened certain paths of resistance and lines of attack and closed others. For rebels, then, the problem of slave rebellion was not to follow courses dictated by the terrain of struggle, but to interpret the obstacles and possibilities embedded within it and mobilize along those lines. Comparing terrains of production and religion sets off the dispersed geography of Southampton in sharp contrast to the both centripetal and centrifugal tendencies embedded in the estates and Bethel Chapel in Demerara. Comparing how slaves navigated the terrains of work and worship with strategies of rebellion in turn offers historians a vantage point to glimpse how rebels worked out strategies of rebellion in the course of everyday routines. Comparative histories of rebels' use of social spaces open a path to get beneath the factors conducive to slave rebellion—where and when rebellions take place—and cultivate deeper understandings of how they are made.

Notes

1. For a convenient timeline of England's wars from 1701 to 1815, see Miles Ogborn 2008: xx).

2. Kenneth S. Greenberg, ed., *The Confessions of Nat Turner and Related Documents* (1996: vii; Schedule A: Estates whose Negroes were engaged in the Rebellion, Schedule B: White persons put in the stocks during the Revolt, Schedule E: Cases in which Fire Arms were actually used and with what effect); *Further Papers Relating to Insurrection of Slaves in Demerara*, in *Slave Trade*, vol. 66 of *Irish University Press Series of British Parliamentary Papers*, 95 vols. (1969: 157–59, 162), hereinafter cited as *Further Papers*.

3. Testimony of Rev. W. S. Austin, *The London Missionary Society's Report of the Proceedings against the late Rev. J. Smith* (London: F. Westley, 1824: 110), hereinafter cited as *Proceedings*. The *Proceedings* are the most comprehensive published collection of the testimony at the trial, conducted in October and November, 1823.

4. On the larger work force required on sugar plantations compared to coffee or cotton, see also Higman (1995: 90–92, fig. 4.6, 68–70, table 3.8).

5. The most penetrating analysis of ecology, the organization of plantation space, and the terms of work and struggle in Guyana is Wazir Mohamed's PhD dissertation (2008), which thoughtfully extends the classic study by Walter Rodney, *A History of the Guyanese Working People, 1881–1905* (1981).

6. For an analysis of Dutch Surinam, east of Demerara, see Gert Oostindie and Alex van Stipriaan (1995: 78–99); they acknowledge the system of irrigation in Suriname as a means of transportation, but emphasize it as a boundary rather than a link between plantations (1995: 87, 95).

7. Testimony of Thomas Robson, M.D., *Proceedings*, 48; Checkland (1971: 185); Rodney (1981: 2, 6, 8); Viotti da Costa (1994: 43–44, esp. 79–81). See also J. C. Cheveley, *The Demerara Rising of 1823*, typescript of extracts, Council of World Mission Archives (CWMA), microfiches 785–92, Yale Divinity School Library, p. 2.

8. Testimony of Bristol, *Proceedings*, 24–25.

9. Testimony of Jackey Reed, *Proceedings*, 51; Viotti da Costa (1994: 80, 99, 79–80, 182).

10. In 1831 only 43 percent of Southampton households in Southampton County owned slaves over twelve years old, and half had no more than three such slaves. Calculated from Auditor of Public Accounts, Southampton County, Personal Property Tax Books, 1831, Reel 323, Frames 463–535, Library of (Richmond) Virginia, hereinafter LVA.

Three-quarters of all slaves lived on farms with ten bondpeople or more, whereas 85 percent in Demerara lived on plantations with over thirty; see also Stephen B. Oates (1975: 2–3); Daniel W. Crofts (1992: 18); Higman (1995: 102–06, tables 5.1–5.3); Viotti da Costa (1994: 314).

11. Entries for Eliza Turner and Thomas Moore, Southampton County Land Taxes, 1823, Book B, pp. 14, 19, LVA; Oates (1975: 13).

12. Sarah Hand Meacham (2009); Edward Ayres (1973: 101–21); Crofts (1992: 19, 78–87, 297, table 1.7). For examples of orchards in Southampton County Deed Books, see Pond to Gray, Jan. 20, 1818, Book 18, pp. 95–96; Vick to Vick, February 12, 1822, Book 19, p. 115; Carr and wife to Williams, June 14, 1823, Book 19, p. 176; Turner to Turner, April 26, 1826, Book 20, p. 75; Cobb Trustee to Strong & Co., Jan. 21, 1828, Book 20, p. 319, LVA.

13. On sugar production, see Sidney W. Mintz (1985: ch. 2). For a reference to a sugar mill as an *ingenio* in British America, see the illustration from Richard Ligon's *True and Exact History of Barbados* (1647) in Russell R. Menard (2006: 14, fig. 2).

14. John Smith Journal, CWMA, microfiches 785–92, Yale Divinity School Library; Viotti da Costa (1994: 54, 60–61 and *passim*).

15. Wesley is a reminder that Britain's struggle with the North American colonies sharpened antislavery sentiment among Tories as well as friends of America; on the latter, see Christopher Leslie Brown (2006, chs. 4–5).

16. South Quay Baptist Church 3 March 1810, LVA. For figures on charges in Baptist church discipline in Southampton, Isle of Wight, and Sussex counties, see Scully (2008: 157–58, tables 8, 9). For figures on charges of drunkenness in Virginia, North Carolina, South Carolina, and Georgia, see Sylvia R. Frey and Betty Wood (1998: 189, 246 n. 20). The two samples overlap but do not cover entirely the same time period. Three of the nine churches in Scully's sample are among the twenty-eight churches in Frey and Wood's, including South Quay. Both samples begin in 1772, but Frey and Wood's ends in 1830, Scully's in 1840.

17. Gill (1956: 236–37); Stuart Piggin (1980: 30); Roger T. Anstey (1981: 43–45); Unfinished Letter of Mr. Smith to the Secretary of the London Missionary Society, Aug. 21, 1823, *Proceedings*, 183–84.

18. Prisoner's Defence, Nov. 1, 1823, *Proceedings*, 63; Jakobsson (1972: 301–2); Viotti da Costa (1994: 126–28, 343 n. 11).

19. Smith Journal, Mar. 1, 1818; Dec. 25, 1818; Jan. 2, 1820; Feb. 12, 1819; Mar. 21, 1819; Jan. 30, 1820; Nov. 2 and 16, 1817, CWMA; Smith Journal extract, May 23, 1823, testimony of Susanna, *Proceedings*, 77, 133.

20. Prisoner's Defence, testimony of Hendrick Van Cooten, *Proceedings*, 63, 71, 95.

21. Smith Journal, Oct. 12, 1817; Feb. 22, 1818; July 5, 1819; Oct. 24, 1819; Dec. 10, 1821, CWMA; extracts from Smith Journal Aug. 30, 1817; Sep. 13, 1817, testimony of Manuel, Philip, *Proceedings*, 5, 17, 23.

22. Prisoner's Defence, testimony of Azor, Prosecutor's reply, *Proceedings*, 63, 73–75, 76, 10, 151.

23. Testimony of Romeo, Manuel, Bristol, Philip, Prisoner's Defence, *Proceedings*, 12–13, 17–18, 23–24, 73–74, 117–18.

24. Extract from Smith's Journal, Oct. 30 and 31, 1819; Dec. 24, 1819, testimony of Bristol, Prisoner's Defence, *Proceedings*, 36–37, 23, 74, 76–77.

25. Testimony of John Stewart, Stewart to the Rev. J. Smith, Feb. 5, 1822, testimony of Bristol, *Proceedings*, 97, 98, 114; Smith Journal, June 29, 1817; Jan. 1, 1821, CWMA; E. A. Wallbridge ([1848] 1969: 55).

26. Smith Journal, March 30, 1817; April 6, 1817; May 25, 1817, CWMA.

27. Smith Journal, April 27, 1817; April 11, 1817; May 18, 1817; July 13, 1817; Nov. 8, 1817; Mar. 5, 1820, CWMA.

28. Smith Journal, Dec. 12 and 31, 1821; Feb. 11, 1819, CWMA.

29. According to the owner of Dochfour, it was approximately fifteen miles from Le Resouvenir, and teachers were named on estates further west of the former. Testimony of Lieutenant-Colonel Reed, Bristol, Seaton, *Proceedings*, 51, 22, 45; Checkland (1971: 186).

30. Prisoner's Defence, testimony of Azor, Jason, *Proceedings*, 63–64, 9–10, 118–19.

31. Bristol, Romeo, Prisoner's Defence, *Proceedings*, 10, 12, 19, 21–22, 28, 118–19, 64; Checkland (1971: 186).

32. Manuel, Rev. Austin, *Proceedings*, 26, 110.

33. Testimony of Joe, Romeo, Manuel, *Proceedings*, 14, 12, 24.

34. Testimony of Peter, Shute, Prisoner's remarks, *Proceedings*, 128–29, 132, 146; examination of Telemachus, Quamina of Nabachlis, Prisoner Jack [Gladstone]'s Statement in Defence, *Further Papers*, 166, 211, 218. Quamina also led the contingent that had appealed to Smith in 1819 about the estate manager's order against attending Bethel.

35. Schedule B: White persons put in the stocks during the Revolt, *Further Papers*, 158–59; testimony of John Stewart, Seaton, Dose, Joe, Smith to Mr. Mercer, Aug. 20, 1823, *Proceedings*, 102, 43, 53, 14, 182–83.

36. For examples of leaders moving between plantations and keeping order, follow the movements of Telemachus and Joseph, two teachers from Bachelor's Adventure, in examination of Biddy Cells, Inglis's Defence, deposition of Barson, evidence of Mingo, *Further Papers*, 153, 154, 177, 212.

37. Deposition of John Bailey, Toney, Liuetenant-Colonel John Thomas Leahy to Sir, Nov. 19, 1823, *Further Papers*, 171, 177, 202.

38. Examination of Phill, *Further Papers*, 174; Cheveley, *Demerara Rising*, 16.

39. On neighborhoods, cohesion, and division among the rebels, see Kaye (2007).

40. They attacked twenty-three households in all, and of the twenty-one found in tax records, ten had at least ten slaves who were twelve years of age or older. Calculated from Southampton County Land Tax Records, Book B, 1831, Reel 309; Personal Property Tax Records, Book B, 1831, reel 323, LVA.

41. Entries for Jesse Porter (R. Porter Gud.) and Thomas Porter, Southampton Land Tax Records, Book B, p. 19; Richard Porter and Thomas Porter, Southampton Personal Property Tax Book B, Mar. 1, 1831, Feb. 14, 1831.

42. Of the seven farms along Barrow Road where the rebels stopped, three adjoined properties with larger slaveholdings. The three properties and the larger adjoining properties (with the number of slaves over twelve years old) were Jacob Williams (4) and William H. Nicholson (14), Rebecca Vaughan (8) and Henry B. Vaughan (29), James W. Parker (13) and James Trezvant (29). The slaveholdings appear in Southampton Personal Property Tax Book B, Feb. 21 and Mar. 3, 1831 (Williams and Nicholson); Mar. 22, 1831 (Vaughan and Vaughan); and April 7 and May 16, 1831 (Parker and Trezvant). The properties are listed as adjoining in Southampton County Land Tax Records, Book B, 1831, entry for Jacob Williams, p. 28; entry for James W. Parker, p. 19. The Vaughans' properties adjoin in Southampton County Deed Book 19, p. 176, Carr and wife to Williams, June 14, 1823.

Works Cited

Allen, Carlos R., Jr.1963. "David Barrow's *Circular Letter* of 1798." *William and Mary Quarterly* 20 (3): 440–51.

Anstey, Roger T. 1981. "Religion and British Abolitionism." In *The Abolition of the Atlantic Slave Trade: Origins and Effects in Europe, Africa, and the Americas*, edited by David Eltis and James Walvin. Madison: University of Wisconsin Press, 43–45.

Ayres, Edward 1973. "Fruit Culture in Colonial Virginia." *Colonial Williamsburg Early American History Research Reports* (RR-84), 101–21.

Brown, Christopher Leslie. 2006. *Moral Capital: Foundations of British Abolitionism*. Chapel Hill: University of North Carolina Press.

Brown, Vincent. 2008. *The Reaper's Garden: Death and Power in the World of Atlantic Slavery*. Cambridge, MA: Harvard University Press.

Checkland, S. G. 1954. "John Gladstone as Merchant and Planter." *The Economic History Review*, n.s., 7 (2): 216–29.

———. 1971. *The Gladstones: A Family Biography, 1764–1851*. Cambridge, UK: Cambridge University Press.

Costa, Emilia Viotti da. 1994. *Crowns of Glory, Tears of Blood: The Demerara Rebellion of 1823*. New York: Oxford University Press.

Crofts, Daniel W. 1992. *Old Southampton: Politics and Society in a Virginia County, 1834–1869*. Charlottesville: University of Virginia.

Dalton, Henry G. 1855. *History of British Guiana: Comprising a General Description of the Colony*. 2 vols. London: Longman, Brown, Green and Longmans.

Daniel, W. Harrison. 1972. "Virginia Baptists in the Early Republic." *Virginia Magazine of History and Biography* 80 (1): 65–66.

Frey, Sylvia R., and Betty Wood. 1998. *Come Shouting to Zion: African American Protestantism in the American South and the British Caribbean to 1830*. Chapel Hill: University of North Carolina Press.

Genovese, Eugene D. 1992. *From Rebellion to Revolution: Afro-American Slave Revolts in the Making of the Modern World* (orig. 1979). Baton Rouge: Louisiana State University Press.

Gill, Frederick C., ed. 1956. *Selected Letters of John Wesley*. London: Epworth.

Gray, Lewis C., and Esther K. Thompson. 1941. *History of Agriculture in the Southern United States to 1860* (orig. 1933). 2 vols. New York: Peter Smith.

Greenberg, Kenneth S., ed. 1996. *The Confessions of Nat Turner and Related Documents*. Boston: Bedford.

Hall, Douglas. 1973. "Absentee-Proprietorship in the British West Indies, to about 1850." In *Slaves, Free Men, Citizens: West Indian Perspectives*, edited by Lambros Comitas and David Lowenthal. Garden City, NY: Anchor Books.

Hempton, David. 1996. *Religion of the People: Methodism and Popular Religion c. 1750–1900*. New York: Routledge.

Higman, B. W. 1995. *Slave Populations of the British Caribbean*. Kingston, Jamaica: University of West Indies Press.

Hilliard, Sam B. 1984. *Atlas of Antebellum Southern Agriculture*. Baton Rouge: Louisiana State University Press.

Howe, Daniel Walker. 2007. *What Hath God Wrought: The Transformation of America, 1815–1848*. New York: Oxford University Press.

Jakobsson, Stiv. 1972. *Am I Not a Man and a Brother? British Missions and the Abolition of the Slave Trade and Slavery in West Africa and the West Indies 1786–1836.* Studia Missionalia Upsaliensia 17. Lund, Sweden: Gleerup.

Kaye, Anthony E. 2007. "Neighborhoods and Nat Turner: The Making of a Slave Rebel and the Unmaking of a Slave Rebellion." *Journal of the Early Republic* 27: 705–20.

Lyerly, Cynthia Lynn. 1998. *Methodism and the Southern Mind, 1770–1810.* New York: Oxford University Press.

Meacham, Sarah Hand. 2009. *Every Home a Distillery: Alcohol, Gender, and Technology.* Baltimore, MD: Johns Hopkins University Press.

Menard, Russell R. 2006. *Sweet Negotiations: Sugar, Slavery, and Plantation Agriculture in Early Barbados.* Charlottesville: University of Virginia Press.

Mintz, Sidney W. 1985. *Sweetness and Power: The Place of Sugar in Modern History.* New York: Viking.

Mohamed, Wazir. 2008. "Frustrated Peasants, Marginalized Workers: Free African Villages in Guyana, 1838–1885." Unpublished PhD diss., Binghamton University, Binghamton, NY.

Mullin, Michael. 1995. *Africa in America: Slave Acculturation and Resistance in the American South and the British Caribbean, 1736–1831.* Urbana: University of Illinois Press.

Najar, Monica. 2005. "'Meddling with Emancipation': Baptists, Authority, and the Rift over Slavery in the Upper South." *Journal of the Early Republic* 25 (2): 157–86.

Oates, Stephen B. 1975. *The Fires of Jubilee: Nat Turner's Fierce Rebellion.* New York: Harper and Row.

Ogborn, Miles. 2008. *Global Lives: Britain and the World, 1550–1800.* Cambridge, UK: Cambridge University Press.

Oostindie, Gert, and Alex van Stipriaan. 1995. "Slavery and Slave Cultures in a Hydraulic Society: Suriname." In *Slave Cultures and the Cultures of Slavery*, edited by Stephan Palmié. Knoxville: University of Tennessee Press: 78–99.

Patterson, Orlando. 1970. "Slavery and Slave Revolts: A Socio-Historical Analysis of the First Maroon War, 1655–1740." *Social and Economic Studies* 19 (3): 289–325.

Piggin, Stuart. 1980. "Halévy Revisited: The Origins of the Wesleyan Methodist Missionary Society: An Examination of Semmel's Thesis." *Journal of Imperial and Commonwealth History* 9: (1): 17–37.

Reckord, Mary. 1968. "The Jamaica Slave Rebellion of 1831." *Past and Present* 40: 108–25.

Reinhart, Theodore R., et al. 1987. *Material Culture, Social Relations, and Spatial Organization on a Colonial Frontier: The Pope Site (44SN180), Southampton County, Virginia.* Williamsburg, VA: Department of Anthropology, College of William and Mary.

Rodney, Walter. 1981. *A History of the Guyanese Working People, 1881–1905.* Baltimore, MD: Johns Hopkins University Press.

Scully, Randolph Ferguson. 2001. " 'Somewhat Liberated': Baptist Discourses of Race and Slavery in Nat Turner's Virginia, 1770–1840." *Explorations in Early American Culture* 5: 328–71.

———. 2007. " 'I Came Here before You Did, and I Shall Not Go Away': Race, Gender, and Evangelical Community on the Eve of the Nat Turner Rebellion." *Journal of the Early Republic* 27 (4): 661–84.

———. 2008. *Religion and the Making of Nat Turner's Virginia: Baptist Community and Conflict, 1740–1840.* Charlottesville: University of Virginia Press.

Vickers, Jason E. 2009. *Wesley.* London: Continuum.

Wallbridge, E. A. 1969. *The Demerara Martyr: Memoirs of the Rev. John Smith, Missionary to Demerara* (orig. 1848). New York: Negro Universities Press.

Watts, David. 1987. *The West Indies: Patterns of Development, Culture and Environmental Change since 1492.* Cambridge, UK: Cambridge University Press.

Archival Materials

Great Britain. Parliament. House of Commons. 1969. *Papers Relating to the Slave Trade, 1823–1824.* Vol. 66 of *Irish University Press Series of British Parliamentary Papers,* 95 vols. Shannon: Irish University Press.

Library of (Richmond) Virginia (LVA). Southampton County, Deed Books, Books 18–20.

Library of (Richmond) Virginia (LVA). Southampton County, Land Taxes, 1823, Book B.

Library of (Richmond) Virginia (LVA). Auditor of Public Accounts, Southampton County, Personal Property Tax Books, 1831.

London Missionary Society. 1824. *Report of the Proceedings against the late Rev. J. Smith.* London: F. Westley.

Yale Divinity School Library. Council of World Mission Archives (CWMA). J. C. Cheveley, *The Demerara Rising of 1823,* typescript of extracts, microfiches 785–92.

Yale Divinity School Library. CWMA. John Smith Journal, microfiches 785–92.

The American Civil War, Emancipation, and Nation-Building

A Comparative Perspective

Enrico Dal Lago

Increasingly, scholars are adopting a "transnational view" in studying the American Civil War, and recent syntheses of American history in transnational perspective have placed the Civil War in the context of contemporaneous events in Europe. Specifically, the central decades of the nineteenth century—the period between 1848 and 1870—saw the unfolding of the classic age of nation-building in Europe, with the rise of nationalist movements throughout the continent during the revolutionary period 1848–1849, followed by the consolidation of two new large nation-states in Italy and Germany. The significant connection between the American Civil War and the latter two events was well understood by Michael Geyer and Charles Bright, who, as early as 1996, had written that "the nation-making, state-creating, industrial and expansive outcome of war . . . makes the middle of the century wars of central Europe and North America similar" and comparable (1996: 620). Essentially, this point is similar to the one that transnational historians would argue in their treatment of the American Civil War as a process akin to Italian and German national unifications. As Carl Guarneri has written as recently as 2007, "the Northerners' plan to unite the states under a strong central government . . . aligned the American struggle with wars of national unification that were occurring in Europe and the Americas in the same decades" (2007: 158; see also Thomas Bender 2006; Doyle 2015).

Yet we cannot forget that despite all these striking similarities, the main difference between the American and European situations is that the Civil War did not merely re-unify a nation, it brought about the emancipation of four million slaves. Indeed, U.S. slave emancipation was such a significant event on a global scale that a number of scholars have focused, for at least the past twenty years, on specific comparisons between the uniquely violent process of emancipation during the American Civil War and the relatively peaceful ending of either slavery or serfdom in other areas of the Americas or in Europe. Currently, there is an ever-increasing scholarly interest in the comparative history of American emancipation, proceeding from Eric Foner's 1983 seminal study *Nothing but Freedom*. Subsequently, studies by scholars such as Steven Hahn, Stanley Engerman, Rebecca Scott, and Peter Kolchin have added a great deal to our understanding of how the ending of slavery in the United States should be seen in the wider context of events and measures occurring in an "age of emancipation"—which also, like the age of nation-building, spanned the central decades of the nineteenth century.

In this connection, it is particularly important to recognize that the "age of emancipation" and the age of nation-building in the Americas occurred as a result of transformations traceable to the making of the *second slavery*. At the end of the eighteenth century, the 1791–1804 Revolution in St. Domingue and the consequent emancipation of Haiti had signaled the end of the colonial system of slave production in the New World. Together with the abolition of the British and American Atlantic slave trades in 1807–1808, these led to the beginning of the "nationalization" of slavery as a major factor of national economic expansion, particularly in the U.S. South with regard to cotton and sugar production, in Cuba with sugar, and in Brazil with coffee. Due to their command of the world economy through their respective agricultural products and due to the particular technologically driven and capitalist-oriented nature of the "national" slave-based economies present within them, the nineteenth-century U.S. South, Cuba, and Brazil were at the heart of the phenomenon that Dale Tomich and Michael Zeuske have called *second slavery*. Such a phenomenon was strictly related to "the world-historical processes that transformed the Atlantic World between the 1780s and 1888" and that resulted in the "formation of highly productive new zones of slave commodity production" (2008: 91) in the U.S. South, Cuba, and Brazil, and, eventually, in their demise through processes of emancipation that happened in different ways and at different times. Essentially, the three regions at the heart of the second slavery went first through comparable, and somewhat similar, processes of "nationalization" of slavery, and then through comparable, though somewhat different, processes of "nationalization" of freedom.

Within this context, we have to think of the American Civil War as a process that, through the creation of a stronger, centralized, and reunified nation-state, led to the implementation of slave emancipation, and thus to the victory of the nationalization of freedom over the nationalization of slavery. If, on one hand, the Republican Party was very much instrumental in this process with its mild policy of prevention of the final "nationalization" of American slavery through its "containment" within the South, on the other hand Lincoln was certainly the one who, through the Emancipation Proclamation, gave the final blow to the Confederate States of America's project of nationalization of slavery. During the Civil War, such a project achieved only a temporary fulfillment with the transformation of the regional and sectional southern nationalism into a Confederate nationalism that led to the creation of a Confederate slaveholding nation separate from the United States. However, as a result of the Union's victory in the Civil War, the Republican project of "nationalization" of freedom achieved permanency within the United States and changed forever the very idea of the American nation, truly unifying it for the first time.

Thus, there is little doubt that the process of nation-building and the process of emancipation as they occurred in the United States through the American Civil War are very much related to one another and should be studied and understood in conjunction. Yet it is fair to say that, despite the fact that the two scholarships—

focusing on one hand on the Civil War in an age of nation-building, and on the other hand on U.S. slave emancipation in an "age of emancipation"—aim at building the foundations of a comparative perspective of two aspects of the same event, the American Civil War, contact between scholars working on these two fields has been scant. At the same time, studies claiming the comparability of one of these two aspects have generally made little or no reference to the comparability of the other aspect as well. With this essay, I intend to suggest possible ways to combine these two approaches, arguing that, to lay the foundations of a thorough comparative history of the American Civil War, we need to take into account, in equal measure and in comparative perspective, both its characteristics as a nation-building process and the significance of the central event of emancipation at its core. I believe that only by directing our investigative efforts toward explaining the multidimensional nature of the American Civil War as a conflict with a clearly global significance can we begin to understand the best and most accurate way to write its comparative history.

In a 1987 article titled "Thesis, Antithesis, Synthesis: The South, the North, and the Nation," Carl Degler used "Hegelian dialectic" to argue that he saw "American history as the interaction of North and South—a Hegelian synthesis that has emerged from the dialectic of a southern thesis and a northern antithesis" (1987: 18). Taking inspiration from that article, I wish to use a similar "Hegelian dialectic" to suggest a possible comparative perspective on the significance of the American Civil War in the nineteenth-century Euro-American world. In particular, I intend to use historical comparisons to elucidate the significance of the following three assumptions, which we should see as thesis, antithesis, and synthesis:

Thesis: the ideology of the Republican Party in the United States until the American Civil War had some characteristics in common with liberal nationalist ideologies in mid-nineteenth-century Europe and liberal ideologies in Latin America, particularly in terms of its "moderate" and nonrevolutionary character.

Antithesis: the occurrence of slave emancipation during the American Civil War was a revolutionary event with radical features that set it apart from all other processes of emancipation from unfree labor occurring in the nineteenth-century

Euro-American world and places it in clear opposition to the mild antislavery policy of the antebellum Republican Party.

Synthesis: the actual process of nation-building in the United States through the reconstitution of the Union during the Civil War—in which Abraham Lincoln played a crucial role—shows a unique feature, in comparison with similar and contemporary processes, in having been the factor that made possible the transformation of the mild antislavery nationalist ideology of the Republican Party into one that allowed more room for Radical Republicans, and thus contemplated the possibility of a revolutionary act such as slave emancipation.[1]

The U.S. Republican Party and Euro-American Liberal Nationalism

As early as 1968, focusing on the universality of the idea of liberty in nation-building struggles, David Potter first argued the comparability of the Civil War era in the United States with nineteenth-century European nationalist movements. However, while many of the points Potter made more than forty years ago are usually included in short comparative treatments by current transnational and comparative historians, Potter's argument on the specific comparability of the processes of nation-building in the United States and Europe in the early 1860s is still only rarely given the importance it deserves (1968). Also, I would argue that, given Potter's emphasis on the liberal aspects of nineteenth-century nationalism, a thorough comparative view of the American Civil War should make reference not just to European, but also to Latin American varieties of liberal and liberal nationalist ideologies as they expressed themselves in the first six decades of the nineteenth century. Thus, when looking at the Civil War era in the United States in comparison with both Europe and Latin America, a question that comes to mind as particularly important is whether the principles supported by the Republican Party, which would guide the Union and reconstitute the American nation, had common traits with the principles of the movements supporting liberal nationalism that sprang up all over the Euro-American world, starting from the early decades of the nineteenth century.

According to Peter Parish, we can best describe the ideology of the American Republican Party in the 1850s as "Republican nationalism"; in his own words, "the key to Republican nationalism may be found in the notion of the Republican Party as a party of improvement . . . [since] Republicans espoused the cause of human betterment and, in the process, linked the idea of the Union to the cause of such betterment" (2003: 118). Similarly to European and Latin American liberals, in fact, American Republicans—akin to their forerunners the Whigs—put the accent on progress, both in material, or economic, terms and in moral terms. Also, comparably to European and Latin American liberals and liberal nationalists, American Republicans linked this progress—of which an essential feature was opposition to slavery—to the very idea of the nation, or, in the case of the United States, to the Union.[2]

In particular, encompassing within itself the different elements of Republican ideology and referring to contemporary ideas that informed liberal nations and liberal-nationalist struggles throughout the Euro-American world, Abraham Lincoln's focus was firmly on the indissolubility of the Union—that is, the American nation—as a thought, an ideal, and a concrete political institution. He best expressed this view in Springfield, Illinois, in 1858, in the "House Divided" speech—his acceptance speech for the Republican candidacy to the Illinois post in the U.S. Senate. In that speech, Lincoln expressed already in definitive form the main guidelines of his thought, which then became the official doctrine of the Republican Party. For the first time on that occasion, Lincoln argued forcefully against slavery's expansion into the western territories, and, referring to a New Testament analogy, he compared the Union to a "house divided against itself," whose situation ought to find a solution either in favor of liberty, as he hoped, or in favor of slavery—as he made clear through the words "this government cannot endure, permanently half *slave* and half *free*" (Johnson 2001: 125, emphasis in the original). With this inspiring analogy, therefore, Lincoln placed at the center of what Ian Tyrrell has termed his "politics of moderate, liberal nationalism" (2007: 87) the integrity of the Union, and focused specifically on the consequences of the problem of slavery's expansion, though not on abolition of slavery, which threatened both the integrity and the commitment to freedom of the American nation.[3]

There is more than one parallel between Lincoln's "moderate" vision of the reunified American nation and the contemporaneous European liberal nationalist movements. To be sure, given the emphasis of liberalism on the individual and of nationalism on the community, at first sight the two ideologies might seem to have proven incompatible; however, the truth was that, quite simply, in nineteenth-century Europe, in the words of Mark Hewitson, "most liberals viewed the nation-state as a natural entity" (2006: 354), to the point that even the never-ending debate over whether their nationalism was "civic" or "ethnic" seems to pale and lose all significance. Like the American Revolution, the French Revolution in its early phase had established that a nation was a voluntary community of responsible individual citizens and that it was to protect the basic individual and universal rights. Together with the important influence of British constitutional thought, these basic ideas continued to be at the center of liberal nationalist ideology for the best part of seven decades in nineteenth-century Europe and to inspire struggles against autocratic rule that demanded the formation of nations based on "freedom of the press, the rule of law, constitutional government, and greater political participation in the affairs of the state"—struggles that would reach their peak with the 1848–1849 European revolutions (2006: 43). However, the 1848–1849 revolutions also showed that throughout Europe, liberal nationalists were not prepared to make concessions to the wider masses in terms of sharing actual governmental power. As a consequence, post-1848 European "liberal national movements," in the words of Stefan Berger, "practiced a range of exclusionary mechanisms directed against the lower social classes" (2006: 43). In this, Europe's liberal nationalists showed that their ideology was antirevolutionary, antiradical, and "moderate" (Hewitson 2006: 353).[4]

Akin to, and contemporaneous with, the evolution of liberal-nationalist thought and practice in Europe, liberalism in Latin America went through different stages, which in similar fashion led to an ultimate conservative involution in most of the countries that had freed themselves from Europe's colonial yoke by the time politics entered the central decades of the nineteenth century. After 1825 and the achievement of independence, with the beginning of the Early National Period (1825–1850), the Creole elites, landowners, and intellectuals who ruled the newly born Latin American republics found themselves with the difficult task of governing countries that were extremely large and diverse and where the majority of the population was illiterate. Still, initially, the liberalism that characterized the elites in power led them to make repeated attempts to create constitutions that initially supported—consistent with the goals of liberal elites throughout the Euro-American world in the first half of the nineteenth century—"enlightened goals which generally favored elections, equality before the law, freedom of speech, educational reform, and industrialization." However, after 1850—also consistent with the general trend of liberal thought in the Euro-American world—as a result of the recrudescence of social division between different classes, the rapid rise of *caudillos* as the guarantors of order and stability, and the continuous rift between supporters of stronger centralized governments and supporters of devolution of power, the elites in power in the different Latin American countries quite simply turned to a more conservative form of liberalism (Fowler 2008: 38; see also Brading 1991; Rodriguez 1998; Lynch 1994).

Comparison between the ideology of the U.S. Republican Party and both European liberal nationalism and Latin American liberalism highlights the similarity between particular features of "Republican nationalism" and liberal nationalist thought in the Euro-American world. Specifically, by the central decades of the nineteenth century, liberal nationalism in Europe and liberalism in Latin America had evolved into conservative, or "moderate," versions of the ideologies that had inspired the European revolutions of 1848 and the 1820s struggles for Latin American independence. By the time both continents had reached the central decades of the nineteenth century, faced with the prospect of a class war prompted by radical programs, the European and Latin American middle classes had closed ranks and focused on a narrow interpretation of the idea of protection of liberties and political participation, effectively excluding the majority of the population. At the same time, though, in both Europe and Latin America, liberal intellectuals and politicians had continued to agitate for constitutional reform and parliamentary representation, while sharing a deep belief in the link between economic and civil progress and nation-building. Keeping in mind the differences due to the existence of universal male suffrage in the United States and its absence in both Europe and Latin America at this time, we can say that these are points of comparison with the ideology of "Republican nationalism" advanced by Lincoln and the Republican Party in the United States. First, there is little doubt that the link between economic and civil progress and the cause of the Union—that is, the American nation—was a top priority in the Republican agenda. At the same time, though, we can link the more conservative or "moderate" features of European liberal nationalism and Latin American liberalism to the ideology of the Republican Party, if we think that the party was committed to a passive opposition to slavery rather than to its abolition, therefore effectively excluding a large section of the American population from the enjoyment of basic liberties and civil rights. This was comparable to the way European and Latin American liberals excluded large sections of the populations of different countries on the basis of property rights and literacy.[5]

Emancipations: Ending Slavery and Serfdom

An immensely important and unexpected outcome of the American Civil War was the 1863 Emancipation Proclamation, which resulted in the freedom of four million slaves. Without minimizing the importance of this event, we should see it in its proper comparative context by noticing that it occurred at a time—the second half of the nineteenth century—when emancipation from unfree labor extended progressively to all the countries where either slavery or serfdom still existed. Building on the important foundations established by the Atlantic abolitionist movements of the earlier part of the century, and by previous momentous pieces of legislation—particularly the 1833 British Act of Emancipation and the 1848 law that freed all the slaves in the French colonies—movements for the abolition of unfree labor gathered new momentum specifically in the four decades included between 1850 and 1890. The Spanish American countries that had not abolished slavery at the moment of their formation in the 1820s did so: in the ten years between 1851 and 1861, all the remaining Spanish American republics—aside from Paraguay, which waited until 1869—proceeded to free their slaves (Benjamin 2009: 615–51).

By the time the American Civil War started, therefore, slavery had disappeared from most of the Americas; it remained entrenched only in Cuba and Brazil, where it had thrived under the second slavery, until it was finally abolished by 1888. Concurrent with this gathering of momentum in the movement for the abolition of slavery, though, was the parallel and contemporaneous movement for the abolition of serfdom, which in this case built on the example of provisions made at the time of the 1848 revolutions to free the peasantry in both Prussia and the Habsburg lands. As a result, by 1860, serfdom still existed only in Romania and Russia, and in the space of five years it would disappear from there as well, as first Russia in 1861 and then Romania in 1864 freed their serfs. It is worth noticing that, despite the fact that by this time it was restricted to these two countries, the emancipation of Eastern European serfdom affected a much larger number of individuals than slavery in the Americas—certainly more than twice as many. In fact, the number of serfs emancipated in the 1860s was well over twenty million, in contrast with the much lower number of slaves emancipated in the period 1850–1890; see M. L. Bush (2000: 177–99).

In the United States, a combination of factors during the American Civil War led Lincoln to support the idea of slave emancipation, in an unprecedented development contrary to the previous mild antislavery policy of the Republican Party. Particularly, the progressive pressure exercised by the growing problem of runaway slaves turning up in Union camps became one of the main factors that created the necessary conditions for the Union government's and Lincoln's gradual inclination toward a more radical position regarding the problem of slavery. At the same time, the views of the Republican Party itself were increasingly radical, also under the continuous pressure exercised in Congress by Radical Republicans—many of whom were former abolitionists—aiming to reach quickly their favored solution: the complete end of slavery. At the same time, Lincoln's views also changed, and on September 22, 1862, after the Union victory at the battle of Antietam in Maryland, he released a first version of the Emancipation Proclamation, which he then modified and released in its definitive form on January 1, 1863. As many scholars have noted, Lincoln's Emancipation Proclamation abolished slavery only in those Confederate territories not yet reached by the Union Army—which, therefore, could not contribute to its enactment—and did not mention the slaves who were already in Union-occupied territories. Still, there is no doubt that it was a revolutionary act of immense significance, not only because, with an unprecedented action, it abolished slavery legally, both immediately and in perpetuity, but also because, wherever they arrived, the Union soldiers now acted as troops of a liberation army, officially instructed by the Union government "to recognize and maintain the freedom of such persons [meaning the slaves]," as the Proclamation stated (Lincoln [1863] 2002: 380).[6]

There is little in the process of abolition of slavery in Brazil that resembles that of the United States; in fact, in comparison, Brazilian slavery ended in a relatively peaceful way. Starting from the mid-1860s, the imperial government started enacting a series of acts against slavery, culminating in the 1871 Rio Branco Law. Similarly to the Moret Law in Cuba, the Rio Branco Law in Brazil freed the children born of slave mothers after 1871. However, it was only in the 1880s that the movement for the abolition of slavery became widespread; by that time, international pressure was reaching an all-time high, since Brazil was the only large-scale slave society still in existence in the Americas, while planters in the northeastern sugar regions began to look for alternatives to slavery. First, starting with Ceará in 1884, different provinces in Brazil took the initiative of abolishing slavery; then, abolitionist organizations sprang up in Sao Paulo and Rio de Janeiro. Meanwhile, the imperial government passed the Dantas-Saraiva-Cotegipe Law, which in 1885 freed slaves who were sixty-five years of age. At the same time, from 1886, an increasingly massive number of runaway slaves, taking matters into their own hands, started to leave plantations and farms, contributing in a major way to forcing the issue of emancipation. Finally, the imperial government acknowledged the de facto unmanageability of the situation and proclaimed the immediate end of slavery throughout Brazil with the Golden Law of 1888. It is interesting to notice that Brazil's Golden Law is similar to the U.S. 1863 Emancipation Proclamation as a governmental decree that freed the slaves immediately and without any form of compensation for slaveholders. Although comparable, the two cases are clearly the results of very different processes, and are both unique in slave societies in the Americas (Costa 1989: 161–213; Schmidt-Nowara 2008: 114–15; Klein and Luna 2010: 295–320; Conrad 1972).

During the same period in which the process of abolition of slavery took place in the last slave systems in the Americas, a parallel process leading to the abolition of serfdom occurred in Eastern Europe. By 1860, serfdom was present almost exclusively in Romania and Russia. The czar promulgated the law that abolished serfdom in Russia on February 19, 1861, freeing at once more than twenty million bondsmen. Extremely long and immensely complicated, the legislation created new officials called "peace mediators," who, even though serf-owners themselves, were supposed to help peasants in their transition from slavery to freedom—a transition that was to be gradual rather than sudden. As Peter Kolchin has remarked, "peasants received their 'personal freedom' at once . . . but they remained under the 'estate police and guardianship' of their former owners" (1999: 92), to whom they continued to owe services either in the form of *barshchina* or *obrok*. Within two years from the 1861 decree, the *pomeshchiki* (landlords) were to draw charters detailing the nature of the exserfs' obligations and of their land allotments. At the end of the two years, house servants were free with no land, while all other exserfs could become free from their temporary obligations only by paying for their land allotments, and therefore becoming proprietors, in a process called "redemption." According to Kolchin, it took twenty years for the majority of the peasants to become proprietors, since only by 1881 did four-fifths of them finally own land. Thus, as in most other situations of transition from unfree labor to freedom—but in complete contrast with both the 1863 slave emancipation in the United States and the 1889 slave emancipation in Brazil—in Russia formerly unfree laborers were still bound by the law to provide additional work for a number of years as a form of compensation to their former owners (1992: 88–95; see also Kolchin 1996: 42–68; Moon 2001).

As Michael L. Bush has written, "the coincidental termination of New World slavery and European serfdom" was "a major event in the history of modern servitude" (2000: 177). From our perspective, though, comparisons between the two concurrent processes of abolition of unfree labor show that slave emancipation in the United States shares only a few characteristics with the abolition of slavery in other parts of the Americas and the abolition of serfdom in Eastern Europe; instead, it has, for the most part, unique features. The main similar characteristic is that, even though recent scholarship has correctly placed much more emphasis on the slaves' agency in the U.S. process of emancipation—as was also the case in Brazil and Cuba—the actual document that decreed the end of slavery in the U.S. South was a proclamation released by the national government, no differently than the abolition of serfdom and all the other cases of abolition of slavery, apart from Haiti. On the other hand—again with the very notable exception of Haitian slave emancipation—the U.S. Emancipation Proclamation of 1863 appears completely different in content from all the other decrees emancipating either slaves or serfs, for two particular reasons: first, it freed the slaves immediately and permanently, and second, it provided no compensation for slaveholders. In contrast, as Stanley Engerman has recently shown, the other emancipation decrees—including those emancipating serfs—always gave guidelines for a process of gradual emancipation, whose main purpose was to provide for some form of compensation to the former owners of unfree laborers (2008: 265–82). Thus, in comparative perspective and in a wider Euro-American framework, the 1863 U.S. Emancipation Proclamation and the subsequent 1865 Thirteenth Amendment to the Constitution appear truly exceptional and significant because of the uniqueness of their radical provisions. In sum, the comparative perspective reinforces the idea that, in releasing the U.S. Emancipation Proclamation, in many ways, Lincoln committed an unprecedented revolutionary act. This is especially true if we think about it also in the context of the antebellum and early Civil War policy of the Republican Party that he headed, which was both "moderate" and mildly antislavery—and certainly characterized by an attitude of nonintervention with regard to the abolition of slavery.

Making Nations in the Euro-American World

When we turn to the actual process of nation-building that occurred through the American Civil War, we cannot help but notice that, until relatively recently, the best-known studies by historians and sociologists on the phenomenon of constructing nations in the central decades of the nineteenth century tended to focus on Europe, and sometimes Asia or Latin America, mostly leaving aside the United States. Only in the past two decades, also as a result of the "transnational turn" in American historiography, American historians such as Thomas Bender, Carl Guarneri, and others have turned their attention to the international context of the nineteenth-century formation of the American nation and have connected it with the historiography on contemporary European nationalist movements. At present, there is a small but steadily increasing number of transnational studies that look at the United States in its transnational context, focusing specifically on the idea of the nation and its use and reception on both sides of the Atlantic.

Valid hints at possible comparisons in this sense can still come from the studies of both David Potter and Carl Degler, who in the 1960s and 1970s pioneered comparative investigation of the United States in the antebellum and Civil War era. To be sure, Degler's studies—and later, the studies of other scholars who came in his wake—dealt mainly with the Civil War as a military event that could be fruitfully compared with the wars for German unification, but in regard to ideology he had to admit that "historians of the United States have not liked to compare Bismarck and Lincoln" (1992: 106) due to the former's illiberal tendencies. On the other hand, David Potter's research, as we have mentioned, focused instead on the political culture expressed in Lincoln's and the Republican Party's view of the nation as akin to the liberal strand of nationalism that pervaded contemporary

Europe. In this sense, Potter found that a better match for a comparative study would have been *Risorgimento* Italy—the nation whose 1861 creation signified more than any other the victory of liberal nationalist principles.

It was really in the 1863 Gettysburg Address that Lincoln's vision for the American nation found its most complete expression. In it, Lincoln reminded Americans of how the Revolution had founded "a new nation, conceived in Liberty, and dedicated to the proposition that all men are created equal" and proclaimed solemnly that "this nation, under God, shall have a new birth of freedom" (Johnson 2001: 263). Therefore, in envisioning the new American nation that was to emerge after the Civil War, Lincoln reaffirmed the validity of the liberal principles of the Declaration of Independence as its foundation and reiterated his own interpretation of the American Civil War as a struggle for national reunification along not just "Republican nationalist," but truly, inclusively, democratic lines. In this respect, it is possible to say that with Lincoln's crucial contribution, the process of nation-building and reunification in the United States led to a novel "invented tradition" of nationhood. This tradition, for the first time, was inclusive of both whites and blacks and, uniquely in the Euro-American world, made possible the combination of the "moderate" principles of "Republican nationalism" and the revolutionary character of slave emancipation.[7]

Despite the very different contexts and concepts of freedom and nation, we can make comparable comments in terms of novelty and an "invented tradition" of nationhood when we turn to Italian national unification, and therefore to the process of nation-building as guided by Cavour and the Moderate Liberals during the Italian *Risorgimento*. Similarly to slave emancipation in the United States, national unification in Italy entailed a combination of factors, some of which were, however, accidental. Even though in 1859 Cavour's plan was for a constitutional Kingdom of Northern Italy, he had struck an alliance with some of the most important democratic leaders, who gathered in the National Society, an organization largely controlled by him and dedicated to achieving national Italian unity under the Moderate Liberals. Among its members was Giuseppe Garibaldi, who decided single-handedly to proceed to the military conquest of the Bourbon kingdom in the Italian south, which he achieved by October 1860. He then handed it over to the Piedmontese king, Victor Emmanuel II, thus ending Cavour's fears that Italy might end up divided in two conflicting northern and southern sections. Shortly afterward, Cavour spoke in Parliament in October 1860 on the subject of ratifying southern Italy's annexation. In his speech, Cavour remarked that "in the last two years, Italy has given a wonderful example of civil wisdom by her attachment to the principles of order, morality and civilization" and advocated as a witness "the impartial voice of enlightened, liberal Europe" (Mack Smith 1988: 326–27), which significantly clarified the decisively liberal and antirevolutionary character of Italy's national unification.[8]

To be sure, a comparative and transnational study of the American Civil War and Italy's *Risorgimento*—the term indicating the actual movement for national unification—would, more than a study of the American Civil War and Germany's national unification, certainly show its primary value as being a test of sorts. Such a test would lead to our better understanding of the ideas and practices of what Peter Parish has called "meliorative nationalism." Parish makes specific reference to Lincoln and the American Republican Party—because of the link between the ideas of progress and freedom at its core—but we could equally apply this expression to the ideology that characterized Cavour and Italy's Moderate Liberals, which was effectively the political movement that guided Italy's process of unification. In short, through this specific comparison, it is possible to investigate the practice of what several nineteenth-century observers thought of as two parallel exercises in "progressive" nation-building on the two sides of the Atlantic in the mid-nineteenth century. In turn, such a study may be particularly beneficial in showing how mid-nineteenth-century American politics were also part of a much wider context—a context as much Atlantic as genuinely Euro-American. In this sense, the United States and Italy were but two of many different parts of a nineteenth-century political milieu that—as C. A. Bayly has shown in *The Birth of the Modern World*—was much more "global" than we once thought (2004; Dal Lago 2015).

At the same time, though, comparison shows clearly that the American Civil War is a case study of nation-building unique in the entire Euro-American world, a case study only partly comparable, in particular, to Italy's national unification. The American Civil War's unique characteristics derive from the fact that it was a nation-constructing process that occurred with the help of a very particular type of nationalist ideology—that which Peter Parish has called "Republican nationalism"—even though it shared some common features with the European type of liberal nationalism that characterized Italy's Moderate Liberals. Unlike the nationalist ideology that characterized Cavour and his allies, though, "Republican nationalism" had within itself the potential for radicalizing, and it did in fact increasingly radicalize during the conflict resulting from nation-building during the American Civil War, to the point that by 1863, it included a major revolutionary element, slave emancipation. In this sense, therefore, comparison reinforces, rather than debunks, the very idea of American exceptionalism in relation to the unique coexistence in the American Civil War of an originally moderate concept of nation-building with a later radical, and even revolutionary, emancipationist idea.

Conclusion

We can look at nationalist ideology, the making of slave emancipation, and the actual process of nation-building as three different elements of a "Hegelian dialectic" that are equally important in understanding the American Civil War. Each of these three elements shows a few remarkable similarities with and some striking differences from other manifestations of nationalism, emancipation, and nation-building in other areas of the Atlantic world and beyond. Such similarities and differences help us to better place the significance of the American Civil War in its proper global context, since it makes it possible to grasp its unique character. To begin with the first element of the Hegelian dialectic—the thesis—comparison with both Europe and Latin America shows that the Republican Party's and Abraham Lincoln's focus on the importance of the American Union as the defender of the principles of freedom and progress has something in common with liberal nationalist movements and liberal ideologies in most of the nineteenth-century

Euro-American world, in terms of both the emphasis on the indissoluble link between national progress and basic civil rights and of the nonradical character of its demands. Instead, comparison with the process of abolishing slavery in Cuba and Brazil, the other two large-scale slave societies in the Americas, and with the process of abolishing serfdom in Eastern Europe, particularly in Romania and Russia, shows that slave emancipation in the United States—the second element in Hegelian dialectic, or antithesis—occurred with mostly unique characteristics, as several historians have already noticed. Those characteristics mainly relate to the much more radical departure that the 1863 Emancipation Proclamation—which decreed immediate and permanent freedom for the slaves with no compensation for slaveholders—represented compared to both the mild antislavery policy of the antebellum Republican Party and the processes of gradual emancipation occurring everywhere else in the Euro-American world.

We would be entitled to see these two elements—the "moderate" type of Union-focused "Republican nationalism" with a noninterventionist antislavery component and the "radical" step of emancipating slaves—as antithetical, as they actually were to a certain extent. However, we should also acknowledge that the actual process of nation-building in the United States through the American Civil War—the third element in Hegelian dialectic, "Synthesis"—succeeded in creating the conditions for their harmonious coexistence in a way that is not comparable to any other process of nation construction in the Euro-American world. This coexistence, though, could not have been possible without the particular characteristics of the Republican nationalist ideology of the Republican Party. This ideology had the potential to transform a moderate appeal to the deepest American national identity into a radical message of inclusive freedom if the circumstances of nation-building turned out to be propitious for such transformation, as happened under Lincoln's skillful guidance. In this sense, the ideology that characterized Lincoln and the Republican Party by 1863 represented a new departure in the idea of American nationhood—one that, even keeping in mind the crucial differences in contents and contexts, is only very generally comparable to the new departure represented by Cavour and the Moderate Liberals in Italy in the same years, despite David Potter's accent on their common traits. In fact, that new departure in the United States created the fundamental preconditions for the making of the exceptional character of the American Civil War as a process of nation-building—a process that joined together, uniquely in the Euro-American world, the "meliorative" and "moderate" brand of "Republican nationalism" with the revolutionary act of slave emancipation.

Still uniquely within the Euro-American world, the revolutionary dimension of U.S. slave emancipation would have led to subsequent equally revolutionary transformations in the concept of national citizenship during the period of Reconstruction (1865–1877). In particular, during the phase of Radical or Congressional Reconstruction, the Radical Republicans who dominated Congress and national politics redefined the concept of national citizenship by acting further on the idea of "inclusive" freedom, not only through officially sanctioning the end of "national" slavery in the United States with the passing of the Thirteenth Amendment (1865), but through making specific legislation that protected the civil rights, and particularly the right to enfranchisement, of the newly freed African American population with the passing of the Fourteenth and Fifteenth Amendments (1868 and 1870). In this respect, in comparison with the postbellum U.S. South, no government in postunification Italy ever implemented policies as revolutionary as the ones of the Congressional Reconstruction. Indeed, as was typical throughout the contemporary Euro-American world, the "exclusive" vision that dominated Italy's Moderate Liberals created a highly stratified new nation, where the concept of citizenship effectively remained the exclusive domain of a small elite of noblemen, landowners, and professionals—in practice, a perfect example of the parable followed by liberalism in both Europe and the Latin American nations during the course of the nineteenth century.

Notes

1. Modern critics have disputed Hegel's actual paternity of "Hegelian dialectic"; see particularly Walter Kaufmann (1965).

2. See particularly Sean Wilentz (2005: 701–02).

3. See also Eric Foner (2010: 99–103) and Richard Carwardine (2007: 76–78).

4. On "civic" and "ethnic" nationalism, see especially Liah Greenfeld (1995); on liberalism and nationalism, Mark Haugaard (2006: 345–56).

5. For some important comparative points, see Nicholas and Peter Onuf (2006).

6. See also especially Foner (2010: 166–206), Ira Berlin et al. (1992: 1–76), Louis Gerteis (2009: 170–194), Michael Vorenberg (2001), and Oakes (2013).

7. See also Gary Wills (1993), Harry V. Jaffa (2000: 73–152), and David Herbert Donald (1995: 460–66). On the "invention of tradition" in relation to nation-building, see Eric J. Hobsbawm (1983: 13).

8. See also especially Luciano Cafagna (1999), Adriano Viarengo (2010), Lucy Riall (2009), and Rosario Romeo (1963).

Works Cited

Bancroft, Timothy, and Mark Hewitson, eds. 2006. *What Is a Nation? Europe, 1789–1914*. Oxford, UK: Oxford University Press.

Bayly, Christopher A. 2004. *The Birth of the Modern World, 1780–1914: Global Connections and Comparisons*. Oxford, UK: Blackwell.

Bender, Thomas. 2006. *A Nation among Nations: America's Place in World History*. New York: Hill and Wang.

Benjamin, Thomas. 2009. *The Atlantic World: Europeans, Africans, Indians and their Shared History, 1400–1900*. New York: Cambridge University Press.

Berger, Stefan. 2006. "Germany: Ethnic Nationalism par Excellence?" In *What is a Nation? Europe, 1789–1914*, edited by Timothy Bancroft and Mark Hewitson. New York: Oxford University Press, 42–61.

Berlin, Ira, et al. 1992. *Slaves No More: Three Essays on Emancipation and the Civil War*. New York: Cambridge University Press.

Brading, David A. 1991. *The First America: The Spanish Monarchy, Creole Patriots, and the Liberal State, 1492–1867*. Cambridge, UK: Cambridge University Press.

Bush, Michael L. 2000. *Servitude in Modern Times*. Cambridge, UK: Polity.

Cafagna, Luciano. 1999. *Cavour*. Bologna, Italy: Il Mulino.

Carwardine, Richard. 2007. *Lincoln: A Life of Purpose and Power.* New York: Vintage Books.

Conrad, Robert. 1972. *The Destruction of Brazilian Slavery: 1850–1888.* Berkeley, CA: University of California Press.

Costa, Emilia Viotti da. 1989. "1870–1889." In *Brazil: Empire and Republic, 1822–1930,* edited by Leslie Bethell. New York: Cambridge University Press, 161–213.

Dal Lago, Enrico. 2015. *The Age of Lincoln and Cavour: Comparative Perspectives on Nineteenth-Century American and Italian Nation-Building.* New York: Palgrave.

Degler, Carl N. 1987. "Thesis, Antithesis, Synthesis: The South, the North, and the Nation." *Journal of Southern History* 53 (1): 18.

———. 1992. "One among Many: The United States and National Unification." In *Lincoln, the War President: The Gettysburg Lectures,* edited by Gabor Boritt and Robert V. Bruce. New York: Oxford University Press, 89–120.

Donald, David Herbert. 1995. *Lincoln.* New York: Simon and Schuster.

Doyle, Don H. 2015. *The Cause of All Nations: An International History of the American Civil War.* New York: Basic Books.

Engerman, Stanley L. 2008. "Emancipation Schemes: Different Ways of Ending Slavery." In *Slave Systems: Ancient and Modern,* edited by Enrico Dal Lago and Constantina Katsari. Cambridge, UK: Cambridge University Press, 265–82.

Foner, Eric. 1983. *Nothing but Freedom: Emancipation and Its Legacy.* Baton Rouge: Louisiana State University Press.

———. 2010. *The Fiery Trial: Abraham Lincoln and American Slavery.* New York: W. W. Norton.

Fowler, Will. 2008. *Latin America Since 1780.* London: Hodder Education.

Gerteis, Louis. 2009. "Slaves, Servants, and Soldiers: Uneven Paths to Freedom in the Border States, 1861–1865." In *Lincoln's Proclamation: Emancipation Reconsidered,* edited by William A. Blair and Karen Fischer Younger. Chapel Hill: University of North Carolina Press, 170–94.

Geyer, Michael, and Charles Bright. 1996. "Global Violence and Nationalizing Wars in Eurasia and America: The Geopolitics of War in the Mid-Nineteenth Century." *Comparative Studies in Society and History* 38 (4): 619–57.

Greenfeld, Liah. 1995. *Nationalism: Five Roads to Modernity.* Cambridge, MA: Harvard University Press.

Guarneri, Carl. 2007. *America in the World: United States History in Global Context.* New York: McGraw-Hill.

Haugaard, Mark. 2006. "Nationalism and Liberalism." In *The Sage Handbook of Nations and Nationalism*, edited by Gerard Delanty and Krishan Kumar. London: Sage, 345–56.

Hewitson, Mark. 2006. "Conclusion." In *What Is a Nation? Europe, 1789–1914*, edited by Timothy Bancroft and Mark Hewitson. New York: Oxford University Press, 312–55.

Hobsbawm, Eric J. 1983. "Introduction: Inventing Traditions." In *The Invention of Tradition*, edited by Eric J. Hobsbawm and Terence Ranger. Cambridge, UK: Cambridge University Press, 1–14.

Jaffa, Harry V. 2000. *A New Birth of Freedom: Abraham Lincoln and the Coming of the Civil War*. Lanham, MD: Rowman and Littlefield.

Kaufmann, Walter A. 1965. *Hegel: Reinterpretation*. Garden City, NY: Doubleday.

Klein, Herbert S., and Francisco Vidal Luna. 2010. *Slavery in Brazil*. New York: Cambridge University Press.

Kolchin, Peter. 1996. "Some Controversial Questions concerning Nineteenth-Century Emancipation from Slavery and Serfdom." In *Serfdom and Slavery: Studies in Legal Bondage*, edited by M. L. Bush. New York: Longman, 42–68.

———. 1999. "After Serfdom: Russian Emancipation in Comparative Perspective." In *Terms of Labor: Slavery, Serfdom, and Free Labor*, edited by Stanley L. Engerman. Stanford, CA: Stanford University Press, 88–95.

Lincoln, Abraham. 2001. "The 'House Divided' Speech" (orig. 1858). In *Abraham Lincoln, Slavery, and the Civil War: Selected Writings and Speeches*, edited by Michael P. Johnson. Boston: Bedford St. Martin's, 125.

———. 2001. "Gettysburg Address" (orig. 1863). In *Abraham Lincoln, Slavery, and the Civil War: Selected Writings and Speeches*, edited by Michael P. Johnson. Boston: Bedford St. Martin's, 263.

———. 2002. "Emancipation Proclamation" (orig. 1863). In *Slavery and Emancipation*, edited by Rick Halpern and Enrico Dal Lago. Oxford: Blackwell, 380.

Lynch, John, and Robert A. Humphreys, eds. 1994. *Latin American Revolutions, 1808–1826: Old and New World Origins*. Norman, OK: University of Oklahoma Press.

Mack Smith, Denis, ed. 1988. *The Making of Italy, 1796–1866*. New York: Palgrave, 326–27.

Moon, David. 2001. *The Abolition of Serfdom in Russia, 1762–1907*. Harlow, UK: Longman.

Oakes, James. 2013. *Freedom National: The Destruction of Slavery in the United States, 1861–1865*. New York: Norton.

Onuf, Nicholas G., and Peter S. Onuf. 2006. *Nations, Markets, and War: Modern History and the American Civil War*. Charlottesville: University of Virginia Press.

Parish, Peter J., Adam I. P. Smith, and Susan-Mary Grant. 2003. *The North and the Nation in the Era of the Civil War*. New York: Fordham University Press.

Potter, David. 1968. "Civil War." In *The Comparative Approach to American History*, edited by C. Vann Woodward. New York: Basic Books.

Riall, Lucy. 2009. *Risorgimento: The History of Italy from Napoleon to Nation-State*. New York: Palgrave Macmillan.

Rodriguez, Jaime E. 1998. *The Independence of Spanish America*. New York: Cambridge University Press.

Romeo, Rosario. 1963. *Dal Piemonte sabaudo all'Italia liberale*. Rome-Bari: Laterza.

Schmidt-Nowara, Christopher. 2008. "Empires against Emancipation: Spain, Brazil, and the Abolition of Slavery." *Review* 31 (2): 114–19.

Tomich, Dale, and Michael Zeuske. 2008. "Introduction, The Second Slavery: Mass Slavery, World-Economy, and Comparative Microhistories." *Review* 31 (2): 91–100.

Tyrrell, Ian R. 2007. *Transnational Nation: United States History in Global Perspective since 1789*. New York: Palgrave Macmillan.

Viarengo, Adriano. 2010. *Cavour*. Rome: Salerno.

Vorenberg, Michael. 2001. *Final Freedom: The Civil War, the Abolition of Slavery, and the Thirteenth Amendment*. New York: Cambridge University Press.

Wilentz, Sean. 2005. *The Rise of American Democracy: Jefferson to Lincoln*. New York: Norton.

Wills, Gary. 1993. *Lincoln at Gettysburg: The Words that Remade America*. New York: Simon and Schuster.

CONTRIBUTORS

ENRICO DAL LAGO—teaches American history at the National University of Ireland, Galway. He is author of several books, the latest of which is *The Age of Lincoln and Cavour: Comparative Perspectives on Nineteenth-Century American and Italian Nation-Building* (Palgrave, 2015).

LUIS MIGUEL GARCÍA MORA—researcher and director of publications at the Fundación MAPFRE (Madrid). A specialist in the political history of Cuba, he has published widely on Cuban and Caribbean history, including *Los ingenios: Colección de vistas de los principales ingenios de azúcar de la isla de Cuba*, coauthored with Justo G. Cantero, Eduardo Laplante, and Antonio Santamaría García (2005). With Alejandro García he compiled and wrote the introduction to *Textos clásicos de la historia de Cuba* (Fundación Histórica Tavera, 1999; CD-ROM), and with Eduardo Torres-Cuevas he directed the electronic edition of *Biblioteca digital de clásicos cubanos: Orígenes del pensamiento cubano*, I (Fundación Mapfre-Tavera, Casa de Altos Estudios Don Fernando Ortiz, 2002; CD-ROM). He has also served on numerous editorial boards, including *Revista de Indias*.

ANTHONY E. KAYE—associate professor of history at Pennsylvania State University, and the Robert F. and Margaret S. Goheen Fellow for 2015–2016 at the National Humanities Center in Research Triangle, North Carolina, where he is writing a book about the Nat Turner revolt. He is the author of *Joining Places: Slave Neighborhoods in the Antebellum South* (2007) and "The Second Slavery: Modernity in the Nineteenth-Century South and the Atlantic World," *Journal of Southern History* (August 2009).

LEONARDO MARQUES—professor of history at Fluminense Federal University (UFF). He is the author of *The United States and the Transatlantic Slave Trade to the Americas* (forthcoming); *Por aí e por muito longe: dívidas, migrações e os libertos de 1888* (2009); and a number of articles on nineteenth-century slavery and the slave trade.

RAFAEL MARQUESE—professor of history at the University of São Paulo and author of *Administração & escravidão: Ideias sobre a gestão da agricultura escravista brasileira* (1999) and *Feitores do corpo, missionários da mente: Senhores, letrados e o controle dos escravos nas Américas* (2004); he is coauthor with Tâmis Parron of *Slavery and Politics: Brazil and Cuba, 1790–1850* (University of New Mexico Press, 2016).

TÂMIS PARRON—research associate at Lab-Mundi, University of São Paulo, and author of *A política da escravidão no Império do Brasil* (2011); editor of *José de Alencar: Cartas a favor da escravidão* (2010); and with Rafael Marquese, coauthor of *Slavery and Politics: Brazil and Cuba, 1790–1850* (University of New Mexico Press, 2016).

JOSÉ ANTONIO PIQUERAS—professor of history at Universitat Jaume I (Castellón, Spain) and author of *La esclavitud en las Españas: Un lazo transatlántico* (2012); editor of *Trabajo libre y coactivo en sociedades de plantación* (2009); coeditor of *State of Ambiguity: Civic Life and Cultural Form in Cuba's First Republic* (2014); and coeditor of the journal *Historia Social*.

RICARDO SALLES—professor of history at Universidade Federal do Estado do Rio de Janeiro; author of *E o vale era o escravo: Vassouras, século XIX: senhores e escravos no coração do Império* (2008) and *Nostalgia Imperial: Escravidão e formação da identidade nacional no Brasil do Segundo Reinado* (2013).

CHRISTOPHER SCHMIDT-NOWARA (1966–2015)—professor of history and Prince of Asturias Chair in Spanish Culture & Civilization at Tufts University. He wrote widely on slavery and antislavery in the Atlantic world, including *Empire and Antislavery: Spain, Cuba, and Puerto Rico, 1833–1874* (1999); *Slavery, Freedom, and*

Abolition in Latin America and the Atlantic World (2011); and most recently, *Slavery and Antislavery in Spain's Atlantic Empire* (coedited with Josep M. Fradera, 2013).

DALE TOMICH—deputy director of the Fernand Braudel Center and professor of sociology and history at Binghamton University. He is the author of *Slavery in the Circuit of Sugar: Martinique and the World Economy, 1830–1848* (1990); *Through the Prism of Slavery: Labor, Capital, and World Economy* (2004); and various articles on Atlantic history and world-economy.

INDEX

Aberdeen Act, 13, 17, 44, 221

Abolicionista, El, 57, 125

abolition of serfdom, 238

Abolition Law of 1880, 132

abolitionism
  Brazil, 162–63
  France, 62
  Great Britain, 2, 6, 19, 49, 59–60, 62, 74, 185, 188
  international, 2, 25, 38, 68, 74, 116
  Spain, 59, 60, 71–72, 74, 117, 120–23, 125, 128, 133, 136
  United States, 52, 60, 70, 74, 238

abolitionists
  France, 61–62
  Great Britain, 10, 29, 32, 38–39, 44, 60, 179, 185
  Spain, 57–61, 67–68, 72–74, 116, 120–21, 139

Adams, John Quincy, 176, 188

African slave trade. *See* slave trade, international

alcohol, 206–207, 210, 218–19, 221

Anderson, Perry, 94, 97

Anglo-Brazilian treaty of 1826, 12, 35, 41–43, 179–80

Anglo-Portuguese Treaty of 1817, 35, 43

antislave treaties. *See* treaties, antislave

antislavery
  Atlantic. *See* antislavery, international
  Brazil, 13, 28
  Cuba, 40, 68
  France, 61, 73
  Great Britain, 1–2, 6, 16, 21, 28, 32, 38–39, 59, 61, 64, 118, 184
  international, 3, 17, 28, 29, 37–39, 52, 58, 68, 71, 74
  morality of, 2, 19–21, 69, 193, 234
  Puerto Rico, 26
  Spain, 26, 28, 34, 40, 58–59, 61, 63–64, 67, 126
  United States, 28, 31–32, 38, 47, 50, 57, 118, 208, 210–11, 233, 242, 246

apprenticeship (British West Indies), 32, 38–39

Arango y Parreño, Francisco, 64–65, 67–68

Argüelles, Agustín de, 60, 73

asiento, 61, 207, 192

Atlantic, 1–10, 14–16, 21, 30, 32, 38, 46, 58–59, 74, 200–201, 231, 244
  Antislavery. *See* antislavery, International
  economy, 8, 17, 74, 201
  North, 29, 45, 173, 192
  slave trade. *See* slave trade, international
  South, 11–12, 44, 179

Austrian Empire. *See* Empire, Austrian
Autonomism, 113, 121, 123–24, 129, 131
Autonomist Party, 119–34, 136

Bahia, 45, 163, 180
balance of power, European, 1, 4–5, 9, 17
Barbados, 59, 199
Barrow Road, 218–51
Barrow, David, 208, 210
Bethel Chapel, 201, 204, 208, 211–17, 221
Blockade, Continental, 5, 10, 30
Blanco White, Joseph, 60–62, 64, 67–68, 71, 73
Bourbon, House of, 9, 61–62, 72, 118, 243
bourgeoisie, 146, 150, 155–56, 168–69
Brazil
    abolition of slave trade. *See* slave trade, abolition of, Brazil
    abolition of slavery. *See* slavery, abolition of, Brazil
    abolitionism. *See* abolitionism, Brazil
    antislavery. *See* antislavery, Brazil
    Conservative Party, 36, 181. See also *regressistas*
    emancipation. *See* emancipation, Brazil
    Empire. *See* Empire, Brazil
    internal slave trade. *See* slave trade, Brazilian internal
    legislature. *See* legislature, Brazil
    National Assembly, 157, 161–62, 169
    Parliament. *See* Parliament, Brazil
    plantation. *See* plantation, Brazil
    postemancipation. *See* postemancipation, Brazil
    proslavery. *See* proslavery, Brazil
    treaties with Great Britain. *See* treaties, Britain and Brazil
British Act of Emancipation 1833, 237
British and Foreign Anti-Slavery Society, 38
British Caribbean
    abolition of slavery. *See* slavery, abolition of, British Caribbean
    emancipation. *See* emancipation, British Caribbean
British Empire. *See* Empire, British

Cádiz, 33, 67–68, 73, 117
Calhoun, John C., 39, 40–42, 48, 51, 193
Campos, Miguel Martínez, 121, 123–24, 126–30
Cánovas, Antonio, 123, 129
capital, 4, 8, 17, 88, 92–93, 95, 105, 107, 114–15, 146
    social, 84, 92, 95, 156
capitalism, 88, 95–96, 116, 146, 149–50, 173, 175, 192
    industrial, 2, 147, 155–56, 168
Caribbean
    British, 27, 32, 35, 38–39, 40–41, 45, 49, 61, 75
    Dutch, 201–203
    French, 27, 29, 61, 75
    plantations. *See* plantations, Caribbean
    Spanish, 27, 59, 61, 63, 74, 84, 87

Cavour, 243–46

Céspedes, Carlos Manuel de, 117

Civil War, American 14–15, 25–26, 28, 47, 51, 57, 70–71, 85, 154, 176, 192, 229–33, 237–38, 242–46

classe senhorial. See master class

colonialism, 16, 20–21, 33, 75, 96, 116

colonies

  France, 4, 8–10, 61–62, 64, 166, 237

  Great Britain, 4–5, 8, 32, 39, 40, 61–62, 64, 124, 202

  Portugal, 4, 9–10

  Spain, 4, 8–9, 30, 61, 62–64, 70–72, 146, 207

Confederate States, 51–52, 154, 231, 239

Congress of Vienna, 1, 4–5, 9–11, 175

Conservative Party

  Brazil, 36, 181. See also *regressistas*

  Spain, 119, 154, 158, 161. *See also* Constitutional Union

Constitutional Union, 119–20, 123, 126

contraband slave trade. *See* slave trade, illegal

Cortes

  Cádiz, 33, 68, 73

  Madrid, 44

  Portugal, 157

  Spain, 60, 119, 121–22, 124, 126, 129, 134, 136

Cortina, José Antonio, 122–23, 128, 133–34

Couto, José Ferrer de, 65–67, 70

Creoles, 17, 61, 65, 68, 93, 116, 118, 199, 236

Cuba

  1868 Revolution, 63, 116–18, 125

  abolition of slavery. *See* slavery, abolition of, Cuba

  antislavery. *See* antislavery, Cuba

  emancipation. *See* emancipation, Cuba

  proslavery. *See* proslavery, Cuba

Cuban Liberal Party, 119, 120, 124, 132

Demerara

  plantations. *See* plantations, Demerara

  Rebellion, 200, 208, 211, 213, 217, 221

Dochfour, 204, 216

Dutch slave trade. *See* slave trade, Netherlands

Dutch West India Company, 203

emancipation, 22, 27

  Brazil, 39, 41, 50, 163, 240

  British Caribbean, 6, 38, 41

  Cuba, 40, 50, 135

  Eastern European serfdom, 238, 241

  Haiti. *See* Revolution, Haiti

  Saint Domingue. *See* Revolution, Haiti

  Unites States, 40, 204, 217, 229–63, 237–71, 243, 245–76, 247

Emancipation Proclamation, 231, 237, 239–71, 246

Empire

  Austria, 39, 145

  Brazil, 25, 27, 35–36, 38, 42, 44–45, 52, 145, 148, 152–53, 164–66

  France, 4, 10, 29, 30, 37, 201

Empire *(continued)*
  Great Britain, 2, 6, 37, 202, 208
  Portugal, 11, 30, 155
  Russia, 9, 39, 145, 148, 238, 240, 246
  Second Spanish, 14, 35, 36–37, 153
  Spain, 30, 49, 50, 60, 67, 74, 176,
    178
Enlightenment, 98, 115

Ferdinand VII, King of Spain, *also*
    Fernando VII, 30, 33–34, 62, 74
flag
  Portugal. *See* Portuguese Flag
  United States. *See* United States flag
Fonseca, Manoel Pinto da, 182, 186
France
  abolitionists. *See* abolitionists, France
  antislavery. *See* antislavery, France
  colonies. *See* colonies, France
  slave trade. *See* slave trade, France
  treaties with Great Britain. *See* treaties,
    Great Britain and France
Fraginals, Manuel Moreno, 61, 89, 93,
    134, 207
free trade, 2, 33, 71–72, 116, 119
"Free Womb" Laws, 26, 117, 154, 163, 239
French Restoration. *See* Restoration
French Empire. *See* Empire, France
French Revolution. *See* Revolution, French
Freyre, Gilberto, 85–87, 102

Genovese, Eugene, 85, 89, 90 91, 97, 98,
    99, 101, 102, 104, 107, 199

Georgetown, 200–201, 204, 218, 221
Germany, 229, 244
Gladstone, Jack, 204, 217
Govín, Antonio, 122, 124
Gramsci, Antonio, 3, 89, 101, 148,
    149–50, 152–53, 154–55, 156,
    159–60, 164
Great Britain
  abolition of slave trade. *See* slave trade,
    abolition of, Great Britain
  abolitionism. *See* abolitionism, Great
    Britain
  abolitionists. *See* abolitionists, Great
    Britain
  antislavery. *See* antislavery, Great Britain
  colonies. *See* colonies, Great Britain
  maritime. *See* maritime, Great Britain
  Parliament. *See* Parliament, Great Britain
  slave trade. *See* slave trade, Great Britain
  treaties with Brazil. *See* treaties, Britain
    and Brazil
  treaties with France. *See* treaties, Britain
    and Portugal
  treaties with Portugal. *See* treaties,
    Britain and Spain
  treaties with United States. *See* treaties,
    Britain and United States
Green, Duff, 39, 41–42
Güell y Renté, José, 129–30
Guizot, François, 151, 159–60, 187
Gutman, Herbert, 97–98, 102, 105
Guyana, British, 220
Guyana, French, 200–201

Haiti
  abolition of slavery. *See* revolution,
    Haiti
  emancipation. *See* revolution, Haiti
  revolution. *See* revolution, Haiti
Havana 45, 61–62, 64, 66–67, 124, 128,
    134, 124
hegemony, 3, 89, 101
  Brazil, 37, 161, 166
  France, 150
  Great Britain, 1–3, 15–16, 19–21, 41,
    174, 192
  imperial, 148, 158
  planter, 91

Iberian Peninsula, invasion of, 11, 30, 33,
    157
Iberian Union, 176
Illegal Slave Trade. *See* slave trade, illegal
industrialization, 7, 145, 158, 168, 236
ingenio, 65, 206
international
  abolitionism. *See* abolitionism,
    international
  antislavery. *See* antislavery, international
  proslavery. *See* proslavery, international
  slave trade. *See* slave trade, international
interstate system, 1, 3–6, 15–22, 27, 37,
    41, 49, 50, 52, 156, 192
Isabel II, Queen of Spain *also* Isabella II,
    57, 116
Italy, 147–48, 150, 155–57, 229, 243–44,
    246–47

Jacobinism, 18, 151, 159, 166
Jerusalem, 200–201, 205, 218, 220
João VI, King of Portugal, 33
Jornal do Comercio, 180, 186
Jorrín, José Silverio, 129–30
July Monarchy, 10, 151, 159

labor, amerindian, *also* indigenous, 62
Labra, Rafael María de, 121, 124–25,
    130–34, 136–37
Leão, Honório Hermeto Carneiro, 37–38,
    43, 50
legislature
  Brazil, 12, 37, 157, 161–62
  Spain, 73, 119, 121–22, 124–26. *See
    also* Parliament, Spain and Cortes,
    Spain
  Virginia State, 208–10
Liberal Triennium, 34, 178
Lincoln, Abraham, 15, 48, 57, 59, 231,
    233–35, 237–39, 241–46
London, 11, 38–39, 42, 50–51, 60, 67, 212
London Missionary Society, 211–12
London, 1841 Treaty of. *See* Treaty of
    London of 1841
Louisiana Purchase, 10, 29, 31

Machado, John Albert, 189, 191
Madrid, 67, 71–73, 116–17, 131, 134
Malê rebellion. *See* rebellion, Malê
Mambises, 117–18, 121, 127
manumission, 127, 133, 135, 149,
    152–53, 159, 210

market, capitalist, 95, 147, 155, 158, 174

maroon wars, 199

Marxism, 94–95, 97–98

master class, 36, 49, 148–49, 151–52, 155–56, 158, 163–66, 199, 205

master-slave relationship, 85, 91, 102–103, 106, 113, 126–27, 130–31, 134, 149, 151–52, 163–65

Maxwell, Wright & Co., 180, 186

Mechanization, 4, 144

mercantilism, 4–5, 7–8, 31, 95

Minas Gerais, 152, 154, 157–58, 162, 181

Mintz, Sidney, 89, 91–93, 101

Missouri Compromise, 31, 36, 47

Missouri Crisis, 31–32

Mixed Commission, Courts of, 11–12, 176, 185, 193

mode of production, 95, 155

Montoro, Rafael, 122, 136–37

Moret Law of 1870, 26, 117, 119, 121, 125–27, 132, 239

Napoleon, 29, 30, 150–51, 166

Napoleonic Wars, 1, 5, 11, 30, 32–33, 145, 155, 174–76

Nat Turner Rebellion, 200, 207–208, 211, 219, 221

Netherlands, The, 61, 176, 202

New World, 26–27, 48–49

Nottoway River, 200, 206, 220

O'Gavan, Juan Bernardo, 44, 50, 63–65, 67

Old Regime, 145, 156, 168

Ortiz, Fernando, 85–86, 91, 102

Palmerston Act, 13, 17, 221

Palmerston, Lord, 20, 38, 45, 50, 187, 191

Paraíba Valley, *also* Vale do Paraíba, 12, 36–37, 74, 152–53, 158, 162, 181–82, 186

Parliament
   Brazil, 35, 38, 41, 46, 153, 158, 180–81
   Great Britain, 185, 202
   Spain, 33–34, 73, 118, 121, 124–25. *See also* Cortes, Spain

Pascual, José Manuel, 122–23

passive revolution, 145, 148, 150, 159–60, 165, 166

paternalism, 87, 91

Pedro I, King of Brazil, 35, 36, 157, 179

Pedro II, King of Brazil, 157–58, 169

Piedmont-Sardinian Monarchy, 156, 244

plantation, 7, 83, 94, 106
   economy, 58–59, 61, 69, 72, 74, 89
   landscape, 204–205, 215, 218, 220

plantations
   Brazil, 126, 146, 158, 181–82, 192
   Caribbean, 61, 84, 88
   Cuba, 60–61, 64, 67, 71, 74, 103, 194
   Demerara, 200–204, 213, 217, 220
   U.S. South, 60, 84–85, 199–93, 205–206, 218, 220

Portugal
  colonies. *See* colonies, Portugal
  slave trade. *See* slave trade, Portugal
Portuguese Empire. *See* Empire, Portugal
Portuguese, Flag, 12–14, 43, 185
Portuondo, Bernardo, 125–28, 130, 132, 137
Proclamation, Emancipation. *See*
  Emancipation Proclamation
Proslavery
  Brazil, 34, 36, 38–44, 50
  Cuba, 65, 67, 74
  international, 25, 29, 38, 39, 51
  Puerto Rico, 72
  Spain, 34, 38, 63–65, 71, 74, 132
  United States, 31–32, 36–44, 47–52,
    67, 209
protests, slave. *See* slave protests
Prussia, 39, 148, 238
Puerto Rico
  abolition of slavery. *See* slavery, abolition
    of, Puerto Rico
  antislavery. *See* antislavery, Puerto Rico
  proslavery. *See* proslavery, Puerto Rico
  slave trade. *See* slave trade, Puerto Rico

Quamina, 213, 217

railroad, 40, 47, 71
rebellion
  anticolonial, 29, 72–73, 158, 162.
    See also Revolution, American,
    Revolution, Haitian
  Malê, 157, 165, 180

slave. *See* slave rebellion
  Turner. *See* Turner Rebellion
Regency, Brazil, 153, 158, 161, 179
régimen de las facultades omnímodas, 34,
  178
Regress, also *Regresso*, 36, 153, 161–62,
  181
regressistas, 158, 161
removal of Portuguese court to Brazil, 11,
  30, 146, 155, 157
republican (political movement), 9, 18, 57,
  59–60, 68, 124, 146, 162, 166, 192
Republican Party, 29, 31, 47–48, 57,
  231–34, 236, 238, 242–77
resistance, slave, 90, 98, 101–102,
  104–105, 152, 165, 221
Resouvenir, Le, 213, 216
Restoration, 145, 151, 155, 159
Restoration, Bourbon, 118, 125
Revista Economica, 123, 134
revolt, slave. *See* slave revolt
Revolution
  1830, 10, 145
  Age of, 3, 22, 208
  American, 4, 8, 21, 74, 145, 209, 235,
    243
  French, 1, 9, 145, 150–51, 155–56
    168, 235
  Haitian, 4, 29, 61, 65, 74, 145, 147,
    176, 207, 230
  Saint Domingue. *See* Haitian Revolution
Rio de Janeiro (city), 13, 48, 157,
  185–86, 239

Rio de Janeiro (imperial court), 11,
    154–55, 157
Rio de Janeiro (province), 152, 154, 161,
    163, 169, 180–81
Risorgimento, 243–44
Rosanvallon, Pierre, 159–60
Royal Navy, 30, 45, 65
Russian Empire. *See* Empire, Russia

Sá, Bernardino de, 182, 186
Saco, José Antonio, 65, 75, 86, 116, 120,
    178
Santo Domingo, 67, 75
São Paulo (city), 239
São Paulo (province), 45, 152, 157–58,
    162, 181
saquaremas, 36–37, 41–42, 44, 46
search, right of, 10, 12–13, 15, 18, 30,
    39, 43, 176, 183, 193
Seaton, 213, 216
Second Party System, 31, 36–37, 166
Second Slavery, 6–8, 27–29, 57–60,
    64, 67, 71, 73, 95, 145, 147–49,
    155–56, 158–59, 167, 173–75,
    230–31, 238
serfdom, 230, 237–38, 240–41, 246
servants, domestic, 41, 84, 240
Seven Years' War, 61
Ships, US built, 15, 43, 180, 184, 186, 190
Sicily, 147
Sierra Leone, 185, 191
slave rebellion, 18, 178, 188, 199, 221
slave resistance. *See* resistance, slave

slave revolt, 33, 90, 95, 158, 163, 165,
    180, 199–200, 202, 204–205,
    207–208, 210–12, 214, 216–21
slave trade
    abolition of, 1–2, 6, 9, 20–22, 32, 33,
        66, 162, 166
    Africa. *See* slave trade, international
    Atlantic. *See* slave trade, international
    Brazil, 12–13, 35, 38, 42–46, 149
        157–59, 173, 179, 181, 189, 193
    Brazil (internal), 45, 174
    Great Britain, 207, 202, 230
    United States, 173–74, 207, 230
    contraband. *See* slave trade, illegal
    Cuba, 26, 38, 44–45, 61–62, 65,
        70, 74, 173, 175, 207, 182, 184,
        188–89, 193
    false flag, 13–15, 43–44, 46, 184–87,
        190–91, 193
    France, 10, 176, 184–85
    Great Britain, 74, 184, 187, 202
    illegal, 34, 38, 43, 45, 51, 173–75,
        178, 187, 192
    international, 1–2, 6, 9–10, 18–22, 31,
        33–35, 38, 42, 44, 47, 51–52, 67,
        149, 153, 157–58, 186, 190–91
    Netherlands, 176
    Portugal, 11, 13, 32, 175, 189
    Puerto Rico, 62, 72
    Spain, 32, 61–63, 66–69, 71, 207, 190
    transatlantic. *See* slave trade, international
    United States, 29, 38, 46–48, 51, 207,
        180, 183–84, 191

United States internal, 29, 38, 46, 174, 205

slavery

  abolition of, 25, 65, 113, 173, 240–41

    Brazil, 154, 164, 239

    British Caribbean, 32, 35

    Cuba, 58, 72, 73, 115–16, 119–20 122–31, 133

    Haiti. *See* Revolution, Haiti

    Puerto Rico, 117–18, 125 130

    Saint Domingue. *See* Revolution, Haiti

    United States, 70–71, 241–42

  nationalization of, 8, 18–19, 230–31

  patriarchal, 85–86, 92

  plantation, 27, 59, 61, 70, 92, 103

slaves, domestic, 83–84, 99

Sousa, Paulino José Soares de, 46, 50

Southampton County, 200–201, 204–11, 214–15, 218, 220–21

Spain

  abolitionism. *See* abolitionism, Spain

  abolitionists. *See* abolitionists, Spain

  antislavery. *See* antislavery, Spain

  colonies. *See* colonies, Spain

  Conservative Party, 119, 154, 158, 161. *See also* Constitutional Union

  legislature. *See* legislature, Spain

  Parliament. *See* Parliament, Spain

  proslavery. *See* proslavery, Spain

  slave trade. *See* slave trade, Spain

  treaties with Great Britain. *See* treaties, Britain and Spain

Spanish Abolitionist Society, 57–60, 71–72, 74, 116, 121

Spanish Empire. *See* Empire, Spain

Stowe, Harriet Beecher, 68–70

Tannenbaum, Frank, 85, 87–88, 91, 93

Ten Years' War (Cuba), 114–15, 117, 125, 136

Texas, 38, 42, 44, 46

Thompson, Edward P., 89–90, 92, 97, 104

Tidewater, 200–201, 206–207

Torrent, Mariano, 65–67, 70

transatlantic slave trade. *See* slave trade, international

treaties, anti-slave trade, 3, 6, 10–17, 39–41, 43, 176. *See also* Congress of Vienna; Treaty of London of 1841; Anglo-Brazilian treaty of 1826; Anglo-Portuguese Treaty of 1817; Anglo-Spanish treaty of 1817; Anglo-Spanish treaty of 1835; Webster-Ashburton Treaty

  Britain and Brazil, 11–13, 17, 35, 39, 41–43, 157, 179–80. *See also* Anglo-Brazilian treaty of 1826

  Britain and France, 10, 39. *See also* Treaty of London of 1841

  Britain and Portugal, 14, 40, 62–63, 126. *See also* Anglo-Portuguese Treaty of 1817, Anglo-Spanish treaty of 1835

  Britain and United States, 6, 14–15. *See also* Webster-Ashburton Treaty

Treaty of London of 1841, 11, 39

treaty, Anglo-Brazilian of 1826. *See* Anglo-Brazilian treaty of 1826

treaty, Anglo-Portuguese of 1817. *See* Anglo-Portuguese Treaty of 1817

treaty, Anglo-Spanish of 1817. *See* Anglo-Spanish treaty of 1817

treaty, Anglo-Spanish of 1835. *See* Anglo-Spanish treaty of 1835

Treaty, Webster-Ashburton. *See* Webster-Ashburton Treaty

Trinidad, 88, 188

Triunfo, El, 122–23, 134

Turner Rebellion, 200, 207–208, 211, 221 (map), 219

Turner, Benjamin, 205–206

Turner, Nat, 205–206, 211, 219–20

Turner, Samuel, 205–206

Uncle Tom's Cabin, 57, 59, 68–69

Union (U.S. Civil War), 47, 51, 57, 231, 233–35, 237–39, 245–46

United States

  abolition of slave trade. *See* slave trade, abolition of, United States

  abolition of slavery. *See* slavery, abolition of, United States

  abolitionism. *See* abolitionism, United States

  abolitionists. *See* abolitionists, United States

  antislavery. *See* antislavery, United States

  emancipation. *See* emancipation, United States

  flag, 13–15, 43–44, 46, 184–87, 190–91, 193

  internal slave trade. *See* slave trade, U.S. internal

  proslavery. *See* proslavery, Unites States

  ships built in. *See* ships, U.S. built

  slave trade. *See* slave trade, United States

  South, 7, 41, 46, 48–52, 74, 188, 230–31, 247

  treaties with Great Britain. *See* treaties, anti-slave trade, Britain and United States

Upper Guinea, 70, 207

Upshur, Abel, 39, 41–42

Varona, Enrique José, 122–23

Vasconcelos, Bernardo Pereira de, 41, 162, 181

Virginia, 29, 40, 48, 90, 166, 200–201, 208–10, 214, 220

Virginia legislature. *See* legislature, Virginia

Vizcarrondo, Julio de, 72, 124

Wanderley, João Maurício Baron of Cotegipe, 153, 163–64, 239

War of 1812, 30, 32, 145, 176, 201

Webster-Ashburton Treaty, 43, 193

Wenceslao Villa-Urrutia, 40, 50

Wesley, John, 208, 211

West Indies, British. *See* Caribbean, British

Whig Party, 31–32, 234
Wilberforce, William, 61–62, 179, 211
workers, Chinese, 114, 120
world system, 3, 50, 95, 156
World War I, 146
World War II, 94

World-economy, 1–4, 7–9, 21–22, 27, 50, 74, 174, 193–94

Zangronis, Juan José, 178–79
Zanjón Pact, 118, 121, 123, 129, 133
Zayas, José María, 122–23, 128